Why You Should Read This Book

One of my favorite things to do to is to talk to people and see what they love to do.

It's so fascinating to look at what people have chosen to do with their life and how excited they get about the ins and outs of their passions.

For example, I just read a Facebook post from a friend who was fervidly imploring people to protect their ears. She went deaf at a young age and now dedicates her life to helping others preserve their hearing.

She can quote all kinds of medical terms, tout the best brands of earplugs, and give you all kinds of hearing advice. She knows hearing inside and out.

I have another friend who loves drinking wine. She absolutely adores everything about the wine process – buying a new bottle, anticipating what it's going to taste like, looking at it, smelling it, swirling it. It's her favorite thing in the world and she'll happily talk to you for hours (and hours!) all about how to properly taste wine.

There are all kinds of people with all kinds of passions in the world. Some people had captivating life circumstances that brought them towards whatever they do while others were always drawn to it.

Regardless of how they found them, it's always interesting to see the world through someone else's eyes. It's a joy to hear the particulars about what someone does, to learn things you never knew before, and to get a momentary glimpse of someone else's life.

This book offers you exactly that.

In the coming pages, you're going to meet people who have all kinds of passions. Some, you may have never even heard of before.

These people have spent a long time doing what they love to do. They're going to give you, in just a few pages, some of the best lessons you can learn in their craft. These lessons took years of experience in many cases – but you'll get them all, easily, just by reading.

By the time you finish the book, you'll have learned new skills in all kinds of areas. You'll learn about emergency food storage, how to have a wonderful marriage, internet marketing, how to give a great presentation – and much more.

To me, this book feels like getting the benefits of going to a dinner party and having countless eye-opening conversations, but without having to get dressed up and leave the house.

As you go through this book, you're going to meet new people, discover new proficiencies, and get momentary insight into peoples' lives.

The skills you'll learn are riveting, the people amazing, and your benefits countless.

It's been an absolute honor to organize this book and I hope you love it as much as I do.

With love,
Rachel Rofé

http://www.RachelRofe.com
http://www.Facebook.com/RachelRofe

Table of Contents

Winning Tips on Overcoming Adversity in Life

By Julio Belson

It is very heartbreaking to be faced with adversity in life, either as an individual or as a business. Many people faced with adversities end up making posomepeopeor decisions in their lives, which eventually lead to more calamities. It is, therefore, essential for you to learn how to overcome adversity when faced with it because it is the ability to overcome our difficulties that define who we are.

Overcoming adversity in life defines the level of your courage and uplifts your spirit. This courage acts as a big advantage when dealing with your next adversity, as it is inevitable to live without adversities. Because life is finite for us humans, we are bound to mourn a loved one at one point or another. This is the most common form of adversity facing humanity today, since it is a daily activity around the world. That is why it is important to treat such adversities as finite too and gather the momentum to move on for as long as you have your breath.

There are many approaches to overcoming adversity, and they all depend on the magnitude of the adversity. It is critical to accept the fact that however unkind your adversities seem to be, you are not picked on by nature to face hardships and misfortunes. This acceptance is the door to successfully overcoming adversities in life.

Overcoming Adversity at Work

Your day could begin with anger propagated by a number of factors sometimes not even known to you. Unfortunately, this is normally transferred to your place of work and, if not tamed properly, it could turn into an even greater adversity. However, do not be worried about what you need to do in such a situation because the following steps will help you to overcome adversity at work in a dignified manner.

• First, you need to accept that you are in a bad mood and avoid fighting the bad mood at all costs. Fighting a foul mood normally leaves you in a circle of even worse moods and completely derails any efforts you may make to overcome your adversity.

• You then need to inform your colleagues that you are not in a good mood because this will assist them in knowing how to relate with you at that particular moment. They will also be assured that whenever you put on your sad or angry face, they are not responsible for making you sad. This then means that they will be able to comfort you as you overcome your adversity.

• Once the people around you have been informed of your situation, you should then proceed to a continuous reminiscence of the good things in your life, beginning with the reason of your current location: your job. A consistent flow of positive thoughts will raise your endorphin levels and naturally get you out of a bad mood.

• With positive thoughts in mind, avoid talking much. Instead, concentrate more on your work and conjuring up thoughts of surpassing your targets and overcoming your adversity by the end of the day. You should, at this point, be telling yourself that if all of the other adversities came and went, then this one will not even last half a day.

• Finally, you should drink lots of water. Yes, the importance of water in dealing with stressful situations has been medically researched and proven to work. Be sure you also eat a well-balanced diet, as the energy levels of your body will automatically keep you in a motivated mood despite the magnitude of your adversity.

These simple and easy-to-apply points will work together to help you overcome whatever adversity you are faced with at your workplace.

Overcoming Adversity in Business

Business people are faced with great challenges of dealing with adversities that emerge from the business environment, as well as from their personal adversities. Successful businesses are managed by people who have continuously overcome great adversities in their businesses. These courageous people keep the following reminders in their minds whenever they are faced with adversities in their businesses.

• The first reminder is that of the business mission and vision. When you think of the magnitude of success you are bound to encounter on your way to achieving your vision, you realize that the adversity you are facing is much less; hence, you divert your energies to completing the business mission.

• The second reminder is that of a "no man is an island" intuition. So, just like you seek the advice of your friends, family, and business associates in sealing business deals, it is very wise to get the assistance of genuine people in your business and personal life.

• Your third reminder in overcoming adversities in business is maintaining a positive attitude towards the business and towards life as a whole. You must always maintain an optimistic view of the future and avoid all negative thoughts.

• A bad day in business does not mean a continuous week or month of difficulties. You should always keep calm and look forward to a successful day and week ahead. That will help you wake up to a much better day in your business.

• If the business is facing failures, you must try again and again. In fact, it is said in business that if you haven't failed or lost, you have not yet succeeded. This is mainly because success in business is defined by the number of many times you are able to pick yourself up when faced with adversities, which in some cases even knock you out of business for a while. Therefore, always try again when you fail, just like you will want to try again when you succeed.

The discipline of applying these tips will ultimately determine the success of your business. The passion and drive that takes you to work every day will also play a key role in overcoming any adversities in your business.

As seen in the steps above, there is a huge similarity in the way these tactics are applied at the workplace if you are an employee or in business if you are the boss. This similarity is even more evidence of the natural form in which adversities of life occur and in how they are overcome.

Books have been written and journals and quotes have all addressed this common issue: overcoming adversity. Real life stories have been told of brave and courageous men and women who have overcome great challenges in their parts of the world. This triumph has created heroes, champions, kings, and queens, yet even at their highest levels, they still face the daily challenges of life.

Adversity in life can be overcome, but can never be eradicated from our lives. And it is this thought that keeps you in the realm of realism because, anything to the contrary is a denial of life itself. The human mind is responsible for very integral processes of our behaviors. The tips above will create an environment of positive behavior that is channeled to your surroundings, which will have a big impact in helping your children overcome adversity.

Helping Children to Overcome Adversity

As a parent or teacher, your behavior towards any children around you directly contributes to the manner in which they manage their adversities. The first thing you need to do is to understand the foundation of resilience and observe your children's behaviors when they are faced with adversity. You need to understand how courageous and resilient your child is to know how to guide him/her when faced with difficulties either in school or at home.

The brain of a child develops according to his/her environment of daily life; therefore, if a child is living in a violent home, he/she is likely to develop a reserved attitude towards people. That is why it is very important for parents to avoid quarreling in the presence of their children. On the other hand, if the child grows up in an environment of courage and resilience towards adverse situations, then they will take the same approach with them as they grow in school and in society. There is a Swahili saying that tells parents that the way you raise your children is the way in which they will live.

We must also teach our children that the resilience of hard times is the mother of the success that they enjoy when they do. By remembering the difficult times in their lives, children will be able to appreciate the fact that the good times only come to those who stay strong in the hard times. This philosophy in their minds will see them overcome any academic and social adversities they face in their lives. The cycle of this kind of behavior amongst children will see their brains develop into strong characters that will end up succeeding by overcoming all of the adversities in their lives.

It is also important as parents or teachers to help our children identify the lessons to be learned in every adversity they face. The realization that the difficult situation occurred for a reason should be the first step here. Let the child understand that in order for him/her to rise, it is sometimes necessary for him/her to fall. When he/she falls, he/she must learn how he/she fell to avoid a similar fall again. He/She will use that to fine-tune his/her skills of being courageous and better overcoming his/her adversities as he/she grows up.

The identification of life lessons in adverse situations will help your child to decide whether he/she will sit on the ground and cry or get up and dust himself/herself off. He/She will be more capable of deciding this if you, as the parent or teacher, are able to help him/her identify the wise move.

Remember that as the parent or teacher, you are also faced with your own kind of adversity when you are in the process of guiding your child in overcoming his/her own adversity. For example, when a child falls and hurts his/her knee, you will be worried about the injury while at the same time trying to guide the child on how to react to the pain. You will soothe the child and assure him/her that all is going to be okay even when you know that he/she is probably going to get a bandage. You have to accept the fact that as much as you will try to overcome the adversity, there will be some effects that may be considered as being even more adverse.

You must assure your children that they can count on you as a parent or teacher to assist them at any time they are faced with adversities. No matter how many times they fail or become scared of even trying, you must be courageous enough to guide them and build their trust for you. It is only when a child trusts you that they can open up to you about issues pressing them in their hearts.

When children feel safe and secure in your arms, they are able to tackle life challenges with more resilience and bravery because they look up to you, and they will want to impress you for guiding them so well. Teach your children that adversity is a part of life; the sooner they accept that fact, the better they will be able to tackle their challenges. At the same time, assure them that just as you have mentors and people you can trust to seek advice, they should also do the same without hesitation.

As teachers, this should be the culture in schools, as it has been proven to work very well in schools where teaching is done with the understanding of child psychology. The same concept is transferred home, where the parents engage in a type of culture that involves mentoring the children in matters of courage and resilience.

Ultimately, it is obvious that the courage to overcome adversity in life is very much valued in society. Learning the exact ways to overcome adversity helps people to face challenges with more courage so that all adversities can be overcome. The most important thing to remember is that as long as you live together with other humans during your lifetime, adversities will always confront you. The key to overcoming them is the key to creating a better tomorrow.

Personal Branding for Entrepreneurs

By Paul David Brand

(www.videosforsuccess.com)

I. Foundations and Basics about Personal Branding

The expression "personal branding" seems to have been used for the first time in 1981 in the book "The Battle For Your Mind," by Al Ries and Jack Trout.

A. Personal branding focuses on your most important asset: Yourself.

Indeed, even if you lost your job, or if your company died, normally nobody could take away from you a powerful personal brand that you would have created.

And this personal brand may help you a lot when looking for a new job or during your process of creating a new business.

B. What is *in concreto* the significance of personal branding?

In his book *Trump University Marketing 101*, Don Sexton writes that brands are a company's most valuable asset, comprising 50% to 80% of its value.

If we do an analogy with personal branding, it's not unreasonable to think that the brand is very important for individuals as well.

Thus, personal branding would apply to individuals via the same advertising and promotion strategies that are used to create a business brand.

These strategies now seem to be affordable and usable by individuals (and not an exclusivity of big businesses any longer) thanks to the new social networks, such as Twitter, Facebook, and LinkedIn.

C. How can we define exactly what a personal brand is?

It's not easy to do it. A lot of people and authors proposed a definition of this complex phenomenon.

According to Robert Brunner, Stewart Emery Wand, and Russ Hall, your brand embodies *"your company's character."* By analogy, we could say that your personal brand embodies your own character.

Steve Cone thinks that a *"brand is a person, a place, or a thing that people recognize readily."*

According to Pascale Baumeister, personal branding is *"all the techniques that enable to identify and promote your own brand."*

David McNally and Karl D. Speak say that your brand is how other people see you and is your personal combination of abilities, style, and conduct.

According to William J. McEwen, a brand is the identity customers associate with a particular product or service.

Ryan Rancatore summarizes the phenomenon of the personal brand in a very accurate and concise way: *"Your personal brand is a combination of who you are and how you can solve someone's problems."*

Finally, Scott Dinsmore proposes what we consider the best definition of all among the ones cited here. According to this blogger, entrepreneur, and expert connector, your personal brand *"is your essence. It is the package that communicates who you are, what you're best at, and how you can most help others in your journey through life."*

We can, thus, notice that personal branding goes beyond the simple fact of managing your digital identity. The goal is not limited to only avoiding reputation damages, but it extends to the creation of a whole identity that is aligned with your character and skills.

D. The previous reflections can help understand what the main goal of personal branding is.

According to Pascale Baumeister, *"personal branding aims first of all to enable one person to have a clear communication about his/her identity [...] so that he/she can stand out from his/her competitors."*

E. Personal branding is, thus, a necessity in our society to be able to differentiate yourself from your competitors and to prosper.

Scott Dinsmore thinks that *"your brand will dictate your success and your ability to connect with the people who matter."*

Today, one of the biggest challenges faced by individuals and companies is the endless and pitiless competition they face.

There are a lot of similar products, services, and talents available in the market today.

The time is over when people bought products and services based exclusively on their quality. The main motivator today is the brand. This is certainly the main reason why Apple has been so successful in the last few years. They produce good quality products, but these are not that different than the ones produced by their competitors. However, their brand clearly stands out and is very powerful.

In our current digital era, it has become a necessity to have a good personal brand, particularly on the Web.

Today, everyone inevitably has a digital identity. It's not possible to avoid it. It's, thus, better to control and manage it so that we are able to convey the image we want.

People who avoid their "duty" to manage their digital identity risk ending up with a very bad one.

It's, thus, a better option to be proactive in this respect.

Of course, the Internet is not the only way to build and manage your personal brand, but it can be a powerful leverage to do that.

Many people think that in our world today, personal branding is much more important than a traditional curriculum.

Indeed, you are less and less judged and rated about your cold curriculum and more and more by (1) what you have accomplished so far, (2) who you know (i.e. your network) and, more generally, (3) by your personal brand in general (which should incorporate the first two elements).

Some people, thus, consider that your personal brand is no less than your modern resume.

F. Now that we have seen that building a personal brand is a necessity today, one could ask what the main benefits from building your own powerful and coherent brand are. They are the following:

1) A greater control on your career and how it evolves.

A personal brand may also bring you new interesting opportunities that are more aligned with your identity and values.

2) A better understanding of who you really are.

You can, thus, discover your life mission and act in this direction.

3) The power to dare expressing who you really are and how to be fulfilled.

As Scott Dinsmore states it, nothing feels greater than knowing who you are, living in alignment with your true self, and being able to share your beliefs and who you are with the world.

4) Align your professional activities (your job and your own business) with your inner values.

You can then choose to be involved only in projects that respect your values.

5) Become more famous.

6) Find your target audience (i.e. your ideal clients) and connect with them.

7) Be successful in what you do and create (ex: in your business).

Some experts in the field of personal branding think that there will always be a market and an audience for someone who has a strong personal brand.

In his book, *Building Brand Authenticity*, Michael B. Beverland states that people seek brands that make them feel validated, understood, and connected. When they find them, they demonstrate their loyalty.

G. A brand can be more or less impactful and beneficial to you, depending on how strong it is.

According to David A. Aaker, a brand is "relevant" when the buyers in a market consider it for purchase after selecting a category; it becomes "exemplar" when it is so strong that it represents in itself a category.

Steve Cone thinks that great brands have four qualities: (1) They inspire people, (2) they can be relied upon, (3) they are essential, and (4) they cannot be replaced by another similar or competing brand.

H. Practically, is there a way to create and communicate a personal brand, and then to make yourself irresistible to your ideal clients (i.e. your target audience)?

Yes, there is a two-step process that is in short the following:

1) Build a strong personal brand (and, of course, a good reputation).

2) Create a strong statement that expresses your personal brand.

We will detail this two-step process in the next section.

Before going on, we should point out that, in this article, we are focusing on personal branding for entrepreneurs. However, the principles and processes described in this article apply to everyone seeking to build a personal brand (ex: students, employees, job seekers, consultants, etc.). In fact, personal branding could be useful to anyone intending to offer his/her services and/or products in the future. It allows him/her to create a unique identity, as well as a powerful, true and authentic image of himself/herself, and it also may help him/her become famous.

II. Create a Strong Personal Brand

A. The Process of Building a Strong Personal Brand.

Strong brands are *"compelling, authentic and relevant."* (Simon Middleton)

1) First step: Know who you really are.

You have to know yourself (in particular, your skills, values, passions, and personality) and what you want to be, have, and experience in your life.

When you have a clear idea of who you are and what you aim for, you can then create your personal brand.

There are nine important blocks that you have to identify and explore in order to discover who you truly are. They will be the foundation on which you will build your own brand.

(a). Your Needs (Maslow's hierarchy).

It's very important to take care of yourself (your body and your mind). Do not overlook your fundamental needs. Sometimes, we tend to be careless in this regard. Do not make this mistake.

You should, thus, avoid working non-stop days and nights on your business and your personal brand without eating healthy, sleeping enough, and having regular physical activity. These kinds of behavior will impact your health in a negative way, your levels of energy will drop, and you will become sick. And, then, it will affect your image and your personal brand. Think long term, not short term.

This first step is not part of the process of creating your personal brand, but as it can affect the latter in a significant way, it should never be overlooked.

(b). Your Values.

They are the core principles that resonate within you.

You should use them as guides to help you make the best decision possible for you any time you have to decide something.

(c).Your Interests and your Passions.

They are very important because they are the activities that motivate and excite you.

Ideally, your business should be aligned with your passions.

As Deepak Chopra said, *"Always go with your passions. Never ask yourself if it's realistic or not".*

(d). Your Big Mission.

It's your ultimate goal (i.e. what you ultimately want to accomplish in life).

Your Big Mission should be aligned with your values and passions.

It will guide you in setting your smaller goals. Indeed, the latter should be aligned with your Big Mission, your passions, and your values.

Remember that to build a great personal brand, you will have to be consistent and coherent in all of your messages (i.e. your explicit communication), but also in everything else you do and create (i.e. your implicit communication).

(e). Your Opinions, your Beliefs, and the Way you Think.

Be bold and confident enough to express your own opinions and beliefs shamelessly.

(f). Your Strengths.

These are the abilities that you have that, when you exercise them, consistently produce good results. One could say that they are your "talents."

(g). Your Uniqueness.

Your uniqueness is not your name, your academic background, your professional experience, your current job, your nationality, or the place where you live.

It's what you will be remembered for long after you have passed away. For example: when we say "Gandhi," what people immediately think about and remember is, "Freedom, non-violence and self-sacrifice."

Your uniqueness is what makes you original and different from everyone else. It's the uniquely added value that you are bringing to the world and your market, and, thus, it's how you are positioning yourself in this market.

This is critical. Indeed, as Simon Middleton said, your positioning determines how people think of your brand relative to other similar brands and, thus, allow you to stand out.

You need to have a unique promise of value, something that can make you different (and in the eyes of your target market, better) than each and every of your competitors. But, of course, you will have to be able to fulfill this promise and deliver on the value you talked about (or even more).

In his book *Married to the Brand*, William J. McEwen points out that a brand promise must be *"credible, compelling and connecting."*

(h). Your Personality.

Your audience wants to know who you are and what kind of person you are. Do not be shy. Disclose all of these personal traits of yours and tell them your story.

(i). Your Curriculum.

Your audience also wants to know what your accomplishments and your competence are. Reassure them by offering them plenty of information about your education, your academic credentials, your professional experience, and your know-how.

The nine above-mentioned elements will enable you to create your own universe (that will be unique and different of the universes of everyone else).

If you need some help in order to discover one or many of these elements of who you are, do not hesitate to ask your family and your friends for feedback in this respect.

They can help you and add details to one or more of them.

Listening to what they tell you, you may also notice that there is a gap between how people currently perceive you and how you want them to perceive you (i.e. the new and real you).

In any case, take enough time to think about all of this and to discover your true self. Remember that your personal brand is one of your biggest assets in your life.

2) Second step: Know who you want to serve (i.e. know your target audience/your ideal clients).

(a). First visualize/dream on who your ideal clients (target audience) are.

For example: Your ideal clients like your products and services, they are loyal customers, they pay for what they purchase well in advance and they never ask for refunds, they refer other dream clients to you, and they promote you (your work and your brand) to all of their friends.

(b). Then find and reach these ideal clients.

Your clients' values should be aligned with yours.

As Simon Sinek said, *"do business with people that believe what you believe."*

Try to determine who your ideal clients are (their values, but also their Big Mission in Life, their story, their needs, and their challenges), and then where you can find them.

However, never forget to be specific, authentic, and honest. Be yourself, and do not try to reach everybody. By trying to please everyone, you will end up pleasing nobody.

3) Third step: Communicate your personal brand and express how you differ from your competitors and how you can create a unique promise (i.e. your added value).

As explained in the first step above, you should know what makes you unique and different.

You have to know yourself very well (your values, your skills, your story, your mission)...

... and then communicate it.

You should have good and effective strategies to communicate your uniqueness.

Be sure to have enough visibility from your market and use this visibility in a clever way.

Know how to present yourself, as well as the unique value you offer.

Dare express your true identity. Do not present yourself as someone you are not, but that you think your target market would like you to be. And do not restrain yourself.

Remember that if you are not 100% honest, your audience will feel it (even unconsciously), and their level of trusting you will drop drastically as a result. It will, of course, affect your personal brand. Another side effect will be that you will feel less happy and fulfilled.

But know exactly what qualities and values you want your personal brand to convey.

Those should never go against your own values, principles, and Big Mission in your life.

But it's possible that you want your personal brand to convey mainly some of your values and focus on them. If that's the case, make sure that your communication and actions further this goal.

Finally, let your audience know what kind of benefits you will give them and how you will give those benefits to them.

Learn about the different ways and methods to communicate your brand and master them.

Oral vs written communication.

Oral communication.

Be enthusiastic in every oral communication. Avoid being boring. You will notice that it is easier to communicate in a charismatic and impactful way when you speak about your passions and when the products and services you offer are in perfect alignment with your fundamental values. It's one additional benefit of creating an authentic personal brand.

Written communication.

Keep a coherent approach in each one of your communications. Do not change your fundamental message, the way you express it, and your unique visual identity (ex: use the same colors, the same logo, and the same profile picture on your website, your blog, and all of your social networks).

Online vs offline communication.

Online communication.

Have a website and/or a blog.

Having a blog and publishing regularly on it is certainly one of the fastest and the most powerful ways to get an audience and engage it.

Pick a domain name (URL) that is coherent with your brand and/or choose an URL (and an e-mail address) that has the following structure:

yourfirstname.yourlastname.com (yourfirstname.yourlastname@gmail.com [or any other serious e-mail provider company]).

Your website should have at least these five different pages:

(1) Your homepage. This page should have your contact information so that the people interested in you, your activities, your products, and your services can contact you easily.

(2) Your portfolio/case studies page. This is a good way to show your potential clients the quality of your work.

(3) Your About page. Inform your visitors on who you are and what you are about. Include a biography and pictures (of you and your team). Here are some examples of information you could include in your biography: your name, your education, your accomplishments, your publications, the conferences you have given (+slides)... and, eventually, some personal things about you, such as your passions, your favorite books and quotes, etc.

(4) Your Testimonials page. It indicates to your potential clients what your past clients have to say about your work and the quality of it. It's a social proof that can reassure your potential clients. Make sure to include pictures of the people offering you their testimonials. This will increase the power of those words of appraisal and make them more credible.

(5) Your blog section. This is crucial. It gives a voice to your brand and allows you to communicate with your target audience (who are your prospects and [future] clients). But, if you have a blog (and you really should have one), be passionate about what you blog and write regular articles on it.

All of your main pages should have the same visual identity (so that your brand is coherent and can be recognized easily).

They should also contain links that redirect to all of the social media sites you are using.

The main social media sites that you can use that can help you a lot when building your brand are the following:

- Facebook (1.15 billion users in September 2013)

- Twitter (200 million users in September 2013)

- Google+ (197 million users in September 2013)

- LinkedIn (147 million users in September 2013)

Your appearance on all of these social media sites should be coherent and congruent.

Your audience should feel this coherence and recognize your brand immediately without a doubt.

Offline communication.

Every interaction in the "real world" is also an opportunity for you to build your personal brand.

Now that you know yourself better and the image/identity you want to convey, try to do it each time you have a conversation and any type of interaction with other people.

Watch out for your words, but also for all of the non-verbal cues, such as the tone of your voice (try to be enthusiastic), your body language (project self-confidence, look into people's eyes, give them a firm handshake), your posture (stand straight), your clothing, and the energy you radiate.

Your appearance, your look, your words, and, more generally, everything that emanates from you must be coherent with your personal brand.

Personalized vs general communication.

Personalized communication includes, for example, the following: phone call, individual e-mail, one-on-one meeting, video conference, etc.

General communication includes: CV, business cards, website (bio), blog posts, social networks, newsletters, taking part in a TV/radio show, writing articles in magazines, writing a book, etc.

Some fundamental principles to keep in mind when communicating (whatever mean of communication you use).

-    Bring quality into your communication. Be clear, concise, and fluid.

-    Be original and unique, but not eccentric.

-    Be enthusiastic and passionate.

-    Be consistent and coherent (both in what you say and how you say it).

-    Have a professional image, but make sure that it aligns with your personality and the values you want to convey (ex: an original look that makes you stand out without making you lose all credibility). Have a unique visual identity, and keep this image in all of your communication (be coherent).

- Insist on your values and what makes you different and unique.

- Always think about ways to fulfill your target audience's needs and solve their problems. For example, listen to what your audience says and what their challenges are. Find ways to help them overcome these challenges.

- That way, you will connect and create rapport with them.

4) Bonus step: Study the people who succeeded and who managed to create a powerful personal brand that is similar to the one you would like to create. Try to emulate them or, even better, get them to help you create your own personal brand.

B. Your Personal Brand Statement.

1) Know your brand (i.e. know yourself and your target audience).

Normally, you should know this information by now and be able to determine what your personal brand will be and to whom you will communicate it.

If you still face challenges when trying to define your personal brand, you could use this simplified process, as proposed by Ryan Rancatore:

Step 1: QUESTIONS. Ask yourself the following questions and find an answer to each one of them:

(a) What are the qualities you have that enable you to do what you do better than anyone else?

(b) What great things do your previous employers think, said, or wrote about you?

(c) What would be the three things that you want someone to remember about you after meeting you?

Step 2: CONSISTENCY. Take a look at your answers and be sure that (a) they reflect who you (honestly) feel you are, (b) they bring solutions to the problems and challenges faced by your audience, and (c) they are aligned with your identity (online and offline). If any of (a), (b) or (c) is not OK, modify your answers (or your current, inaccurate identity).

Step 3: SYNTHESIS. When you are sure that your brand and its elements are consistent with who you are and can easily resonate with your audience and the challenges they face, create a statement that summarizes the fundamental essence of your brand.

2) Summarize your personal brand in a short and memorable statement.

Create a statement that includes the main elements of your identity and, thus, of your personal brand.

In order to do that (and in addition to all of the other keys and questions indicated above), as Scott Dinsmore says, keep in mind the three following questions:

(a) Who are you?

(b) How do you stand out?

(c) Why should others care?

Your statement should be short (one to three sentences) and clear.

For example, it could have one of the following structures:

Structure 1: "I am [insert your name] and I am [insert your job and what aspects of it you are really passionate about (these aspects should help solve an important problem of your audience, in a unique way if possible)].

Structure 2: "I am [insert your name] and I love [insert what you love to do (which should be related to the product/service you sell) and that you are really passionate about and that should help solve an important problem of your audience, in a unique way if possible)].

Structure 3: "[Insert your name] is [insert what you are most passionate about or your main characteristics that you think best describe you]. He/She is committed to [insert your main mission to help your target audience]. He/She is doing that by [insert the way you will help your audience, with your products and/or services for example].

III. Mistakes to Avoid while Building your Personal Brand

A. Thinking that it is too early or too late to create your personal brand.

Don't seek bad excuses for not acting today (ex: saying that you are not ready). Your personal brand is a very important matter, and thus, you should not procrastinate in this respect. Start creating your personal brand today and begin to reach your audience and engage them. Just follow the steps and process described above. As Scott Dinsmore says, "*the best time to begin was likely years ago, but the second-best time is right now."* Will your personal brand be perfect immediately? No, of course it won't. But you will improve it as time passes and as you evolve and learn more about the way to develop, manage, and express a powerful, coherent, and unique personal brand.

B. Not being authentic in your communication.

Being yourself is critical here. You cannot build a sustainable personal brand by trying to be someone else than the true you. Authenticity cannot be faked, or, at least, not for a long period of time.

C. Not being consistent and coherent in all of your messages.

And the need of being coherent and consistent doesn't apply only to your communication, but also to everything you do.

Remember that your actions speak louder than your words. You should then embody your message and walk your talk.

And be aware that everything you do (even your most insignificant actions) builds your personal brand and may influence the way others perceive you (in a good or in a bad way).

D. Not being crystal clear in your communication.

In each and every one of your messages, make sure that your personal brand has been clearly expressed and can be understood easily.

Remember that the greatest leaders in history were also great communicators.

Thus, improve your communication (both oral and written).

E. Having no visibility.

Even though you have built a great, authentic, and coherent personal brand statement, it won't have any impact if nobody hears about you and your brand. You should, thus, always look for opportunities to strengthen your brand (ex: write an article in a journal or on another blog; speak at an event; take part in an important seminar in your field of activity; being interviewed; etc).

F. Not being unique and, thus, not standing out.

If you want your personal brand to be recognized and impactful, it's a necessity that you differentiate yourself. Create an original personal brand that is aligned with your personality, your values, and your goals.

G. Not triggering your audience's emotions.

To be effective, your brand has to create an emotional connection with your target market. Without this connection, the power of your brand is diminished. As Simon Middleton explains in his book, *Build a Brand In 30 Days*, people buy a brand when it aligns and connects with their needs and feelings. Branding is an emotional process.

H. Not being involved and committed.

Be brave enough to shamelessly express your strong opinions. You will certainly be hated by some people. They won't like your message. But, in any case, you do not want to connect with these people. Dare to connect in a bold way with people who think like you do and have the same convictions as yours (but who often don't dare to express them).

I. Not evolving and progressing.

According to Tom Peters, the more you invest in personal renewal and growth, the better your personal brand will do. It's, thus, really important that you constantly update your knowledge in your field of expertise (read books, write articles and books, speak at events, etc.). The creation of your personal brand is an endless and evolutionary process; you will, thus, repeat your message and, when you evolve, modify your message so that it adequately transmits the new, updated, and better you. Also, monitor the way people perceive you and make sure the image they have from you is aligned with the one you want to convey.

However, you should not forget the original identity of your personal brand. Branding creates a bond with your audience. It's, thus, advisable not to alter your personal brand in a critical way without having very good reasons to do that (you would risk losing a big part of your audience if you did).

J. Not delivering on your promise.

Your brand will have a strong promise to help your audience solve their problems and overcome their challenges. Of course, you will have to then deliver on your promise and propose good solutions.

K. Giving up.

As we said before, personal branding is a perpetual process. Moreover, it takes time to see the results of your personal brand-building efforts. Be patient and persistent. It will pay off in the long run.

L. Doing bad things for your reputation.

Obviously, you will avoid at all cost bad behaviors that could result in hurting your reputation and your image.

M. Bonus: Other mistakes to avoid in order to have success with your personal brand and in all aspects of your life in general.

1) Not connecting today with like-minded people who you appreciate and also with people you admire.

These people could support you today or help you in the future.

They will help you grow and strengthen your personal brand.

They could be partners in your business.

Remember that it is more about who you know and not that much about what you know when it comes to success in business.

Build your network and your tribe.

In his book *The Brand You 50*, Tom Peters writes that making yourself into a brand takes a lot of people and, thus, you have to reach out and build.

2) Not constantly delivering value to others.

It's a universal law in life that you have to give first, then you will receive. Make it a habit to give first and help other people (ideally, it should be on your daily to-do list to give and help at least one person). It's also true for personal branding. Never stop offering great value to your audience. Let them be sure that you care about them and that the simple fact of being your loyal reader and customer brings a lot of value to them.

You can bring value to your audience in different ways. For example: (1) gratitude. When you express gratitude to one or more members of your audience or when you praise and acknowledge them (even better, do it publicly), you make them feel great; (2) solution. Listen to your readers' and customers' challenges and help them overcome their challenges. You can provide your own solution (ex: writing an article on your blog to help them solve their problem or answering their e-mail with a solution) or find someone in your network that you are convinced could help them; (3) connections. Be a connection facilitator. Be generous and help different members of your network to connect, making sure that this connection will be beneficial to both of them (win-win).

3) Not constantly trying to evolve in all areas of your life.

Your personal development is very important. Read a lot of good books, apply the good advice you get, and try to eliminate bad habits and create good ones (at least one each year). And do not forget to adapt your personal brand to the new and better you.

4) Not overcoming obstacles and challenges.

Don't be paralyzed when facing challenges. These are opportunities for you to progress. And the way you managed to overcome big challenges could be a powerful opportunity to upgrade your personal brand and a good story to tell to your audience....

5) And finally... not asking for help.

Everyone needs help to succeed. And asking for help could be an excellent way to connect with the person who helps you (and who could later support your projects and your brand in other ways).

To learn more about the principles of success, visit:
http://videosforsuccess.com/.

The Dream Clarity System

By Sheila Brown

www.SheilaKBrown.com

Have you ever found yourself stuck, confused, or just plain frustrated because you can't figure out what you want in your life? No matter how much you meditate, write in a journal, talk to friends, etc... you simply cannot figure things out. Well, I've been in that place a number of times and it is completely frustrating!

My name is Sheila Brown, and I am known among my friends as "the woman who can manifest almost anything." I have used my gift of manifestation to get cars, free trips, jobs, lucrative consulting contracts, online biz success, first-class airline tickets, TV show appearances, boyfriends, hot dates, etc.... At times, it is like playing a game in which I am guaranteed to be the winner.

I first learned about the power of manifestation at the same time most people did, in 2007, when I was first introduced to the DVD *The Secret*. I do not even remember how I acquired my first copy. I do know that I have since gone on to purchase more copies than I care to admit to and have given them away to friends that I felt could use them.

When I first viewed the DVD, it all sounded very familiar to me, but I didn't fully grasp the magnitude of what they were teaching until a year later. It took several viewings and discussions of it over the next year for me to finally begin to "get it" and then believe in what the DVD was teaching. Also, one year after I first viewed the DVD, I picked up my well-worn copy of *Think and Grow Rich* by Napoleon Hill to re-read for the fourth time. I read that amazing book every year, and each time I do, it is as if I am reading a new book for the first time. With each reading, my level of consciousness is different, and I am able to "see" and "hear" concepts that I completely missed in previous readings.

This time around with *Think and Grow Rich*, it all seemed very familiar to me, and it was not because I had read it several times before. I realized that what was in the book was almost everything discussed/taught in *The Secret*!! It was as if they had put *Think and Grow Rich* on a DVD! It was at that point in time that I began to understand just how powerful my mind was at controlling things in my life and being able to invite what I wanted in my life via the power of manifestation.

Armed with this knowledge, I became a manifesting beast. In January 2005, I manifested a release from a job that was sucking the life out of me. I got laid off and walked away with a huge severance! I then manifested a very lucrative career as a consultant; my first client was the one movie studio in Hollywood that

I wanted to work for, and they came after me! I then went on to manifest multiple lucrative contracts with many other studios over the years. All came easily & effortlessly. I was able to manifest huge chunks of money to pay for personal development courses, multiple first-class vacations all over the world and a new car. I was invincible, or so I thought.

It was during a 22-month financial freefall that I experienced from 2009-2011 that I perfected what I call my "Dream Clarity System." For those 22 months, I remained positive and constantly worked on ways to figure out how to get back to financial abundance again. I found that, during this period of time, I was unable to visualize as I had in the past, which meant that my manifesting gift had gone away as well. I would write in my journal, write business ideas, and read daily to keep my mind focused and sharp. It was during this period that I re-read my copy of *The Four Hour Workweek* by Tim Ferris. In it, Tim outlines his "Dreamlining" process in which he shows you how to price out your big dreams to make them more attainable in a certain period of time. This got my head spinning. I was unable to determine what my dreams/goals were. It used to be so easy for me, but now I felt powerless.

I had an idea to regain my clarity that combined writing in my journal with the process of mind-mapping. This idea eventually evolved into my "Dream Clarity System," or DCS, for short. I have used this system extensively to now be able to manifest my new dreams.

Here is how the process works:

I decide on a dream or goal I want to manifest. I then pull out my journal and write everything I can about it: My "why," what it will look like, and feel like. I put in as much detail as I can possibly extract from my mind. I also write about the outcome I want to attain as a result of achieving it, including how I will react when I attain it. I then begin the "Dream Clarity Process," which is,

1. Take a clean piece of 8½" by 11" paper.

2. Draw a circle in the middle of it that is 2×2 or 3×3.

3. In the middle of the circle, write your name and the dream/goal you are working on. For example, "Sheila Brown – My Dream House."

4. Moving around the circle, draw lines going outward like spokes on a wheel.

5. At the end of each line, write one word or phrase that describes an aspect of the dream. Staying with the dream house example, if you draw 10 lines, you might put:

- 2-story oceanfront, wraparound porch

- Big backyard
- Quiet, safe neighborhood
- AAA+-rated schools
- Great neighbors
- 3-car garage
- Big deck
- Beautiful landscaping
- Etc....

6. Make as many lines and entries as you need to until you cannot think of one final detail. When complete, your picture should look like a wheel with the hub being the circle with your name and goal/dream written in it. The lines will look like spokes, and the words and/or phrases you wrote will be coming off of the ends of each line.

7. Now go back and read out loud what you wrote. "Sheila Brown's Dream House has...." List out all of the points you wrote.

8. Add more if more details come to you. The more detailed and clear you are, the better.

9. Now, close your eyes and allow yourself to "feel" and "see" what you just wrote. Draw a picture or make a movie in your mind of what you "see." Include each and every detail that you just wrote or spoke. This is your vision of what you want, and this process allows you to anchor your vision into your subconscious mind so that it knows what to work on for you.

10. Now, it is time to add more detail. Go back to each point you wrote for each line and ask yourself if you can go deeper. Draw lines/branches off the end of the word or phrase you originally wrote and add more detail. For example, for "2-story house," you could add the following:

- Red door
- Spanish tile roof
- Stucco finish
- Plantation shutter windows
- Custom wood work throughout
- 4br, 5ba, full basement
- Etc....

You want to go really deep with detail here!!

11. Add in the extra detail branches for each spoke that needs it until it is completed. Your page should be full.

12. Repeat the process where you go back and read out loud what you have

written in your wheel, but this time, with the extra specific details.

13. Now close your eyes and visualize and anchor the enhanced vision.

Do you see how by following this process for each and every one of your dreams or goals, the probability of you being able to manifest them increases exponentially?? You will be shocked at how powerful this process will be for you. You will realize two things.

1. You have never gone into this much detail with your dreams before.
2. You probably never imagined that your dreams or goals could have so much detail.

I coach my students that manifesting your dreams/goals is the equivalent to placing your order with the Universe. It cannot and will not give you what you want unless you are specific. The Universe does not discern what you do or do not want. It gives you exactly what you ask for every time. If you say, "I want a man/woman in my life," you need to be VERY specific!! You will get a man/woman all right, but he/she will more than likely lack the fundamental things you want in a partner. BE SPECIFIC!!

Think about this example. You pull up to a McDonald's drive-thru and the cashier says, "Hi, welcome to McDonald's. May I take your order?" You then say, "Yeah, I want a burger, fries, and a drink!". There will be silence as the cashier waits for you to be specific on which burger, what size fries, and what drink you want because no one comes to McDonald's without ordering a specific type of sandwich. He/She will then ask you which ones you want, to which you say, "I want a Big Mac, extra pickles, a large fries, and a Coke."

Specificity is the way that McDonald's or any other restaurant will be able to give you what you want, and this same specificity is the only way that the Universe will give you what you want! The "Dream Clarity System" is the best way I know how to get crystal clear specificity on what you want in life to be able to communicate it to the Universe in order to receive it.

There are three final keys to this process that I want to share with you. First, please keep in mind that this process is strictly used to determine and get clear on the "What" and not the "How." It is not our job in manifesting what we want to be concerned with "How" something will show up. That is the sole responsibility of the Universe to work out. Our job is to say "yes" to opportunities that arise and to take deliberate, immediate, massive, consistent action when the "how" does appear.

The second point is that you have to completely detach from what you wrote and the outcome. By "detach," I mean you must have total belief and faith that what you have asked for will eventually show up for you either in the way you describe it or in an even better form than you laid out. Be patient, have faith, and do not stress about the "how" or the "when." Detachment is the secret elixir that makes this all work!

The third point I want to make is once you finish the process, move straight into a space of total gratitude for receiving what you have asked for AS IF it has already shown up. Literally allow yourself to react exactly as you would AS IF you were currently experiencing it. How will you feel when you turn the key and enter your dream house for the first time? Will you cry? Will you smile so hard your face will hurt? Will you scream as you run from room to room? Will you dance and jump for joy? Whatever your reaction will be, do it! You can simply visualize it, but I recommend actually getting up and screaming, jumping, or actually saying what you would say. While doing it, give thanks to The Creator and The Universe for manifesting this dream for you!! Act AS IF!

This process really does work!! Since January 2011, I have gone from being completely broke with $10.00 to my name to:

1. Landing a lucrative six-figure consulting contract with a studio at a time when no one was hiring. It was the exact studio I wanted to work for, and every detail I mapped out came to fruition.

2. Took my 14-year old niece on a $10,000 Parisian vacation.

3. Took 19 luxury, international and domestic vacations in 2012, all of which were self-funded by me.

4. Moved to my dream luxury oceanfront home on an island where I run a thriving coaching business and Internet business.

I used the exact Dream Clarity System I laid out for you to manifest all of this and more!

Try it today. It works!!
Sheila Brown

About Sheila Brown

Sheila Brown is a powerhouse World Traveler, Business Consultant, and Internet marketing coach who helps aspiring and veteran entrepreneurs build more income streams to enjoy lives of Freedom. Prior to dedicating herself full-time to coaching and teaching her students, Sheila Brown worked as a top executive for Fortune 500 companies like Pepsi Cola, Gateway Computers, The Walt Disney Company, and Activision and as a Consultant for movie studios & entertainment companies for 18 years. In 2009, she decided to leave corporate America and her

Beverly Hills lifestyle behind and pursue her passion for International travel full time. In making that decision, Sheila found herself in a 22-month long financial tail spin that, at her lowest point, she found herself in the welfare line in South Central Los Angeles. Through her positive thinking and consistent implementation of her business goals, she was able to build a new life of complete financial freedom and has, since, gone on to travel to over 34 countries, 130+ cities, and has relocated to both Thailand and the beautiful Dominican Republic where she is currently living her oceanfront dream life!

As the co-founder of Portable Incomes (http://portableincomes.com/enroll), a six-module online course that teaches how to create portable income streams to have a portable life, she's taught product creation strategies, business branding, outsourcing, and traffic generation to students all over the world that has enabled them to build lives of freedom for themselves.

Her personal website is: http://sheilakbrown.com

Social Media Links:
LinkedIn: http://www.linkedin.com/in/sheilakbrown
Facebook: https://www.facebook.com/sheila.brown2
YouTube- My travel videos:
https://www.youtube.com/user/Theonyxtraveler/videos
Email to reach me: info@portableincomes.com

Emergency Food Storage

By Emily A. Cabot

Introduction

The following guide is all about how you can secure yourself and others in your home by using a good amount of emergency foods. The right emergency foods can make all of the difference in the event of a serious emergency, when resources are scarce and you potentially ending up stuck somewhere.

The foods that you can use include a variety of options. There are more than a hundred different things to use, for instance.

In fact, you can dry, seal, freeze, or can different foods to make things last for a while. You'll learn in this guide about how you can dry and can foods, as well as how you can use different storage methods to your advantage for all sorts of specific foods.

The particular kinds of foods that you can prepare on your own and store for later use are especially interesting. You can learn here about how you can cook, prepare, and store foods of all types while using very specific rules for getting individual options ready.

The need to keep you and your family healthy and safe in an emergency is critical. That's why the foods listed here are safe and healthy for everyone without creating more risks than needed.

This guide could save your life if you use it right. Be sure to refer to it and to prepare your emergency plans around the ideas listed here.

The Importance of Emergency Food Storage

During wartime or a natural disaster, food scarcity and an absence of electricity or natural gas for cooking purposes requires a great deal of improvisation and reliance upon the basic cooking tactics used by our forefathers. It is a well-known fact that apart from water and shelter, food is the most important item that you would require in a surviving situation. Despite that, we often come across people who react with confusion or downright scorn when told about the need for having an emergency supply of food. To them, it's like - "Why do we need to do that? What is the government for?"

In any case, that's a pretty fragile argument. Apparently, what they fail to comprehend is that the government as well as the local administration may not be in a position to offer immediate aid to the affected citizens during a devastating disaster. So, to get rid of that false sense of security, one must observe the underlying facts associated with disasters of epic proportions.

The fact is that many disasters can be extremely catastrophic and can cause serious damage to any place. They can cause roads to become impassable, communication signals to fail, and can even make it harder for you to leave your home in some cases.

These serious problems can range from floods and hurricanes to tornadoes and earthquakes. Terror attacks can be even more devastating when you consider some of the weapons that are often used against people in attacks.

The threat of what could happen in the event of an emergency is far too important to ignore. You need to prepare yourself in the event that there ever is an emergency that gets into your area and puts your life and the lives of others at risk.

So, Why Do We Need Emergency Food Storage?

The world as we know today is increasingly becoming more and more uncertain. A casual look over the week's headlines will allow you a sneak peek into that bitter truth. Nature's fury, pandemics, war cries from hostile nations/terror groups, etc. - there are numerous ways how disasters (man-made or natural) can all of a sudden paralyze the society we are accustomed to in our day-to-day lives. Probably, it's not a case of IF, but WHEN. We will never know that until the day a tragedy befalls us. Can you afford to take risks with your and your family's lives at stake?

For those whose survival plan almost exclusively relies on government aids, you clearly have to think about what could happen if the disaster ends up disrupting all available civic amenities in the region, including power plants, water supplies and communication channels. What if a sizable portion of the country falls victim to the tragedy, making it almost impossible for the government to redirect its resources to all affected areas simultaneously?

Worse yet, during such disasters, the local administrations will probably be as badly affected as the citizens themselves. So, assuming that the Federal Government is still intact and functioning normally, it may take them several days or even weeks before finally reaching the affected population in certain regions. Until then, you will have no other options for survival outside of whatever you have.

It's a cold and harsh fact that under such a tragic scenario, natural selection will step into action, and only those with adequate preplanning and preparation will have the highest probability of survival. You clearly have to be prepared if you are to actually survive such a serious problem in the future.

Do We Need to Store Food to Survive a Pandemic?

While it's relatively easy to understand the significance of emergency food storage plans to survive large-scale natural or man-made disasters such as tsunamis, floods, tornadoes, and war, among other risks, most people don't consider pandemics as a potential threat to food or water supplies. It makes sense too - after all, how can a bacteria or virus-borne disease - no matter how widespread - result in food shortage (unless, of course, it's a zombie pandemic)? Trust us - you should not underestimate those microscopic threats. They are as capable of disrupting your food or water supplies as any other outside threat can.

Now, we are not suggesting that you should stockpile a multiyear supply of beans and rice in your store room or basement. However, we do believe that a two- or three-month supply will do you good to help you get through any large-scale pandemic.

There are a couple of scenarios where having adequate food supplies at home may offer you some serious advantages.

First, if the pandemic is really widespread and thousands of people are falling sick with every passing day, having a decent storage of food at home will allow you the luxury of not requiring yourself to go to the grocery store. If the news is mostly comprised of stories such as rising death counts and overwhelmed hospitals, avoiding the crowd will probably be the best way to protect yourself from the disease or the infection.

Secondly, if the situation gets out of control, the government is likely to shut down all non-essential businesses and establishments and probably would ask citizens not to leave their homes unless absolutely necessary. While grocery shops won't be treated as non-essential businesses for obvious reasons, you can easily predict that the number of open shops will be too low to take care of the entire population. Therefore, you should have food on hand so you don't have to worry about the risks that come with a certain event or situation.

So, there is a high probability that the situation will turn hostile, and people will be ready to do almost anything to get themselves and their families the basic supplies they need. Riots and looting will be inevitable under these circumstances. The only way you can avoid such mass chaos would be by stockpiling a good amount of emergency food at home.

Moreover, it is also possible that there could be a long-term scarcity of certain staples if farmers are unable to harvest crops or deliver them to the market because of fuel shortage and/or quarantines. Fuel shortages are bound to happen if the government issues a travel restriction during the pandemic.

The crux of the matter is that disasters don't come knocking on your door. Therefore, if you have not already done so, now is the right time to start stockpiling your emergency food.

What to Buy

Emergency food storage is not just about storing random food items in your basement or store room. Rather, it's more about selecting the right food items that can not only stay fresh and edible over a prolonged period, but can also help you stay healthy and fit.

In this current chapter, we will draw a brief outline of the composites of an ideal emergency food storage program. The details on the different food items mentioned in this overview will be covered in the subsequent chapters.

Water

The human body contains approximately 65 percent water and, therefore, is one of most important nutrients that our bodies cannot survive without. According to Rubner, a renowned German physiologist, an animal can survive even after losing nearly all of the fat and glycogen in its body plus up to 50 percent of the body's protein due to starvation. However, the same animal would die due to the loss of only one-fifth of its body's supply of water.

The primary sources of water for our bodies include:

1. Fluid foods in diet
2. Solid foods in diet
3. Water produced by the body through the metabolism of energy nutrients.

The loss of water from the body occurs by the way of skin (perspiration), kidneys (urine), intestinal tract (feces), lungs (expired air), and eyes (tears).

As per the guidelines issued by the Center for Disease Control and Prevention (CDC), one gallon of water per day per person should be enough for emergency considerations.

One plan for storing water would be to use a tablespoon for every 15 calories consumed in a day. Therefore, an average 2,200-calorie diet would entail 10 cups of water.

How can you store water? There are two things that you could use:

- Small jug-sized 1- to 2-gallon containers
- Large 50- to 100-gallon reservoirs attached to larger devices

It does not take much for you to transport a small container. Large reservoirs are a completely different story. These larger items are often linked to a potable water system in order to keep the flow of water into your home working as effectively as it can.

While drinking water can be useful for storage, you should be aware of how long this water can last. Many forms of water can last for years after they are bottled or stored. Of course, this is provided that the water is actually stored in a secure manner and has not been exposed to any outside threats.

Appropriate Food Supplies Based on Nutrition

There are a number of different foods that can be used in your diet to keep your body healthy. These include foods that have been suggested by the USDA in its famed food pyramid. As you can see, the food pyramid includes many foods dedicated to providing you with the nutrition you need to keep your body healthy and safe.

As you will notice, you have to use a large amount of bread, pasta, and grains in your diet to keep your body active. This is to provide your body with a regular digestive system while also providing you with the necessary energy that you require.

Fruits and vegetables are especially important because they relate so heavily to keeping your body healthy. They contain plenty of vitamins, minerals, and fiber to keep your body healthy and safe.

Meats and proteins are always important, as are dairy-based products. However, these products can wear out after a while and might contain more fat than what your body can afford.

The top of the pyramid is where all of the fats, sweets, and oils in your diet would go. You clearly have to use as few of these as possible if you are to keep your body safe and under control.

Vitamins

It might also help to have plenty of vitamins on hand for your needs. This is not necessarily a type of food, but it is something that should give you plenty of protection for your body's needs. Supplements like multivitamins may provide you with the nutrients that you might not have easy access to in the event of an emergency.

Canned Products

Canned food products are especially helpful when it comes to keeping your body healthy and providing you with enough foods in an emergency. The canning process has become popular in foods that can be preserved and secured inside sealed containers that do not have to be refrigerated.

Canning works when foods are boiled, pasteurized, frozen, or dried out and then placed in a can. Water may be added to the can in some cases to keep things soft. The can will then be sealed off with a secure lid that can only be opened by using an appropriate can opener or a pop-top lid.

The amount of time a canned product can last for will vary, but you could find some products that will last inside of their cans for years. This is a huge benefit because, it makes sure you actually have something that can be used for your diet in the long run.

Dried Food

Dried food may also be used in the event of an emergency. This is a kind of food that has gone through a dehydration process after it was prepared. It can easily be prepared for consumption by adding warm water. You will learn more about dried food later on in this guide.

All of these foods are valuable items to have in your pantry in the event of an emergency. They are not only important to your life and your health, but are also capable of keeping you protected in the event of an emergency.

Foods for Family Members

Don't forget to find enough food for family members that have special needs. Baby foods and baby formula are important, as is pet food. Everything should be in secure piles and ready to eat or serve.

Canning Foods

Canning is a great procedure that is used to preserve the foods that you've already got. As we just recently mentioned, canning entails your foods being stored in protective jars and then sealed off with secure lids to keep them fresh for years. You can keep certain foods in your home for years after they are appropriately canned.

However, canning can be a risky endeavor due to the threat of bacteria getting into the food. This can cause diseases to spread and even make it so that the foods inside of your cans will no longer be useful. However, this can be controlled if you use the right safety measures when storing canned foods and also while getting your foods canned on your own.

Why is Canning So Great?

Canned foods have become a huge staple in many emergencies. Emergency food supply centers even swear by these foods. That's why you see so many of these in the food shelters that you often read about in the news. Canned foods are very useful for several reasons:

1. Canned food is safe to use because it has been appropriately heated before processing. This means that the bacteria and other harmful materials that can get in the way of a can will be removed before things are stored.

2. It is hard to tamper with foods stuck in a can or jar. The glass, tin, or steel in a can or jar will keep foods intact and safe from outside harm.

3. The nutrients inside of canned foods will be easier to preserve than if the foods were out in the open for a while.

4. The total amount of time that canned foods can last for may be a while. The reason why so many food drives require people to bring canned foods above all else is because they do not wear out as easily as others. You might expect a can of something to last for two or three years before it goes bad.

Canning Foods on Your Own

While it is always a good idea to order canned foods from any supermarket, it might be an even better idea to can your own foods. Here's a simple procedure that you can use in your own home to can foods the right way.

1. Check each jar to see if there are any scratches, dents or cracks in them. These should not be present in your jars because scratches and dents can not only keep foods from being sealed, but can also be places where bacteria can get in the way.

2. Place all of your jars and lids in a vat of boiling water and heat them for about ten minutes. Boiling water can kill off any particles or pieces of bacteria in your jars and lids. Include any rubber bands around the lids..

3. Add vinegar to any foods that might not be acidic enough. Lemon juice may also be added if you don't have vinegar. You need a slight bit of acidity in your jars to preserve the foods.

4. Place a clean funnel over the can or jar so nothing can get in touch with the sides of the jar as the food is being placed in it.

5. Insert your food into the can or jar and secure it as tightly as possible. The lid must not be bulging or flat, nor should it spring up or down as you push on it.

6. Heat the cans or jars in about one to two inches of hot water. It does not have to be boiling all of the way at this point. It just needs to be enough for the water to be appropriately heated.

Canned Food Safety

Although the benefits of canned food are plentiful, there are a few critical standards that must be used with food safety in mind.

You must always store your food in a safe place where temperatures will not be much of a burden. Sticking your canned foods in conditions of about 75°F is always best..

Make sure you replace your canned food stock every two to three years. While it's true that canned foods can last a while, the acidic nature of some foods might wear off, thus making them prone to bacteria.

Always dispose of any cans or jars that have dents, cracks, or other damages to their physical bodies. They may not be as fresh as you might want them to be.

Overall, canned food is always useful for whatever you plan on having in your pantry.

Dried Food

Dried food is a little different from canned food, but it's still a good type of emergency food product worth considering in your pantry. Dried food is a type of food where the water content inside of it has been removed.

The odds are that you've seen dried food in stores in the form of something like beef jerky or banana chips. There are many companies that are also dedicated to manufacturing and selling different kinds of foods that can be dried up and stored in packages to be heated for later use.

In fact, it does not take much to start up dried food after you have fixed it up. You just have to add an appropriate amount of hot water to your dried food to plump it up. Of course, some foods like beef jerky do not require water for them to become edible.

How Are Foods Dried?

Dried foods are created through a process known as food dehydration. A few simple steps can be used to get foods to lose their moisture and be stored for later use. In fact, your foods will continue to taste great well after they have been dehydrated if you use these easy-to-use steps to get everything ready.

1. The foods that have to be dried will need to be inspected. First, fresh fruits and vegetables can be examined to see if they are ripe and have no bruises on them. In addition, any meats that have to be dried should be fully cooked and tested before anything can start. Everything also has to be washed or, else, bacteria and other harmful materials might get into the food.

2. All foods can then be cut up into any kind of serving pattern that a person wants. For example, pineapples can be sliced into flat rings. It's often best to make sure everything is about one-quarter of an inch thick or less so it will be a little easier for things to dry up.

3. An appropriate dryer has to be added to the process. It will be responsible for heating everything up and keeping moisture from being stuck inside of the foods you have. You can learn more about the types of drying devices you can use in a later part of this chapter.

4. Keep an appropriate temperature up and running. You have to use a temperature of about 130°F on average to not only heat up your food and dry it, but to also keep the texture and flavor of your food from being lost. This temperature should be enough to keep the food from hardening and being too difficult to eat.

Storing Dried Food

You have to store dry food in a space that's about 65°F to 75°F on average. It's a condition where the food will not wear out or become weak.

In addition, while dried food can be effective and can prolong the lives of different foods, you might have to use these foods within six to twelve months after they have been prepared. They can still be used beyond that, but they might lose their flavors or textures.

Don't forget to also see if your food is actually drying. It might help to check that your food is actually dry.

Vacuum

A vacuum may be used for storing your food. A vacuum will be used after a food has dried, stored in a bag and then treated with an appropriate vacuum seal. This seal will not only create a secure link for food to be stored, in but will also make it so there will be no oxygen left in the package. This means that the food could last a little longer.

This can be used for meats, breads, and other easily perishable items after they have dried out. You will have to get a separate vacuum sealer to make this possible.

Dehydrators

A commercial dehydrator is by far the most popular choice. This will create a sealed environment that uses an ideal temperature and plenty of covers that will collect the moisture from food as it drips out.

It will be good to have dried food if you want things that can last for a while in the event of an emergency.

Food for Freezing

You can freeze the foods in your home. This is done by keeping the foods at a condition that is below zero degrees Celsius, the point where liquids start to solidify and become frozen.

Frozen foods are likely to last for a while. In fact, some of these might end up staying fresh in a freezer for at least an entire year.

In addition, the nutritional properties of your food should be the same when they are frozen. The inherent properties of your foods should remain if you preserve them in a safe environment where the temperature is consistently freezing.

What Goes In?

The things that you can add into your freezer can include all sorts of items that relate to what you want to use for your dietary needs in the event of an emergency. However, there are so many different kinds of foods to consider that it might take a while to set up an appropriate space to fit everything into.

You might consider adding cooked meats into the freezer. You can always cook different meats, seal them inside of vacuum containers, or wrap them in protective materials and then store them inside of your freezer. This will keep the meat from wearing out too quickly.

It's also a good idea to use a freezer for fresh fruits and vegetables if you also seal them in proper containers. These can be stored and heated for later use without losing any of their properties. Any bacteria that might cause these foods to spoil or wear out will become dormant, as it is below freezing.

Watch the Freezer

You have to be careful when using a freezer in this process. There are a few things that are worth doing to keep your freezer working right.

You have to make sure you are using a generator in the event that the power goes out for any reason. You have to use a generator to keep a freezer powered up so it will continue to operate for hours or even days after the power goes out.

Try to use a freezer that is large enough for your needs, but don't go too big. You need to find a freezer that can be transported from one place to the next in the event of an emergency. A freezer that has about ten cubic feet of space should be good enough.

Take a good look at the space in your freezer and figure out where you are going to place everything so it will be ready.

Remember, your freezer is a huge key to keeping your foods safe and controlled in the event of an emergency. You need to make sure that you use a freezer that will keep all of your foods protected in the event of an emergency.

Food Sanitation

Food sanitation can be best explained as the practice of following some specific rules and procedures to prevent food contamination. Many jurisdictions around the world have laws to regulate food sanitation in addition to the regulations and guidelines created by public health agencies. These laws are to be followed by companies that make food products for sale. They are critical to the safety of the consumer and can particularly be duplicated at home on your own.

The importance of food sanitation can be comprehended from the fact that it is strongly recommended at virtually every single step of the supply chain in the food industry - from the workers in crop fields to the waiters in restaurants. In its simplest form, the phrase "food sanitation" refers to the rules and procedures meant to keep our food healthy and safe to eat. "Food hygiene" is a more commonly used term to refer to "food sanitation" at the consumer level, such as in the home kitchen and other spaces.

During an emergency, storing enough food for yourself and your family is not the sole factor that you should be concerned about. There are other important things to consider as well, including how to keep the stored food fresh and edible over a prolonged period of time. It must be keep clear and controlled if it's to be edible.

How to Protect Your Stored Food

First and foremost, you should always make it a point to store your emergency food supplies in a cool, clean, and dry storage area. Avoid storing food in open containers on shelves.

The lids and other spaces in your foods must be kept secure. That means that any lid you have for your foods must be sealed and secured so nothing can get in the way of your food. This must be done right so there will not be any spoilage risks coming into your food as you are using it.

Keep food storage areas free from spilled food and food particles. It only takes one small bit of something for insects to get into a spot and to start harvesting on that food, thus causing your place to become infested.

You have to store your foods in cold conditions if you're in a place that is prone to insect infestations. A rule of thumb would be to go towards something that's very close to freezing, but not that far down. The best strategy would be to go at a level of 35°F to 45°F to keep everything intact. In fact, any condition that might be less than 65°F will be good enough. This is strongly recommended if you live in a place where insects tend to thrive and are likely to actually get into your property.

Canned foods should be treated a little differently because it's easy for them to wear out and develop bacteria if they are not stored in the right conditions. It is often best to go with a temperature of around 75°F when storing canned foods.

Dried food has to be stored in a space that's similar to where your canned foods will go. It's especially important to make sure they are placed in a dry area.

Oxygen Absorbers

You should look for an oxygen absorber to keep the effects of oxygen from being too dramatic or worse than they might already be.

An oxygen absorber is an interesting product that can be added to the food sanitation and protection process. An absorber is used to take in the oxygen that comes into a container or other space, thus keeping your foods from being likely to wear out from oxygen exposure.

The truth about oxygen is that while it is a vital part of the air, it is also something that can cause many foods to spoil over time. It can cause different foods to wear out and age quickly. Therefore, the need to have an oxygen absorber in a space is important. This will particularly be helpful for sanitation procedures because oxygen can cause some bacteria to grow on some foods if they are not treated properly.

A simple absorber will be made with a packet of powdered iron pellets or sodium chloride to keep the moisture in a spot under control. These ingredients are used in an absorber to reduce the amount of air and moisture in a package.

You can easily place several of these absorbers inside of food packages, storage bins, freezers, and other places. However, you should use a few simple rules for getting these absorbers to work right:

- Do not place an absorber in a wet spot or, else, it will dissolve.
- Never use an absorber that is open or punctured.
- Do not eat the contents of an absorber.
- Do not heat the absorber.

This type of material is useful for sanitation simply because it keeps your foods from developing bacteria that can cause them to feel dirty. You must use an absorber to make sure your food will not be at risk of harm from the air.

101 Emergency Food Items

Now that you know why it is so critical for you to get emergency food items in your daily life and how you can easily store them and use them, you have to be aware of some of the different kinds of foods that you can use. Here's a look at 101 of the best foods that you can add to your emergency pile. These come in many forms and are suitable for many different members of the family. Either way, you must use these in your emergency room:

1. Peanut butter
2. Crackers
3. Trail mixes
4. Multigrain cereal - preferably, individually-packaged servings
5. Raisins
6. Dried banana slices or banana chips
7. Dried pineapple rings
8. Dried apples
9. Canned tuna
10. Canned salmon
11. Green beans in cans
12. Canned soups
13. Sports drinks
14. Powdered milk
15. Beef jerky
16. Beans, both dried and canned
17. Dried vegetables
18. Cooled raw vegetables

19. Jelly
20. Sugar
21. Salt
22. Pepper
23. Instant coffee
24. Instant tea bags
25. Fruit cocktails
26. Hard candy, preferably without a large amount of salt already in it
27. Honey
28. Salad and food dressings
29. Vacuum sealed meats
30. Dried corn
31. White rice
32. Bouillon products
33. Ready-to-cook pasta
34. Cooked ground beef to store in a freezer
35. Vegetable skins
36. Meatballs to freeze
37. Ice cubes; these may be used for not only preparing foods, but also for keeping a freezer secure and being less likely to overheat
38. Canned vegetable juice
39. Canned tomato juice
40. Energy bars
41. Granola
42. Millet
43. Chia seeds
44. Sprouts
45. Protein bars
46. Cheese spray
47. Dried salmon
48. Freeze dried chicken
49. Dried turkey
50. Organic tomato sauce
51. Tomato paste
52. Organic chips
53. Rolled oats
54. Quinoa
55. Green lentils
56. Sealed cookies
57. Bread mix
58. Flour
59. Wheat germ
60. Salsa
61. Curry powder
62. Cured salami
63. Dried bacon

64. Summer sausage or other preserved meats
65. Dried apple chips
66. Dried carrot pieces or slices
67. Powdered ice cream packets
68. Freeze dried chocolate bars
69. Mints
70. Powdered garlic
71. Coconut powder
72. Dried and shredded coconut
73. Baker's chocolate
74. Barbeque sauce
75. Dried bread pieces, particularly croutons
76. Smoked fish
77. Roasted beef
78. Sealed cheese slices
79. Pork rinds
80. Wheat cookies
81. Canned sardines or brisling
82. Frozen peas
83. Frozen carrots
84. Chilled spinach
85. Dried or sealed lettuce leaves
86. Baking soda
87. Miso powder
88. Vinegar
89. Bottled club soda
90. Canned asparagus
91. Canned baby carrots
92. Vitamins for all members of the family
93. Energy drinks; it's best to use ones that don't have sugar in them
94. Nuts inside of their shells; make sure you have a nutcracker just to be safe
95. Fruit bars
96. Fruit snacks
97. Meal replacement cans
98. Shake powders
99. Baby food (if you have a baby)
100. Baby formula, preferably something that is ready to serve out of a container
101. Pet food (if you have a pet)

You don't have to use all 101 of these foods, but it's still a great idea to consider them when starting an appropriate collection of foods that you can store in a place for safe use in the event of a serious disaster.

Emergency Organic Food

Everyone seems to be talking about organic food these days. They all love organic food because they know that it apparently contains loads of healthy ingredients, isn't harmful, and all that other stuff that the news says. The fact is that organic foods might actually work perfectly in the event of an emergency.

One of the biggest reasons for this is because organic foods do not have some of the same artificial ingredients and preservatives that you might expect to find in typical foods. The fact is that artificial ingredients are often added to preserve flavors and to keep the textures of some foods intact. The problem is that they may not be good enough with regards to keeping these foods working for a while after they have been made.

What's more is that many of the artificial ingredients that claim to be useful can actually be harmful. MSG and artificial sweeteners are among these ingredients that can hurt your body when used in the long run.

Even the artificial colors that are used in foods can be problematic. They often get in the way of the natural flavors that you should be enjoying when making your food.

What's even more interesting is that your body might be easier to protect if you use enough organic foods in its diet during an emergency. Organic foods are known to do a better job with protecting the body's immune system, thus keeping it secure from all sorts of outside problems that often get in the way of a healthy diet. It's especially critical to keep your immune system healthy during an emergency because a weak system will cause you to become more likely to suffer from various medical emergencies.

The types of organic foods that you do prepare in your diet should be considered as well:

- Whole grains are always useful when it comes to finding healthy foods. You can keep millet or buckwheat in your pantry, for instance.

- Natural seeds may also be added to keep your body healthy. Chia seeds are especially useful for their fatty acids.

- Powdered milk is especially important considering how it will have an extensive shelf life. However, you have to make sure it comes from cows that are not treated with growth hormones, antibiotics, and other harmful artificial materials that many places have been using over the years.

You need to consider these organic foods if you want your body to stay healthy in an emergency. Organic foods are not only useful and natural, but are also likely to give you the nutritional benefits that you deserve while you are trying to take care of yourself in an emergency.

Emergency Food Bars

The nutritional bar has become a staple of many diets. A good nutritional bar can include all sorts of valuable nutrients and ingredients that are dedicated to giving you a well-rounded diet filled with all sorts of important nutrients to keep your body active and healthy.

You can particularly use emergency food bars in your emergency shelter to make sure you have something that will provide you with plenty of protection for keeping your body active and healthy at all times.

So, what should you find in these bars? There are many different things that have to be considered when getting things that can be used.

You have to start by taking a look at the ingredients found in such a bar. These include more than just the foods that are added to a bar to give it the flavor you might expect out of it. They also include the types of bases used to keep the bar intact. A good bar might include things like wheat or granola to keep things together.

Dried fruits or nuts can also be added to some bars. These are to give the bars a little more flavor. Not every bar can have these flavors, but it is still a good idea to think about them.

Speaking of which, the flavors that come with a bar should also be checked on carefully. These flavors include fruit and nut flavors for the most part. Some of these bars may even include chocolate. The flavors should be naturally safe and easy to enjoy.

The number of calories that come with a bar should also be factored into everything. While it's true that many companies that make nutritional bars tend to throw in a few hundred calories into their bars, some emergency food companies will actually make bars that can handle thousands of calories.

This does not necessarily mean that you absolutely have to use a bar like this in order to stay healthy and nourished. However, it certainly helps when you have such a bar with a good amount of energy on hand.

The specific directions for eating a bar can be listed right on the package. These directions might include the need to eat one or two of these bars in a day for the best results. Also, you might have to add water to some bars or even eat them in small bits.

The amount of time you have with which to consume a bar should also be checked. Today's emergency bars are prepared to where they can last for years.

The final consideration to see is the nutritional label. The label should include information on how many nutrients it has and how much of a daily supply of protein, fat, carbohydrates, and critical vitamins and minerals are included in a product. The total amount will vary by each product, but it can still be very useful.

Conclusion

Let's close this out with a reality check – we all don't want to think that bad things are going to happen. The truth is, there is always going to be a serious risk of a major disaster coming into our lives.

Here's a good consideration to think about. This guide was written in May 2013. In the two to three months surrounding this time period, there have been massive tornadoes in Oklahoma, a huge fire in rural Texas, and a bombing in downtown Boston that resulted in the city being shut down for nearly an entire week.

The recent emergency shutdown of a nuclear power plant in North Carolina, the recent government shutdown in Congress, and the ongoing threat of snow in some of the northern parts of the United States only show that emergencies can happen at any time and that the threat of an emergency can be just as bad as a real one.

And that is not including some of the stories that we've heard about over the last few years. People are still talking about Superstorm Sandy and the devastation that it left. There are even places on the Gulf Coast that look as though Hurricane Katrina went through it just last week.

Remember, your life might be in the balance during an emergency.

I hope these thoughts help your lifestyle in the ever-changing world events of our society.

Emily A. Cabot

Request Information from Emily by contacting her at:
emily@greenmountainpress.com

A personal note from Emily

I live with my two sons, Asa and Eli, and my husband Mark in Northern Vermont. My real passion is writing children's books, and I became convinced that after reading to my two sons each evening when they were young, I had to write cute and funny bedtime stories for others to read. There are life's lessons to learn in all of my writings, and my books are educational for kids. I can also remember when my Mom and Dad read to me every night before bedtime. In fact, my Dad used to change his voice for the appropriate character he was reading to me. I used to laugh and laugh.

As an added bonus, I am including an audio link to my first book, *The Adventures of Crog the Frog Prince*. **Please follow the link on the last page.**

You and the children in your life might enjoy:

http://www.amazon.com/Adventures-Crog-Frog-Prince-ebook/dp/B00EX790PC/

http://www.amazon.com/The-Adventures-Crog-Zog-Children-ebook/dp/B00GNBA9D8

FREE BONUS: *The Adventures of Crog the Frog Prince* **Audiobook**

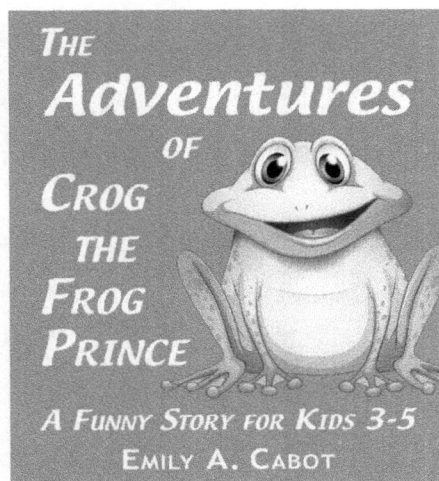

THE
Adventures
OF
CROG
THE
FROG
PRINCE
A FUNNY STORY FOR KIDS 3-5
EMILY A. CABOT

If you'd like to listen to a FREE Audiobook of my new book on "Crog," you can download it for free for a limited time by clicking on this link or pasting this link into your browser:

http://www.greenmountainpress.com/crog_the_frog_signup/

Enjoy,

Emily

5 Core Elements to Writing Fiction

By Cherry-Ann Carew

Writing is about using the full breadth of your imagination. Dare to use it. "Think, believe, dream, and dare." ~Walt Disney

One of the most remarkable things about us, human beings, is our capacity to be creative, and that creativity can define us in a way that changes lives. Any kind of writing is a form of creativity in my opinion, but writing fiction is in a league of its own that is deceptively simple, yet immensely complex.

A tiny idea, for instance, can become the book that changes our view of the world. A trivial story can light up the eyes of a person in need of hope and bring them happiness beyond our scope of understanding, and a written account of a specific moment can be so poignant that it changes the entire course of one's life.

Naturally, your reasons for wanting to write fiction are entirely your own, and you will have questions galore. One of the biggest of these questions is, "How long should my story be?"

There are some hard and fast rules when it comes to the length of a story, so picking your body of work can be as difficult as conceptualizing your idea. Nevertheless, there are three principal formats when it comes to works of fiction. These formats include the short story, the novella, and the novel.

Let's start with the short story. The short story usually has a well-developed theme because there's not much character development or depth, nor is there any rising and falling tension that you would find in a novel. The average number of words is around 7,500, which can easily be read in one sitting.

Then, there's the novella. Though it is longer than a short story, it can also be read in one sitting. With a novella, however, you'll have more opportunity to develop characters and conflicts.

These books are not divided into chapters and can run anywhere from 17,500 to 40,000 words.

The novel: Ah, now this is the dream for many aspiring writers of fiction - we'll go into more detail as to what constitutes a novel shortly. But for now, the minimal length is 40,000 to around 100,000 words. If it goes beyond 100,000, it is usually a historical novel, and should it exceed the 150,000-word mark, consider making it into a sequel or trilogy.

I know I said above that there are three principal formats when it comes to works of fiction, but there's another: the novelette. And though it's not especially popular, I would be remiss if I omitted to mention it. The novelette is longer than a short story, yet shorter than a novella, with a word count of about 7,500 to 17,500.

Okay, now that you have a gist of the different formats, you probably have no end to the number of ideas that's rummaging through your head from a dream or nightmare you had, perhaps, or you read something in a magazine or newspaper, or someone said something that sparked an idea for a story.

However, like any worthy endeavor, the starting point is often the most difficult. Nevertheless, before you put pen to paper or fingers to keyboard and take on the journey of writing, you need to be clear about what kind of story you want to write. In the grand scheme of things, you want to entertain, but you first need to nail down in what genre you intend to write. For instance:

- Do you want your readers to go on a 'Who Done It' *mystery* tour?
- Bite their nails from *suspense* until a secret is revealed?
- Go deep into the bowels of a *fantasy* world where good overcomes evil?
- Sit on the edge of their seats through a *thriller* chase?
- Take them into the world of science, i.e. a *futuristic* realm.
- How about a *romantic* journey, where they live happily ever after?

Once you are clear about the genre, you can then get into the rudiments of writing your novel, which usually begins with a lead-in. The beauty of writing a novel is that it allows you plenty of time to develop your characters and explain the setting(s), among other things. You can fuel your imagination to broaden your idea by creating believable characters, realistic scenes, a compelling plot, theme, and style – all to entertain readers, and these elements are what you'll use as your tools (along with others, but these are the fundamentals) to structure your novel.

In essence, the structure of a novel follows a defined pace that includes the lead-in, the precipitating incident, an escalation of action, one or more reversals and escalations, the climax, the falling action, and, finally, the denouement, as is shown in the 3-Act Structure Model below that is commonly used by writers and screenwriters.

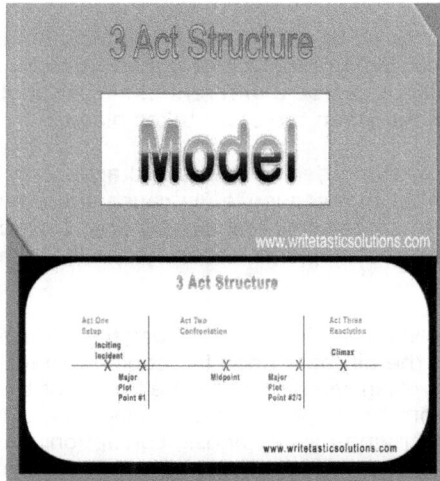

3 Act Structure

Model

www.writetasticsolutions.com

3 Act Structure

Act One
Setup
Inciting
Incident

Act Two
Confrontation

Midpoint

Act Three
Resolution

Climax

Major
Plot
Point #1

Major
Plot
Point #2/3

www.writetasticsolutions.com

Let's take a look at what these five essential elements denote in a story:

- Your character is the *who.*
- The setting represents *where and when.*
- The plot is the *what.*
- The theme is the *why*.
- The style is the *how*.

Let's take it one step further and explore their functions:

A character, in short, is a participant in a story, and is, generally, a person. However, a character can also be any persona or entity. In addition, there are different types of characters. For example:

A point-of-view character is a character by whom the story is viewed, and who does not necessarily have to be the main character in the story. A protagonist is the main character of a story, while the antagonist is the character who competes, or opposes the protagonist.

Then there are minor characters who interact with the protagonist. These minor characters assist in helping to move the story along.

The aim when creating your characters is to make them three-dimensional. In other words, they need to be as real as you and me. Aim to create characters whom readers can identify or affiliate with. Explore and expose their fears and secrets; give them quirks and backstories to motivate their actions, thereby creating powerful conflicts.

The setting, sometimes referred to as 'milieu,' is the location and the time where the story takes place. It can be a real place or a made-up city or country within our own world. Additionally, it can be a different planet or another universe. The setting is basically where and when the story takes place.

The plot, a.k.a. storyline, is the order of events and actions of a story, especially as they relate to one another in a sequence via cause and effect. Here's a big tip: Avoid plotting your story in an episodic fashion. By this, I mean that you should not write 'this happens and that happens.' Your story will lack rhythm and pace and will bore the reader.

The theme is the core meaning of the story and usually transpires as you write. For instance, the belief in the ultimate good in people or that things are not always what they seem is often referred to as the 'moral of the story.' Your theme can be anything from the importance of family, lack of trust, the death penalty, war over peace, striving for happiness, corruption, guilt, lust, greed, racism, injustice, love, etc. Some stories do not have any theme at all. Similarly, some are so thinly veiled that they're left to the reader's imagination or they're open to interpretation.

Style includes the various choices you'll make, consciously or subconsciously, as you create your story. They include the overall picture, such as point of view and narrative voice, along with structure, tone, dialogue, imagery, grammar, punctuation, word usage, sentence and paragraph length, etc. These combinations serve to bring out your unique voice and your unique writing style.

In addition, there are elements of style that include the narrator, who tells the story and point of view - from whose perception the reader sees, hears, and feels the story. The common points of views used in fiction include:

- First-person: The story is relayed by a narrator who is also a character within the story. Therefore, the narrator reveals the plot by referring to this viewpoint character as 'I' or 'we.'

- Third-person narration provides the greatest flexibility to the author and is, therefore, the most commonly used narrative mode in fiction writing. In the third-person narrative mode, each and every character is referred to by the narrator as 'he,' 'she,' 'it,' or 'they,' along with his/her/its name.

- Third-person, subjective: The third-person subjective is when the narrator conveys the thoughts, feelings, opinions, etc. of one or more characters.

- Third-person limited: If it is only one character, it is usually referred to as third-person limited because the reader is 'limited' to the thoughts of a particular character (most often the protagonist), much like the first-person mode, except that you will still use personal descriptive pronouns such as 'he,' 'she,' 'it,' and 'they.'

- Third-person, omniscient: This usage is very common in classic novels, such as *Pride and Prejudice* by Jane Austen and *Oliver Twist* by Charles Dickens, for instance. A story in this narrative mode is presented by a narrator with an overarching point of view, or what is usually referred to as 'godlike.' This means that everything that occurs within the story world, including what each of the characters is thinking and feeling, is all-seeing and all-knowing.

The climax of the story is when the conflict of the plot is resolved and is deemed the most exciting part of the book. This is where the protagonist will face the antagonist, and she will do whatever she has to do to triumph, if this is what you decided will happen at the outset.

There are many, many elements you will implement when writing your story, but these are the five core ones that form the basis.

Now, I know writing your novel may be intimidating when you set out to write such a large body of work, especially if you are a novice writer, but you get a lot of flexibility and it will definitely be an exercise you will never forget. In addition, it can open the door to many future stories. So, shelf your intimidation and have a go at it.

Okay, let's put all of what I covered together. To give you a visual, here's a chart that breaks down the 3-Act Structure sequence in more detail:

Traditional 3-Act Structure Sequence

Example 1
Beginning <-> Middle <-> End
Within this structure, there is what is referred to as a 3-Act sequence.
Example 2
Act 1 <-> Setup (Beginning) Act 2 <-> Development (Middle) Act 3 <-> End

Now we go one step further, whereby in Acts 1 and 2, there are Major Plot Points that drive the story forward.
Example 3
Act 1 <-> Setup <-> First Major Plot Point
Act 2 <-> Development <-> Mid-Point/Second Major Plot Point Act 2 (Second Half) <-> Third Major Plot Point
Act 3 <-> Climax/Resolution

Side Note: Plot Points are where the conflicts take place.

Act one is the setup. This is where you introduce the protagonist and the main characters that will play a relevant role in the story. If your story dictates, this means the villain, too, whether a person, thing, or a natural disaster.

Introduce the inciting incident—that is, the problem, be it relational, inner, or situational. Introduce the setting. You may have multiple settings; however, set the scene.

In this first Act, the protagonist will react to whatever unpleasant events that has disrupted her life. Readers will learn about her and form a relationship with her. Will they connect with her or her dilemma? Will they root for her to overcome the conflict that she encounters? Will they care? Perhaps they connect with the villain instead, because his story is more appealing. Whichever it is, work hard to set the groundwork to lead into Act Two and hook and engage the reader.

Act Two – here, you raise the stakes. In this act, and from the inciting incident, the protagonist tries to make sense of what's going on, usually at the beginning. In essence, the stakes are raised by barriers, obstacles, additional complications, and situations, leading the protagonist to react.

Add new twists. Make the protagonist act in unpredictable ways as she tries to get her bearings. Do what is necessary to stimulate and grip the reader. You can inject backstory that was not evident in Act One, and the protagonist can use evidence or knowledge as she strives to solve the problem(s). This is where she encounters setbacks. At the same time, the villain is trying to counteract, giving the writing more drama.

However, the protagonist reaches her lowest point. All her efforts seem useless. She feels defeated and goes through a 'dark period.'

In the second part of this Act, the protagonist makes a decision on how to deal with the conflict/events.

In Act Three, the final obstacle/hurdle, climax and resolution happen here. The protagonist fights like a crazy woman to put an end to the problem. She will come face-to-face with the villain and come out the winner if the purpose is for her to be successful. You then tie up the loose ends by answering any central questions, sub-plots are resolved, and morals or themes may become evident. Any lessons learned from the events also become apparent.

I write both fiction and nonfiction, and I can tell you that fiction is challenging to write, but it is also extremely rewarding. You will need desire, discipline and dedication. Oftentimes, you will need to step outside of your comfort zone because you will look at the world at a deeper level. Fictional works tend to draw more from the imagination, though the drudgery of research cannot be dismissed. And, you'll visit the most strange and intimate places.

Time spent writing fiction can also lead to a greater understanding of yourself. As you watch your story unfold, you might see themes or characters that reoccur often in your life. Maybe you will identify with your protagonist, or maybe you will see your family or friends in a different light.

Writing fiction gives you the tool to reach the hearts and minds of other people – even if it is a temporary escape. It can touch people in such a profound way that they talk about it for years to come.

Fictional characters are often some of the most beloved of all. These characters enter the hearts and set up residence there. Everyone can remember a novel that they have read that startled them, caused them to see things in a new way, or even changed their view of the world. I'm pretty sure you can remember characters that have influenced you in some way.

The first and most important step in writing your novel is making sure that you appreciate the story. If you work only to please your audience, you are going to lose what makes the story exciting to you. Writing for someone else is extremely difficult, though some writers have become very good at it.

Remember that your novel is yours, first and foremost. Of course, you want it to sell well, so strive to strike a balance and enjoy the journey.

A great book should leave you with many experiences, and slightly exhausted at the end. You live several lives while reading. ~William Styron

About Cherry-Ann Carew

Award Finalist & Bestselling Author, Cherry-Ann Carew | Book Coach | Developmental Editor | Founder of Writetastic Solutions is passionate about helping Authors, Speakers, Experts & Service Providers bring out their creative expression to write, publish, and market their books. Discover how her Coaching and Editing services can help you *Write It, Work It, Publish It*™ at: http://www.writetasticsolutions.com/services/

Connect with her on Social Media:

Blog: http://www.writetasticsolutions.com/blog/
Google+: https://plus.google.com/+CherryAnnCarew/
Twitter: https://twitter.com/CherryAnnCarew
LinkedIn: http://www.linkedin.com/in/cherryanncarew
Pinterest: http://www.pinterest.com/CherryAnnCarew/
Facebook:
https://www.facebook.com/WritetasticSolutions.EditingandCoachingServices?v=app_4949752878
Facebook Power Write Group Page:
https://www.facebook.com/groups/PowerWriteYourBook/

Creating Quality Content For Internet Marketing

By Joe Chengery

http://www.joechengery.com

My name is Joe Chengery, and I am an Internet marketer, copywriter, copyeditor, content creator, and author. I started copyediting way back in 2002 for well-respected Internet marketer John Delavera, creator of the well-known newsletter, *TurboZine*, and Internet marketing commerce platform, Delavo.

John wanted copyediting of his text, being that English is not his first language. I was one of his *TurboZine* subscribers, and he noticed my ability to copyedit from some emails we passed back and forth to each other. He asked me if I would copyedit his *TurboZine* newsletters and emails, to which I agreed. We have been friends since.

I have also done copyediting, article writing, copywriting, and blog posting for other Internet marketers, including Paul Kleinmeulman, Gabor Olah, Erwin Goh, Donna Walsh, mentorees of Rachel Rofe, and more. I am honored to be a part of Rachel's Rolodex of Trusted Outsourcers. I have been doing similar projects for Julie-Ann Amos' Exquisite Writing site since 2009. I have also learned from the aforementioned Internet marketers and others when it comes to Internet marketing, copywriting, email marketing, Kindle publishing and more.

Being that I have either done Internet marketing or have done various aspects of Internet marketing for others for as long as ten years, I have a pretty solid foundation of how to go about creating content and making sure that your website visitors enjoy the content you provide.

Creating Quality Content

What exactly is quality content?

Many people ask this question, whether it's new website owners who are just starting out or experienced website owners who experience a case of writer's block and are unsure of what to write next for their sites and/or blogs.

The best way to produce quality content in your niche is to check out what is going on in the world regarding your niche or industry. This means researching current events and issues affecting your industry. There are many ways you can go about doing this:

- Examine other notable sites and blogs related to your industry and see

what topics are being commented on the most, shared on social media, and are prominent on the front page or industry-related pages.
- Watch news programs that pertain to your industry; whether that is CNN, CNBC, MSNBC, Travel Channel, etc. Again, note what topics are being discussed first and what social media comments/feedback are shown on air.
- Related to above, also make sure to check out their respective websites and blogs regularly, as well as subscribe to email lists and/or RSS feeds.
- Check out Magazines.com and MagazineLine.com for ideas on what magazines and publications are available related to your industry. In addition, check out the title covers; topics on these covers are likely to be very popular that people want to read about right now.
- Subscribe to magazines and publications that relate to your industry. You can subscribe to digital and/or physical versions; in fact, it's sometimes beneficial to subscribe to both because there is often content in one version that doesn't appear in the other.

Once you do the above, be sure to check in at least one to two times per day in order to learn the latest news and what is trending. Read the articles and blog posts to see what is being discussed and what comments are being made to see what you can write about.

Now, instead of writing the same or similar piece on your blog or site, try looking at the story from a different angle and writing from that perspective. It helps to utilize the questions that reporters will often use to create their stories:

- Who?
- What?
- Where?
- When?
- Why?
- How?

For instance, if you have an Internet marketing site, and you read on other sites that video marketing is effective, come up with some statistics on how effective it is and some challenges Internet marketers face when it comes to marketing effectively with video on the Web, as well as how you can overcome those challenges.

You could write one long article, or better yet, write multiple articles. You could even write a short report or ebook to offer for free to visitors to your site in return for their contact information. After all, the main key is to build your list. After your business is established, you could even sell the short report or ebook at a low price, or could even offer it as a one-time offer to another of your products/services.

This works in niches outside of Internet marketing as well. For instance, if you are running a weight loss or nutrition site, and other sites in your industry are talking about the latest diet plan, take a different perspective and list the pros and cons of such a diet and the factors a person must take into consideration before beginning such a diet plan. Especially take into consideration different members of your target market, such as busy moms-on-the-go, senior citizens, those who are obese, those who have health issues or complications, etc.

Note that you can utilize the information you gathered from other blogs and sites and utilize it in the information you present (though write it in your own words first; if you do quote anything directly, be sure to give proper credit to the appropriate source or sources). However, don't just regurgitate what other sites and blogs are doing; your site will never stand out this way and never separate itself from the rest of the industry, exactly what you want your site to do.

Yes, this will take some research and some time, but remember, you want to write quality content, and you want your site to stand out, so just writing what everyone else is doing is not going to get the job done. Take the time, make the effort, and really make your content shine.

PLR (Private Label Rights)

Some website owners want to utilize PLR to create the content on their sites. This can work IF you or a trusted outsourcer modifies the PLR content in such a way where the content is really unique and valuable.

NEVER, EVER use PLR as is; there are several reasons why:

1. Many PLR articles, ebooks, etc. have outdated information in them. If you post that unchanged on your site, you will not be looked upon as an authority because you're putting up information that might have been relevant two, three, five years ago, but that has been outdated for a while. Keep in mind that each post you make on your site is time-stamped, so if you're posting that information in 2013 and trying to pass it off as being new and relevant to today's industry, your reputation and credibility will take a hit, which will impact sales.

2. PLR that is unchanged likely will not have your "voice." By "voice," I mean your own writing style, your own personality when writing. This is what you want to establish over time on your site, as your subscribers and customers will come to know you and connect with you better as time goes on. Keep in mind that the better the relationships you make, the more they will trust you, and hence, will be more likely to purchase your products/services and the products/services you recommend. Just using PLR on your sites that doesn't have the same "voice" as your own writing will stick out like a sore

thumb; this is another reason why PLR must be modified to gain the maximum benefit from it on your websites.

3. Many PLR articles, ebooks, etc. have spelling and grammar mistakes in them. As the next section will explain further, this will only damage your credibility and reputation if you use them as is, and thus, will hurt your ability to make sales and become a leader in your industry.

4. There is debate over whether you can use PLR and it will or won't damage your site's search engine rankings. What is likely though is that your site will not stand out from the competition if you are using the exact same other articles as other sites. Many sites are willing to use PLR as is without any modification; therefore, if you (or a trusted outsourcer) are willing to put in the effort to modify your PLR, you stand a much greater chance of your site and business standing out in your industry.

Spelling and Grammar Mistakes

One thing that is CRITICAL: You CANNOT afford to make simple spelling and grammar mistakes. Some think that they can gloss over this, that online content can have spelling and grammar mistakes and that it's perfectly acceptable.

The truth is, with more competition in your respective niche (and most niches nowadays have significant competition, with it growing all of the time), this means that you cannot give your prospects any reason to doubt your authority and make them look elsewhere for what they are seeking. Spelling and grammar mistakes make your content, and your business, look amateurish.

In addition, spelling and grammar mistakes make your content much more difficult to read, and anything that distracts your prospect from reading your content and being convinced of your expertise is going to encourage them to look elsewhere for the information they seek. This is exactly what you DON'T want, especially in this day of increasing competition.

You have one or more websites in order to profit from them. This means that you want to appear as professional as possible when you present content to them. After all, you want to establish yourself as THE authority, the go-to company in your niche that people will turn to when they have a problem or they are looking for information in your niche. To do that, you have to establish a consistent track record of providing quality information and products/services to satisfy your website visitors and turn them into customers.

In fact, as I am writing this selection for this book, an email came into my inbox, referring me to an eMarketer article titled, "SMBs Lean on Content for Lead Gen."

The article showed how white papers, Webinars, and other content marketing pieces can lead to your business gaining new leads for additional profits and greater reputation in your industry. This shows the importance that your content has in gaining leads for your business.

However, if that content looks unprofessional, how will that reflect on your business? Not well, certainly, and not the top choice for your target market. Instead, they will turn to a competitor in your niche, exactly what you don't want.

Now, how do you go about keeping grammar and spelling mistakes out of your content. Many would say that a spellchecker in your word processing program is enough. While it can catch some of the more obvious spelling and grammar mistakes, spellchecker will often miss mistakes that can be noticed by your audience.

For example, check out the following example:

"I ate a lot of deserts."

Now, you may know the meaning of this sentence, but take a careful look at it. Can you spot what's wrong with it?

The error in this sentence is the word "deserts." A "desert" is an arid landscape, such as the Sahara Desert or the Mojave Desert. Yet, that's not what we're talking about in the sentence above, is it? Certainly, it is not, being that we don't eat "deserts."

Instead, we were looking for this word: "desserts"

"I ate a lot of desserts."

A "dessert" is a sweet concoction, usually eaten after a meal. Brownies, pies, cakes, crepes, muffins, puddings, and other sweet foods are common foods that are often classified as "desserts."

Certainly, the sentence above now makes sense for all who look at it. You may have known what you wrote, but that doesn't mean that others will know what you wrote. Even if they can figure out what you meant, the fact that you wrote it incorrectly doesn't make you or your business look good.

After all, if you messed up content on your website, does that mean you messed up content in your ebook, software, or other offer you are presenting on your website? You may think (even know) that you took more time to carefully construct your ebook, software product, or other offer, but what will your prospects think?

They may get the impression that if you are careless about the content on your site, you will be just as careless about your product offers, and if they think this, you can bet that this will negatively impact sales, as they will turn toward your competitors instead for the information they seek.

Now, try the following: Using your favorite word processor, input the sentence we mentioned above:

"I ate a lot of deserts."

Do you get a red line going underneath the word "deserts"? Chances are, you likely don't. Now, try using your spellchecker program to see if it catches it. What's the result? It probably didn't catch it, right?

As you can see, spellcheckers alone can't protect you from all spelling and grammar mistakes. Therefore, you need to keep some guidelines in mind to help you limit the mistakes as much as you can.

1. Say the sentence you want to write. (You can say it under your breath if you wish, but be sure to have your mind focus on each word). Just because you know what you mean does not guarantee that your prospects will know what you mean.
Additionally, your mind will often get ahead of your fingers when typing on a keyboard, so if you're not careful, you will leave out critical words that are needed to have the sentence make sense. Plus, as we've seen, a spellchecker will not always protect you from mistakes that you should catch. This is why it's vital you focus on every word you plan on writing, even if you need to speak the words outloud. Remember that every misspelled word or poor grammar mistake can impact on your credibility as a reputable and knowledgeable company.

2. If possible, try to not wait until the last minute to produce your content. When you do this, you tend to rush, making it more likely you'll make spelling and grammar mistakes in your writing. In addition, your content likely won't come out as clearly as you intended it to, which will make it more difficult for your visitors to absorb the content, utilize it, and see the value of it. Plus, you'd like to put it aside and go back to it after a break to see if everything flows as smoothly as you intended it to. Plus, you will often think of other topics you can include in your article to make the quality of the content even better.

While it's not always possible to do #2 where you can put your writing aside for a bit and come back to it, it's easier to accomplish this if you set aside a time for writing your site or blog content for several days or even a week in advance if you utilize a scheduling feature that you find in popular blogging platforms such as WordPress. This way, you won't feel the strain, stress, and rush of a deadline by waiting until the last minute to post content, thereby limiting the amount of mistakes your content will have.

3. Hire a quality copyeditor, which we will discuss in the next section.

Hiring a Quality Outsourcer

Certainly, as your site grows over time and you publish more and more content and produce more products/services for more and more clients, things can get more hectic. As a result, it's harder to keep up with everything. Outsourcing can be a great way to get the quality content you need, IF you can find one or more quality outsourcers for your writing needs.

You should keep the following things in mind to help you find that perfect outsourcer or outsourcers:

1. How much does he/she cost per article? Don't just go for the cheapest outsourcer you can find. There are other factors to take into consideration besides price.

2. Can he/she write fluently in English to where it makes sense and sound well?

3. Is he/she good at adhering to deadlines?

4. Is he/she willing to transfer all rights to you with no complications or
5. problems?

6. Is he/she able to display enough writing proficiency to emulate your voice? (Look to **PLR** section #2 above for more information on voice and why it's important to consistently display your own voice on your sites).

With finding quality copyeditors, questions 1, 3, and 4 apply, plus the following questions:

1. Does the copyeditor show how many words per page he/she charges? Be sure to know how many words your copyeditor considers as one page. After all, if a project has very small font, there will be more words on a page, whereas with larger fonts, there will be fewer words on a page. Many quality copyeditors will indicate how many words on average is on one page (the average is usually considered to be between 250-350 words for 12-point font in Times New Roman or Verdana font).

2. Is the copyeditor capable of emulating your own voice to appease your target market? It's imperative to find a quality copyeditor who can not only edit your work to where it flows smoothly and is grammatically correct, but that it emulates your voice and speaks to your target market effectively.

3. Sometimes, it takes time to find one or more quality outsourcers, but it is vital to help expand your business because, you, yourself, can only get so much done in one day. To expand your efforts and leverage your time to the maximum productivity of your business, it is vital for you to find one or more quality outsourcers you can trust to deliver the best quality content for your business.

About Joe Chengery

I own the copyediting/article writing/blog posting/copywriting site *JoeChengery.com*, a site that has been online since 2004. I am familiar with many aspects of online marketing, since I have also done online marketing and affiliate marketing since that time. This includes

- Copyediting
- Article writing
- Blog posting
- Copywriting
- Ebooks
- Info-publishing
- Email marketing
- Kindle publishing
- Press releases
- White papers
- App text publishing
- SEO
- Content creation
- Social media marketing
- More

I plan on writing books about different aspects of writing and online marketing in the future. If you wish to stay updated on my future books and plans (including info-publishing), please head to *JoeChengery.com* and sign up to the list there.

In addition, please feel free to connect with me on social media:

Facebook: http://ow.ly/pDXaO
Twitter: http://ow.ly/pDXgd
Google+: http://ow.ly/pDXlL
LinkedIn: http://ow.ly/pDXB9
Pinterest: http://ow.ly/pDXTe
Instagram: http://ow.ly/pDY9v (search for "joechengery" without the quotes)
Empire Avenue: via (e)JOECHENGERY

My Sites

http://www.joechengery.com – my article writing/blog posting/copyediting/copywriting site (Will be revised and updated in late 2013, early 2014; you can sign up for updates at the aforementioned link).

http://adcopysecrets.com – Coming Soon! Copywriting Tips and Services.

http://www.electronician.com – Coming Soon! All about technology and more.

http://jchengery.wordpress.com – *Digital Marketing Times* blog. All about how digital marketing is affecting our world today in terms of business, retail, and more.

More sites to come in the future. Connect with me and stay updated.

My Books

I am publishing on Amazon Kindle, and am also planning to publish via iBookStore, Google Books, and traditional publishing as well.

Please sign up to the list on JoeChengery.com, and I will keep you updated!

Personal Note

I was the copyeditor for this book in which you read these helpful techniques related to writing, marketing, publishing, personal development, and more. My personal thanks to Rachel Rofe for giving this honor to me.

Thank you for reading, and I hope to connect with you in the near future. Take care!

The New David & Goliath Battle – Small Business in the Internet Age

By Michael Claasz

They are lean, mean, and hungry for success... small businesses are on the move everywhere. Never before in history have opportunities for small business been greater. Examples abound of enterprises that grew from very humble beginnings and have blossomed into multimillion dollar companies in a very short period of time.

Michael Dell started selling computers he built in his College dorm room as a 19-year-old, reportedly with an initial cash investment of around $1,000. Today, Dell Computer Corporation is worth in excess of $50 billion dollars.

Mattel Inc., the makers of Barbie, set up shop in their garage in California, initially selling picture frames.

Although small businesses generally have limited resources available and a restricted ability to enjoy economies of scale, they do enjoy some significant advantages over their larger counterparts:

1. They are more agile and flexible – they can respond more readily to changes in market conditions or customer demands. This gives them the ability to tailor their offerings to meet individual customer needs. They are free from red tape and governance by committee; the owner, operator, or small management team can change tactics quickly as the need arises.

2. They are able to provide a more personalised service. A small business operator has more personal interaction with all aspects of the business than the nameless, faceless corporate personnel behind the façade of big business.

3. They are better able to establish authentic community connections, which can help to establish a fanbase and grow their business by word of mouth.

4. Their cost of operations can be lower, although small businesses are unlikely to exert the same negotiating power with suppliers.

5. The lack of red tape in operations provides an environment more conducive to creativity and innovation.

6. The ability to specialise and focus on market segments that may be too insignificant for large operators.

7. The sky is the limit. When starting from a small base, there is plenty of room for growth.

Despite these advantages, life is certainly no bed of roses for small business operators, and statistics on the rate of small business failure make for depressing reading. Nevertheless, there has probably never been a better time in history to be involved in small business.

The advent of the Internet has changed the small business landscape dramatically and irrevocably!

No longer is a small business restricted to a physical storefront, limited to serving customers in a small geographical area over a small number of hours each day. The businesses that grow and prosper are those that harness technology to their advantage.

A small business is no longer constrained by its geographical location. With a simple website, it has the ability to reach customers all around the world day and night. This may not seem like a significant advantage to a local business such as a restaurant or the local pet store, which by the nature of their products and services would still appear to be limited to serving the local area. However, a little thinking outside of the box may enable even these businesses to break out from a local business to a national or even an international operation. While it may not be feasible to deliver takeaway meals, goldfish and hamsters overseas, even these businesses are capable of developing spinoffs that could transcend local or national boundaries. For example, a restaurant could develop a series of recipe books that can consolidate and build its brand, while the pet store can produce pet training videos or other information products to complement its furry and feathery stock.

The Internet has caused many aspects of life to change dramatically and at a very rapid rate. Businesses that identify new, previously unknown opportunities and capitalise on them will reap the greatest rewards.

A lot of the technology required to take advantage of these changes is available cheaply or at no cost. This is another great advantage to small businesses. While a multimillion dollar company may spend thousands of dollars developing a corporate website, a small business can have a website up and running within hours or days at surprisingly little cost.

In the good old days, channels for broadcasting marketing messages were limited to print media, television, radio, or direct mail. These invariably involved considerable cost. However, today, there are countless avenues to promote small businesses online, many of them free or at low cost. Social Media has exploded in recent years, and many small businesses that have harnessed the power of word of mouth via positive social media have rocketed from obscurity to overnight mega successes.

Some of the most popular Social Media sites in no particular order are the following:

Facebook – http://facebook.com – With over a billion users, you'd probably have heard of Facebook even if you lived under a rock. No doubt, there will be Facebook-enabled rocks in the not-too-distant future. :-) Although Facebook has the reputation of a place to hang out and keep in touch with friends, it is nevertheless a place where serious business takes place as well. Businesses can set up fan pages at no cost on Facebook, providing a medium for customers to interact and leave feedback, "Likes," and recommend the business to their friends. The advantage of such social proof is that it is viewed as more authentic when coming from a friend – far more valuable than paid advertising. Facebook also provides the means to engage in very targeted advertising campaigns, which can be extremely economical if you know what you are doing.

Twitter – http://twitter.com – While this short messaging service provides bite-sized (140 characters or less) bursts of information on anything ranging from news to inane updates about the personal lives of its millions of users, it does serve a useful function if used appropriately. The ability to retweet messages can lead to rapid propagation of messages and the ability to reach audiences of several thousand if not millions in very short time frames.

YouTube - http://youtube.com – One of the most visited sites online. The love affair with video is very much alive. This is not just a site to watch cute cats and drunks trip over themselves; it's also where serious businesses establish and consolidate their brands and communicate with their markets. There are many success stories on YouTube. Perhaps one of the more well-known is the rise to popularity of the singer Justin Bieber. However, YouTube success is not restricted to the music industry; it can be used to benefit any business looking to get its message across.

Other popular social media sites include the following:

LinkedIn – http://linkedin.com
Pinterest – http://pinterest.com
Google Plus - http://plus.google.com

A common element in all of these social media sites is the ability to connect with large numbers of people quickly, easily, and relatively inexpensively. While social media can be invaluable to spread marketing messages and build brand recognition by creating a positive buzz, it is important to remember that negative feedback can also spread like wildfire through the same channels. A few negative comments can often outweigh a multitude of positive ones. Therefore, it will not suffice to maintain a haphazard approach to social media and reputation management. A structured and proactive social media strategy is vital to amplify the positive messages while minimising the damage from any negative ones.

One of the impediments to growth that a small business encountered in the past was a lack of skills in crucial areas of business and technology. This has once again been largely mitigated by the Internet. It is now no longer necessary to have all of your staff working within the same office or geographical area. Depending on the task, it may be possible to outsource across the globe to employ the most relevant skills needed at the best rates possible. Not only does this minimise staff costs, it also reduces the need for office space and infrastructure. Furthermore, online services such as Google Docs (http://docs.google.com) and Dropbox (http://dropbox.com) enable collaboration on tasks across the globe. Other services like Skype (http://skype.com) enable communication across the world and assist in monitoring staff progress.

More information about outsourcing can be found at: http://newbieheaven.com/outsourcing

Technology can also help to reduce or eliminate the drudgery of repetitive tasks. Relatively inexpensive software tools can be purchased for this purpose, or one of many online services can also help. One such service which has exciting potential is, "If this then that" - https://ifttt.com/ - which does exactly what the name suggests. If a particular defined condition is met, then another action that can also be defined will be performed automatically. For instance, every time a new post is made on the business blog, this could automatically be tweeted and posted to Facebook. While this may seem insignificant, the time savings can be substantial when these actions are performed frequently.

Needless to say, the Internet has simplified research. Information is available for product as well as market research often at the click of a button. However, ease of access to information can be a double-edged sword. The sheer volume of data can be overwhelming, and it may sometimes be hard to extract the bits of useful and relevant information amidst all of the irrelevant "noise." Small business survival is all about staying relevant and meeting the evolving needs of customers. For instance, with the proliferation of online video rentals and digital downloads, the old-fashioned DVD video rental store will quite likely need to reinvent itself and reposition its value proposition if it is to remain relevant and survive.

The Internet makes it possible for small businesses to specialise in micro-niches. In the pre-Internet age, when customers were drawn from a limited geographical area, it was harder for businesses to focus on very narrow niches because the small number of customers made it uneconomical. However, with a global Internet audience, even very specialised niches can have sufficient customers to make it feasible and economical for a business to serve them.

Much of the cutting-edge technological advances have become widely available online. These are no longer secrets reserved for the big operators alone. Hence, small business needs to be an early adopter of new technology if it is to maintain its competitive edge.

One such technological change is the increasing popularity of mobile devices. Consumers are increasingly relying on mobile devices, such as Internet-enabled phones and tablets, to browse the Net. In the "Always online" world we now live in, an ever-increasing percentage of searches are performed on devices other than desktops and laptops. This percentage varies from country to country, but statistics indicate that the percentage is consistently higher than 50%, and it is growing. Not only does this pose new challenges for small businesses, but it also opens up new opportunities. Challenges primarily arise due to the smaller-screen sizes of the mobile devices. A website that is optimised for standard desktop and laptop screens appears quite differently when viewed on a mobile device. Actually, the problem isn't so much that it appears differently; it's that very little of it appears on the screen at all, making scrolling and navigation extremely tedious. Visitors have very short attention spans, and tedious navigation is a real "no-no."

A website that isn't responsive or optimised for all devices will result in lost visitors and, consequently, lost business. On the other hand, a visitor using a mobile device presents an opportunity to the business. The visitor is already on a mobile phone a great deal of the time; the website should do all it can to entice him or her to take the next step and actually make phone contact. In order to achieve this, the mobile site should make navigation as simple as possible and prominently offer the ability to call the business by presenting a "tap to call" button, for instance. Optimising websites for multiple devices might sound complicated, but it isn't. Get a free assessment by visiting http://ausmobilesites.com/freeassessment.

Clearly there are significant advantages for small businesses operating in the Internet age. Those who choose to embrace technology and change with the times will prosper, while those who stubbornly resist change will struggle to survive.

Perhaps the small business owner's prayer should emulate the words of Reinhold Niebuhr: "God grant me the serenity to accept the things I cannot change, the courage to change the things I can, and the wisdom to know the difference."

About Michael Claasz

Michael Claasz is an accountant with over 25 years of experience and has a special interest in business process improvement and automation.

List Building Success Tips – Your Path to Consistent Online Income

By Paul Counts

One of the biggest questions I get asked is how you can generate stable, consistent income online. I always reply that focusing on building an email list is one of the best things you can do to generate income that lasts online. The largest online retailers use email marketing as a huge part of their online income. It has proven to be effective in about every niche market online and business model, including information products, services, and physical products.

Regardless of what you may have heard about the death of email marketing, it is still a vital way to reach people consistently. Email marketing will not be going anywhere fast either. New social media sites have made it easier than ever to reach more people and even help you build your email list up.

Although Facebook, Twitter, Google Plus, Pinterest, YouTube, mobile marketing, and many other opportunities have sprung to life lately that give you as a marketer great chances to reach more people, it doesn't replace email marketing. When you consider that all of these sites actually use emails to get you back onto their sites, that should be proof enough. You have probably gotten email notifications for new friend requests, new follows, new posts, and new photo groups that match your interests. They use email themselves because they know it is where people are located.

New technology has made it easier than ever to get your emails read as well. With all of the smartphones, iPhones, iPads, tablet computers, netbooks, and more, people can leverage email literally anywhere and on the go. Oftentimes, people get notifications on their mobile devices, letting them know new messages have arrived.

Step #1: What You Need to Start Building Your Email List from Scratch

The first step to building your email list is to make sure you have the right services and tools ready to go. You will need a domain name, Web hosting, an autoresponder, a HTML editor, and a FTP client software. If that confuses you, don't worry a bit. I will explain each part below.

Domain Name

A domain name is your website's name or online address. It is whatever goes before the .com, .net, or .org that you see on websites in your address bar. For example, the domain name for Amazon is Amazon.com.

You can acquire your domain name from a variety of sources. The two more popular places to go for domains are GoDaddy.com or NameCheap.com. You can also do a search for "domain names" on your favorite search engine.

Some things to look for in a domain name include being memorable, descriptive of your offer, and short without using more than one dash. You want to try to get .com domains first, but .net names are also good ones to look at.

It is not required to include your keywords in the domain, but can help tell your audience what it is you offer. It no longer is a huge benefit for search engine ranking purposes to have your keyword in your domain name. So, don't get too caught up in finding keyword-rich domains.

There is a neat little tool found at www.namemesh.com that allows you to put in your keywords, and it pieces together some domain name combinations to consider. They help you find some good domain names from your keywords that aren't taken yet. They also give you some nice domains to use that are fun to help create brands around your phrases.

Another place to not rule out for finding quality domain names is GoDaddy Auctions. You can visit https://auctions.godaddy.com/ and search for domains that are expiring soon. Just click on "Advanced Search" to narrow down your search to prices of say, $5 to $15, to find quality domains at good values. Use the keyword field to try and find domains that are related to your niche. Another option to consider checking is only those domains that offer a "Buy It Now" option. That means you could immediately buy the domain and end the auction before someone else gets it.

Web Hosting

Web hosting is where you store your website files to bring them live on the Internet. Just like you would pay for rent in a storage unit, you are paying a Web hosting company a set amount to rent Web space and to deliver your content to the Web.

Top Web hosting companies to consider include HostGator.com, BlueHost.com, and GoDaddy.com to name a few. There are many other Web hosting companies to consider. The main thing I look for when choosing a Web hosting company is 24/7 live customer support. I also would recommend looking at reviews online in webmaster forums to get honest opinions. Searching on your search engine alone oftentimes returns results for people promoting hosting as an affiliate. So, try to get the honest answers if you do research.

Another consideration you should look for is an easy-to-manage control panel.

HostGator and BlueHost have one that is called cPanel, and GoDaddy has their own easy-to-manage area. Also, look for Web hosting companies that offer accounts with multiple domains or unlimited domains, as well as those that offer a lot of space for a good price. Don't get stuck paying $50/month for Web hosting. You should be paying about $10 to $20 a month for a good shared hosting plan.

If you stick with the three companies above, you should be good.

Autoresponder

An autoresponder is a service that allows you to capture customer and subscriber emails, automatically promote to them, and also send them mass emails. The top companies stay up with the new changes and requirements in email marketing, which means more of your emails get seen and read by the audience you are targeting.

The two most popular companies used by online businesses include AWeber and GetResponse. You will also find some shopping cart companies like Nanacast or 1ShoppingCart that also include their autoresponders as part of their shopping carts.

I personally use AWeber, though, for my email marketing efforts. You want to look for an autoresponder company that allows you to set up multiple lists without charging more, as well as one that lets you send unlimited emails during the month. Some limit you to, say, 5,000 emails for the entire month. That may sound like a lot, but if you have an email list of 2,500 people, it means you can only send out twice before you are charged for every email after that.

Make sure you set up an account. These two recommended autoresponders will get you going for less than $20 the first month, and the price increases with the amount of subscribers. The good thing is that your expenses will grow minimally as your list does. So, you won't have to stress about not having the money because your list will be large enough to justify paying more.

Make sure you get an autoresponder because you will find later on that it is the number one investment you can make. If there was one payment that I would say I couldn't afford to miss each month, it is my autoresponder.

HTML Editor

You will want to get an email editor so you can create your landing page or squeeze page that will be used to generate visitors to your website. An HTML editor allows you to use a point-and-click software to create and edit Web pages without having to know how to do website coding.

At www.kompozer.net, you can get a free HTML editor that works on both PC and Mac computers. This is an open-source software that is completely free, and it is more than adequate for what you need it for. You will find it is comparable to many paid options.

If you visit www.paulcounts.com/template you can download a free squeeze page HTML template that can be used inside of KompoZer.

FTP Client Software

A FTP Client software, in a nutshell, transfers the files you work on from your computer to your Web hosting company so they can go live online. It is not essential, as some Web hosting companies let you upload files individually from within their control panel. It does make your life easier for uploading your sites, files, and content, however.

You can get a free FTP client called FileZilla by doing a search on your favorite search engine for "Filezilla download." This version works on both PC and Mac computers. So, it is everything you need.

Step #2: Creating Your Free Offer

The second step to building up your email list is to have a free offer, or an "ethical bribe," as it is sometimes called. It doesn't matter what your business model is; you need to give people a reason to opt into your email list. You can't simply ask them to sign up for your newsletter. People need to know what benefits they are getting.

You can use a newsletter as a giveaway, but it should be content-filled with real benefits to the person who gets access to your newsletter. You also need to be able to portray the benefits. Here are some ideas for what would work as a free giveaway product:

- Short Report – This can be a 7- to 15-page report that teaches people a specific topic within your niche market.
- Video Training – Give people access to a short 10- to 15-minute video training that helps people in your niche market. PowerPoint videos work well here. You want to try and give away some of your best content possible because it will quickly get people to see the value you can provide.
- Content-Filled Newsletter – Give a 10-part email series loaded with valuable content.
- List of Resources – Compile a list of different things in a PDF to peak people's interest: "Top 10 Ways to Save Money At The Grocery Store," "Top 5 Fat-Fighting Foods," "Top 25 WordPress Plugins"; you get the idea.
- Coupon Code – This works really well if you sell physical products in your

own store. You can give people a coupon code to save them money on a purchase in exchange for giving you their email address. This also can work for information products and services, but the idea giveaway for those business models is mentioned above.

Step #3: Creating a Converting Squeeze Page

Now that you have the tools and services you need, and you have your giveaway offer created, it is time to create your landing page or squeeze page. It is commonly referred to as a squeeze page because the goal of it is to "squeeze" information from the visitor.

The main function of a squeeze page is to give the website visitors two options. They can either grab the free offer you are giving to them or they can exit the page. You don't want to clutter a squeeze page with extra navigation beyond the necessary disclaimers below.

Good Headline

Your headline is super important. It is arguably the most important part of your squeeze page. The headline is what draws people into your squeeze page and helps entice them to put in their email address. Without a good headline, people will most likely bounce off of the page without taking the action you wanted.

When working to improve your opt-in rate, the best thing you can focus on is your headline.

Your headline should be easy to read and understand and include a desired benefit for those opting in. Typically, your headline is in bold red font so it stands out. Here are just a few examples of quality headlines that you could consider using.

"How to Get Rid of Tonsil Stones Naturally and Never Deal With Them Again..."

"Free Insider Video Reveals How to Generate Massive Video Traffic & Exposure Using YouTube"

"Instantly Save 15% Off of Your Next Purchase!"

Bullet Points

Bullet points do a really good job of summarizing your offer in a concise manner. The main thing about a high-converting squeeze page is that you keep it short after the headline. So, bullet points are just short, descriptive sentences that highlight certain elements of the offer you are giving away for free.

You only need three or four bullet points. You can do something like this:

Inside this free report, you will discover:

- How to finally lose that extra belly fat once and for all.
- What 5 super foods you should be eating on a daily basis to increase your metabolism.
- The one exercise I do 3 times per week to get me real results fast.

After your bullet points is your opt-in form.

Opt-in Form

The next element after your headline and bullet points is your opt-in form. To get this, you will use the code provided by your autoresponder service. Just follow their on-screen instructions to integrate this form. If you have a difficult time with this step of creating your opt-in form and placing it on your site, you can find someone on a site like www.fiverr.com to do it for you for a low cost. You can also find any number of videos on YouTube on this process.

Disclaimers

The final part of your squeeze page is your disclaimers. This section is below your opt-in form. It would include your "Privacy Policy," "Terms & Conditions," "Disclaimers," and "Contact Us" pages. Those are best found at the bottom in smaller font that is visible and readable, but not standing out. You will find having those extra pages not only protect you, but they also have been proven to increase your conversion rate.

If you want to download a squeeze page template that you can use to incorporate these elements, just go to www.paulcounts.com/template.

Step #4: How to Get Traffic to Build Your List

After you get your squeeze page loaded to your Web hosting company, it is time to start driving traffic to it. Without traffic, you won't get new leads that you can market to later by email. There are many different strategies for getting website traffic, but I have listed below a few of my favorite methods. If you want more traffic generation methods, you can download my free "25 Proven Traffic Methods" video course at www.paulcounts.com/proventraffic.

To accelerate your list building you want to use multiple traffic generation methods. Again, there are many other traffic methods, but these are a few of my favorites to use. Paid traffic strategies will almost always be quicker than free traffic methods. I am going to give you a variety of each. If you decide to include a one-time offer or introduce a special offer after they opt into your email list, you could really see how the paid methods would be worth it.

Blogging

Placing an opt-in form on your blog in the sidebar is another excellent way to get new subscribers. Another idea is to use a Lightbox pop-up that automatically opens up when people visit your site. You can get details on that within your favorite autoresponder service.

Even though we just talked about the importance of using a squeeze page, you don't want to forget to place an opt-in form on your blog. Another side tip is to link to your squeeze page from the navigation. Just have a link up there that says "Free Offer." It can link to your squeeze page.

This way, people can sign up on the sidebar form on your blog, as well as see it in the navigation.

The key to having a successful blog is to write relevant content on a consistent basis. It could be weekly, daily, or every other day, for example. The most important part is that the content is really good. Try for posts that have between 500 and 1,000 words. Try to embed YouTube videos or pictures you have rights to use into your blog posts to increase their appeal. You are better off to post a really good weekly post as opposed to a daily post with thin content.

Also, consider writing opinions on hot topics in your industry. You should keep up on news as it pertains to your marketplace. If there are new diet fads, you should critique those. If there is a big product launch in your niche with lots of attention, you can write a blog with an honest opinion on the offer. That review could generate you commissions and send traffic to your blog.

Just don't forget to build your list on your blog. You could be losing a lot of people if you aren't.

Facebook Pages and Ads

Facebook has just too much traffic to not be using it in your marketing efforts. There are a couple of things you want to do for getting traffic with Facebook. The first thing is that you want to set up a Facebook Page that goes with your niche market. On that page, make sure you include a link to your squeeze page.

Make relevant posts about your niche, and don't be shy about linking to other articles, blog posts, infographics, or videos that you find interesting. You want content to be on your page before you start promoting it too heavily.

You can start running Facebook ads straight to your Facebook page. Another thing to experiment with is sending paid traffic from Facebook ads directly to your squeeze page. Test to see which option gives you the best conversion rate and traffic for the cost.

Really focus on targeting people who have expressed an interest in your marketplace. Be careful with this form of traffic, as you can spend a lot of money without meaning to. Just experiment and keep an open mind.

Pop-Under On Sales Pages

This is one of the fastest and easiest ways to get targeted traffic to your squeeze page. You can use a pop-up software like Exit Splash that generates a pop-up window when people leave, asking them if they want to see a special deal.

When you are launching a product and have JV partners sending you large amounts of visitors, it only makes sense that you capture some of those people leaving your site. Let's say you get 10% of the people who exit to end up opting-in. So, with 1,000 visitors you will get 100 new subscribers. If you don't add your squeeze page as a pop-up offer on your sales pages, you are missing out in a big way.

Solo Ads

Solo ads work really well in the home business and Internet marketing niche, the fitness and health niche, and in the investment market. You can easily find solo ads in these niches, and you can find them in other niches as well. A solo ad is where you pay someone with an email list to send out your offer to their targeted subscribers.

You can buy solo ads based on clicks or just based on how big their subscriber list is. Solo ads work well for sending traffic to a squeeze page because the clicks are targeted. Typically, you will get between $0.30 and $0.50 per click. That is not bad for paid traffic, and the fact that you can generate lots of long-term income from your email list can make solo ads worthwhile.

To find solo ads, you can run searches on your favorite search engine with your niche name and the phrase "solo ads." You could also join a paid directory like the Directory of Ezines to find more.

Like any other paid advertising, it is good to test your results. The nice thing about solo ads is that you can start slowly and work your way up.

Video Marketing

Video marketing is an excellent way to generate traffic to your squeeze page. As you know, YouTube is one of the most popular sites online, and lately in search results, you are finding videos showing up in the top spots.

To effectively do video marketing, you should create 10 or so topic-based videos using PowerPoint slides and something like Camtasia (paid option) or CamStudio (free option). Keep the videos short, but informative. Use your keywords in the title of the video and in the description. Also, in your description, you should put the link to your squeeze page at the beginning. It should look like this: http://www.yoursquezepage.com. Make sure you include the "http://" in front of the link, as that makes it clickable below your video. It will drive you more traffic that way.

Google Alerts

This is an awesome traffic strategy. You may want to create a separate Gmail account before you start this. The method involves setting up Google Alerts for your main keyword phrases. Whenever new content is posted online about these topics you will get an alert. You can then quickly go to the site where the new content was posted and see if you can leave a comment. Most of the time, it is a blog post or something that allows you to leave a comment.

You would leave your comments about the content and include a link to your site in the field where they ask for the website. You can also mention in a few of the comments that you found the information in this report, video, etc. helpful and link to your squeeze page.

The key thing here is to be one of the first to comment. That will ensure you maximize your exposure. It is still a valid way to get lots of links out there.

Document Sharing Sites

You can take some of the PowerPoint content that you used to make the videos and turn the slides into a PDF. You can easily convert it by just saving the PowerPoint as a PDF. Make sure you include your squeeze page link in the PDF as well.

After you are done making it a PDF, just upload it to document sharing sites like www.docstoc.com and www.slideshare.net. Use your keywords when posting.

Forums

All niches online have forums. The key thing here is to find forums that allow you to include a signature line below each of your posts on the forum. You can get involved by answering questions people have. Of course, you can't just point them to your website in the thread, but your signature line below will include your link to the squeeze page. It is easy to get stuck on forums, so don't get too carried away here. Focus on spending like 15 minutes per day replying to threads and helping people. You will be surprised how fast it can add up to a lot of posts.

There are many other ways in which you can get website traffic. The key is to constantly be promoting that squeeze page using whatever methods you can think of. As your list grows, you can even consider doing promotional email swaps with quality businesses within your niche. This is where you pick a date and time to each send out each other's offers. So, find someone with a relevant offer, a good responsive list, and see if he/she will swap with you. It is a great, free way to generate new leads.

You don't want to do this method with just anyone though, as your leads could become pretty diluted.

Traffic is the key to growing that list up. Once you start getting traffic also, take a note of your conversion rate by going to the Web form section of your chosen autoresponder. It will often tell you how many impressions the form had and how many opt-ins it generated.

Generally, you want to aim for a conversion rate between 35% and 50% on your squeeze page. This means that if you get 100 targeted visitors, you should be getting 35 to 50 new subscribers.

Step #5: How to Create Long-Term Profits from Email List

It is really important that you have a plan to send emails to the people who are subscribing. The best thing you can do is to set up a series of follow-up messages that let people know who you are, deliver quality content to them, and, of course, present relevant offers that you found helpful. It could be your own products or products that you are promoting as an affiliate.

Also, look for opportunities and offers that you can promote as an affiliate. A few good networks to find affiliate offers for digital products are www.jvzoo.com and www.clickbank.com. Use the broadcast message feature to send broadcast messages to your list to profit.

The key thing to remember is that building your email list is one of the most important steps you can take to create a stable and consistent online income.

How To Present Your Ideas Convincingly

By Kristina Cunningham

www.kristinacunningham.com

Every time you want to introduce something at work, you have to sell someone on your idea. You have to talk or write about your idea so that other people can understand it and see the benefit of it. You have to come up with a proposal, either formal (in writing) or informal (conversation or presentation). You have to include enough information in your proposal to convince your readers or listeners that your idea is worthwhile, but not contain too much information so that they feel overwhelmed. How do you walk this tightrope and guarantee that *your* idea will get the go-ahead?

Your idea may be a new product, system, or process, or it may be a change to an existing product, system, or process. It may be a new way of doing business or even a new business itself.

Heilmeier's catechism provides a framework for you to distil the most important information about your idea so that you can convey it clearly and convincingly to your audience.

Heilmeier's catechism was developed by George Heilmeier when he was Director of the United States Defense Advanced Research Projects Agency (DARPA). He developed this standard set of questions for his program directors to use when reviewing new research and development projects and funding proposals. Heilmeier had a long history in technology development, having worked at RCA Laboratories on the development of the liquid crystal display (LCD), as well as significant periods with the United States Department of Defense overseeing long-range research and development planning. After leaving DARPA, Heilmeier also used his catechism when he moved to Texas Instruments and Bellcore. It has become a well-respected checklist for justifying ideas and new approaches.

Heilmeier's catechism consists of nine questions, which are generally written as:

1. What are you trying to do? Articulate your objectives using absolutely no jargon.
2. How is it done today, and what are the limits of current practice?
3. What's new in your approach, and why do you think it will be successful?
4. Who cares?
5. If you're successful, what difference will it make?
6. What are the risks and the payoffs?
7. How much will it cost?
8. How long will it take?

9. What are the midterm and final "exams" to check for success?

Each question, although simply asked, is a powerful trigger to help you encapsulate your idea.

What are you trying to do? Articulate your objectives using absolutely no jargon

Jargon gets in the way of communicating your idea. You use a word and assume other people know what it means or interpret it in the same way as you do. So often, this is not the case. People are often unwilling to ask for clarification if they don't understand completely. If they are then unsure what your idea is actually about or understand it to mean something else, they are unlikely to be persuaded to support your idea, let alone champion it.

While at DARPA, Heilmeier concentrated on six main themes:

1. Create an "invisible aircraft"
2. Make the oceans "transparent"
3. Create an agile, lightweight tank armed with a tank killer "machine gun"
4. Develop new space-based surveillance and warning systems based on infrared focal plane arrays
5. Create command and control systems that adapt to the commander instead of forcing the commander to adapt to them
6. Increase the reliability of our vehicles by creating onboard diagnostics and prognostics.

Imagine if the first objective had said, '*Create a "stealth aircraft",*' as it is now known. Possible things that they could have investigated meaning "stealth" are a silent aircraft or a small, super low-flying aircraft. Instead of using a potentially ambiguous word, they focused on the actual facet they were working on - creating an aircraft that was, in effect, invisible, that could not be seen by other technologies.

As well as not using jargon, it is vitally important that you can explain your idea simply. Only when you have grasped what is really important about your idea can you explain it in a clear, concise manner to someone else. It's like teaching someone else to do something. When you start explaining it, you realise all of the assumptions and unnoticed steps you take to do the job. To teach someone else thoroughly, you have to be aware of every tiny step in the process, understand where it fits in, and be able to communicate the whole process.

How is it done today, and what are the limits of current practice?

Before you can move anywhere else, you need to know where you are now.

Because where you are now sets the criteria for the first steps you can take.

Questions to think about here are

- Why are improvements needed?
- What currently works?
- What doesn't work?
- What could work better, and how could it work better, if we changed things?
- What are the consequences of doing nothing?

The aim is to define *why* something needs to change, to provide the reason to move from the current state. If everything works fine, why change it? In Australian colloquial – "If it ain't broke, don't fix it."

What's new in your approach, and why do you think it will be successful?

Some versions of Heilmeier's catechism write this question as "why now and not last year or 10 years ago?" This question aims for an understanding of the outside factors that may affect your idea. You need to do your research and provide evidence that this is the right time and place for your idea to come to fruition.

Has your idea been tried before and failed? What happened? If it failed before, why will it work this time? What has changed? Is your idea or approach sufficiently different so that it will succeed this time?

If someone has already succeeded with your idea, do you need to continue? Is your idea different enough to warrant proceeding?

If no one has done it before, why not? What has kept other people from coming up with a similar idea? What particular combination of circumstance, timing, technology, and any other relevant factor has contributed to the idea being feasible now?

If your idea requires certain technologies or products, are they available and in ready supply?

If your idea requires input and support from other people, are they available, do they have sufficient training, and are they willing to support you in this?

You may need to consider doing some preliminary work, potentially doing a small-scale proof of concept.

Getting to the heart of "why this idea?" and "why now?" can require a significant amount of research and soul-searching. However, when you have done it, you have taken a large step towards justifying your idea.

Who cares?

Who is going to be positively impacted by your idea? If the idea has no benefit for anyone or doesn't make anyone's lives better in any way, then what purpose does it have?

Define everyone who will gain some kind of benefit from the implementation of your idea. This could be

- you
- your team
- your business
- your customers
- the good of society
- anyone else you can think of.

If appropriate, use individual names. You should be able to present the benefits of your idea to these people and gain their support. The more champions other than yourself that your idea has, the easier it will be to convince other people of its benefits.

If you're successful, what difference will it make?

The angle that this question is coming from is to look at not just what the new implementation will do, but to bring out the positive outcomes to the users who are being impacted by it. You're looking at more than the features and functions that your idea offers. This is where you define the real benefits that your idea will bring when it is fully implemented. Other questions that can help you to define this are

- What does success look like?
- How will we know when we've implemented this properly?

Too often, people make changes to things without really defining what their endpoint is. Without knowing where you're going, you will never know if you have successfully arrived there or not.

List all things that will be improved as a result of your idea being implemented.

Be as concrete as possible. Instead of saying, "people will be more productive," quantify it in some way and provide evidence. For example, "the accounts team will be 20% more productive, as they do not have to maintain data in two different systems, which currently accounts for 25% of their time."

Sometimes, you may not have hard data, or your idea may be for something so new that it will completely revolutionise how people do things, such as the first iPod, for example. In this case, tell a story. Build a visual picture around how people will interact with your idea, showing the potential benefits.

What are the risks and the payoffs?

Identify the risks of implementing your idea. Also, identify any mitigation strategies that you can put into place to reduce the impacts of these risks. Risks can cover all areas, such as

- financial
- time frame
- reputation
- technology
- business impact

It is also relevant to consider the risk of *not* implementing the idea. What impact could it have on your business if everyone else is doing something similar and you do not? Sometimes, there is little risk in moving forward and significant risk in doing nothing.

As well as the risks, you must also identify the rewards, the payoffs, that will result from the idea's implementation. These may not be purely financial. Any area where there is potential for risk also has potential for reward. Make sure you consider all of them. It may still be beneficial for your business to implement an idea at reasonable financial risk, yet with potential to build your reputation as an innovator and gain new sources of customers.

Demonstrate why the potential rewards are worth the risks. Consider identifying alternate strategies as a means of reducing the risk while still achieving a reasonable payoff.

How much will it cost?

What is the cost to implement this idea? And even more importantly, what is the cost of *not* implementing the idea?

Remember, costs are not just about money. They cover

- time
- money
- people
- opportunity cost

If you're finding it difficult to come up with concrete costs, research how much similar projects like this one cost. You can look for ballparks within your own business or across your industry.

How long will it take?

This can often be a difficult question to answer. If you don't have definite figures, provide a range of times. Include any assumptions that you make in defining your time frames.

In the same way as cost, you can look at how long projects like this one have previously taken.

What are the midterm and final "exams" to check for success?

The longer the time period to implement your idea, the more important it is to check along the way that you're on the right track. There's no point waiting until the very end before you find out that you didn't hit your objective.

Make sure that you factor in key points along the way where you can review your progress. At each of these key points, you must include a set of criteria that you can review your progress against. If you haven't set criteria, and you just look at how far you've come, then you're wasting your time. Your criteria must be SMART.

- Specific – the criteria must be clear and unambiguous. It needs to identify what the criteria is, the reasons why it needs to happen, who evaluates the criteria, any location where it needs to happen, and any requirements or constraints.
- Measurable – you must be able to determine whether you met the criteria or not, and if not, by how much.
- Attainable – the criteria should be a stretch, to encourage you to put effort

into reaching it. However, it must not be so far out of reach that it becomes a disincentive.

- Relevant – the criteria must be relevant to the outcome you want to reach. If you are aiming to build an invisible aircraft, setting criteria to build a faster car is not relevant. The criteria must also be appropriate for where you are in the implementation. When you are at the design stage, it is not appropriate or helpful to measure your progress against a manufacturing criteria.
- Timely – the time frame in which the criteria must be met. You are already doing this by assigning your criteria to key points in your progress.

Conclusion

When you can successfully answer all the questions in Heilmeier's catechism, you are well on your way to presenting a convincing story that will have people acting on your ideas. You will know intimately why this idea is needed and relevant, what benefit it will bring to people, be able to explain it clearly and succinctly with no jargon, and be able to answer any question put to you.

Convincing people that your idea is worthwhile is about giving them the information they need, in as simple a way as possible. And then being able to back it up, by answering all their questions. Heilmeier's catechism allows you to do that.

Next time you need to present an idea, use Heilmeier's catechism as the basis for your proposal.

About Kristina Cunningham

Kristina Cunningham loves helping people find better ways to communicate and put forward their ideas. Using her skills in writing and business analysis, Kristina wants to help you present your ideas as convincingly as possible.

Kristina works across the whole spectrum of business – enterprise level, business, and system analysis. She knows just which dial must be adjusted to maximise performance. Kristina makes sense of the world, pulls it apart, sees a better configuration, and creates it.

Professionally, Kristina has been working in the IT industry in the areas of analysis, testing, user interface design, and technical writing. Kristina works with systems and processes, both human- and computer-based.

Kristina is based in Canberra, Australia. To contact Kristina, please visit http://www.kristinacunningham.com.

Become The Authority And Double Your Business!

By Krizia (Miss K) de Verdier

In a hyper-competitive marketplace that has no borders and that runs full steam 24/7, the only way for business owners to remain on top is by becoming that type of authority that dethrones all competition.

It's not an easy task because there are so many moving parts to creating a strong brand presence and establishing yourself as the authority. That said, if you put in place a solid marketing plan and you execute it, you'll have created the catalyst that will take your status in your industry to levels you never thought possible.

It's one thing to build a business (even if it's a very successful business); it's quite another to become an authority.

If your goal is to serve your ideal clients while churning a hefty profit, you'll really want to devise the type of strategic plan that will ensure that you become the "only logical choice" in the mind of your ideal clients.

With that in mind, you'll have to structure your business very differently from other business owners who don't have the desire to be seen as the trusted and credible source in their respective industries.

If you've been in business for a while, and you're looking to redefine yourself and start earning the money you deserve, you'll gain by fine-tuning your marketing and brand strategy to help set you apart.

Think about it: In every industry, there's a leader – that person who stands out, that person who gets called by the media, that person who gets paid to speak at major events, that person who really doesn't ever have to chase after clients because their authority status has clients flocking to them.

If you were to close your eyes, I'm sure there are faces that pop up immediately in your mind.

There Are Many Reasons Why You Would Want To Establish Yourself As The Authority

If you're like most business owners, you dislike having to "sell yourself," but selling is intimately tied to your ability to own a profitable business.

When you establish yourself as an authority, you don't have to deal with a lot of the concerns less successful business owners have to deal with. It's that simple.

By being seen as the authority in your industry, you'll take advantage of the following perks:

1. Never sell yourself again. The beauty about being recognized as an authority and credible source is that you no longer have to keep "selling" yourself or your business. Once you're perceived as that authority, people will automatically assume what you sell or offer is the best, and they'll buy in droves!

2. The media loves to quote authorities. The media is always looking for authority figures for quotes to give credibility to hot topics. By clearly establishing yourself as the authority in your field, you make the media's job so much easier, and they'll reward you by inviting you to share your expertise.

3. People won't question your prices. People will penny-pinch a low-cost product or service, but if you start charging several thousands of dollars for your services, people feel like it's money well-spent because they'll be buying from "an authority."

4. Charge more. Once you start being quoted by bigger media outlets, you can easily double the prices of your services.

5. Sell way more. When you get interviewed by major media outlets, you'll quickly notice a serious spike in your sales activity because viewers will be scrambling to quickly find you on the Internet and buy pretty much anything you're selling.

6. Get more speaking engagements. The Internet has created many successful businesses because it's not only easy to reach ideal buyers on the Internet, but it's also quite easy to open yourself up to the world. That said, you create serious bonds when you speak in front of an audience; there's nothing quite like it. Once event organizers start seeing you as the authority in your field, they'll invite you to speak at more events, and you'll be exposed to a brand new group of potential clients.

7. Get paid to speak. You know your authority status has hit a fever pitch when you start getting paid to speak at events! That's when magic happens because, you'll be seen as the "well-respected" speaker who will dazzle a crowd, and the event organizers who invite you to speak will do a major marketing push to ensure they sell out of seats for the event and, therefore, allow them to justify your fees. All this publicity and marketing will only be beneficial for you in attracting a brand new crowd of potential clients.

8. Exclusive invitations to powerful mastermind groups. This might be the most understated benefits of becoming an authority. Once you start establishing your mark, you'll get approached by other very successful people in your industry who want to invite you to join their exclusive mastermind groups. These groups usually recruit the smartest minds in your industry, and the knowledge you'll gain, as being part of these types of groups, will transform your business.

9. Get invited to be a part of lucrative promotions. These exclusive mastermind groups you'll be invited to will give you the opportunity to create new business partnerships that can help promote your products or services to a much wider audience.

10. Never have to chase after new clients ever again. This is one of the biggest perks of being seen as "the authority" – clients literally are tripping all over themselves to work with you. You no longer have to "sell" yourself or "sell" the reason why you're the best person for the job; your authority status speaks for itself! Imagine getting loads of emails and voice messages every day from prospective clients, dying to work with you. That's the typical day of business owners who are seen as the authority in their respective industries.

How Do You Become An Authority?

Becoming an authority has its definite perks, but the question that remains is, "How exactly do you go from being an average business owner to becoming an authority?"

World-class performance coach Anthony Robbins has said that *"success leaves clues,"* and nothing could be truer when it comes to finding ways to establishyourself as an authority.

The fastest and easiest way for you to become that instant authority is to model what other very successful people in your industry do to build their business.

If you dissect the business model of the top industry leaders in your sector, you'll notice a few very distinctive elements to their business that have helped establish themselves as the authority.

12 Ways Successful People Become The Authority

1. Strong Web presence. I don't want to sound harsh or critical, but the reality is that there are plenty of businesses out there running websites that do a serious disservice to their brand image. Whether it's because their designs haven't been updated in the past decade, their sites don't render properly in a mobile environment, or their sites are not set to capture leads to help build their databases, it's important to be aware of the pitfalls that affect both beginner and more experienced website owners.

Although there are hundreds of mistakes most site owners make, the top ones include:

a. Outdated site. A site that looks like it was created in 2004 will not instill confidence in your potential clients that you're keeping up with the trends. You won't get too many members of the media knocking at your door because your site does nothing to showcase your credibility. You might think it's a minor thing, but your website is one of the first interactions people will have with you and you want to make sure you send out a strong message.

b. Not capturing leads. This is a crying shame! When you build your database of raving fans, it becomes a lot easier to connect with them and to continue to foster a solid relationship with them. If you want your website visitors to do something (for example, buy your products or sign up for your email newsletter), you've got to tell them to do it! Adding strong call-to-action messages to support your site's primary goal (capture the name and email of your potential ideal clients) is an important part of running a profitable website.

c. Not having a video. Nothing brings to life a website than a video! You can spend a lot on a professional video, or you can simply start by shooting a quick welcome video using your own equipment. A video brings a dimensionality that a photo cannot. Your video will also make it easier for your potential clients to better connect with you and, that, in the long run, boosts your credibility factor.

d. Making it difficult for people to reach you. Not having a clear way for people to contact you is honestly like telling the world you really aren't interested in expanding your business. Make sure to include a way people can call, email, or start a service ticket in order to reach you.

e. Colour combination that's impossible to read. If your site has a black background and red font, it's like saying to people, "I really don't want you to get to know me." The colour and font combination is a crucial element in terms of creating a website that establishes you as an authority and serves as a client magnet. You always want to have a clear and professional site that speaks volumes about your authority status, and the best possible combination is a white background with a black font. Make sure the font is big enough that it's easy for anyone to read!

f. Using a Flash intro. A flash site looked really cool in 2006, but that's not the case anymore. Flash sites can be quite distracting and often lower the visitor's experience (this is another way of saying, "People won't stay on your website for too long"). Flash might sound fancy, but it's annoying, and it's not the best if you want people accessing your site via their mobile devices (currently, most people access the Internet via their mobile devices, and you don't want to alienate that audience). Creating a simple and clear website on WordPress will better serve your business.

A website should be way more than a brochure. Your site needs to be engaging, it needs to let people know why you're the authority in your industry, and why it is so important for them to want to learn more from you.

2. Cohesive presence online. Once you've established the type of brand identity (a.k.a. look and feel) that serves your business, you need to make sure it's the same on every single platform you use to market & promote your business – from your business card, to your social media presence, to your offline marketing efforts. Nothing will kill a brand faster than having different identities. Think of Nike – you no longer have to see the "swoosh" to know it's a Nike advert. There's a look and feel to everything Nike does. The same goes for Apple. Apple has been a leader in establishing a clear distinctive feel for its company, and its brand is reflected in every aspect of its marketing and customer service.

3. Brand presence on social media. Your brand presence on social media doesn't stop with a few banners and photos. It also encompasses the type of content you share on social media. As the authority in your field, there's a certain expectation your raving fans have of you, and they expect the content you share on social media will reflect your in-depth knowledge in your field.

4. Pick one or two social media platforms of choice. As an authority, you have a busy schedule, and that means you won't be able to be proficient at engaging with your fans on every new social media platform that pops up. I'd recommend you follow Guy Kawasaki's example and focus only on one or two social media platforms of choice and outsource activities on your other platforms. The person who takes care of your other social media platforms can simply follow the style you've established on those platforms where you are very active. This strategy allows you to have a strong presence on the most important social media outlets without having to spend half of your day posting on them.

5. Master email marketing. Social media is quite powerful, but it doesn't trump the relationship you build with your list of raving fans and clients. Email marketing is extremely important in helping you communicate on a regular basis with your audience, and this will have extremely positive effects on the growth of your business.

6. Show appreciation to clients. People want to be acknowledged! It's one of the fundamental needs we have as humans. Your success is attached to your being able to show your appreciation to your clients. It doesn't have to be complicated. It can be simple emails or you can get a designer to create a cool graphic you can share on social media. A heartfelt "thank you" goes a long way, and it also separates you from the rest. When you stand out for doing exceptional things, you build your credibility factor faster.

7. Rely on strong JV partners to help expose you to new raving fans.
When you work with Joint Venture (JV) partners, they'll showcase you as an authority that deserves the attention of their own fanbase. This is a powerful way for you to be seen as the authority in front of a brand new crowd of potential fans and buyers.

8. Turn extensive knowledge and experience into lucrative products. One of the fastest ways of sealing your authority status is by educating others on what you know and master. Digital products and live conferences are excellent ways for you to package and sell your knowledge.

9. Leverage offline marketing opportunities. Direct mail might not be as "cool" as it once was, but a lot of very smart business owners are establishing a new level of authority by popping up in their ideal clients' mailboxes. The advantage of leveraging direct mail, personal phone calls, and networking events is that you bypass spam filters, Gmail's new policy of filtering promotional emails. Add in the fact that catching people's attention online is trickier today than ever before, and utilizing offline marketing opportunities wherever possible will differentiate your business as being the authority in your industry.

10. Find ways to become newsworthy and attract the attention of big media. There are many ways for you to leverage current news to increase your likelihood of becoming newsworthy. If you see a major event taking place in the media, turn that to your advantage by sharing your opinion on video and sharing that video to the widest possible audience.

11. Speak and connect with a live audience as often as possible. You cannot ignore the potential viral power of establishing a strong online presence, but you also must continue to leverage speaking opportunities whenever you can. People are likelier to quickly want to work with you when they meet you in person and when they get to hear how your expertise can help them improve their lives or businesses.

12. Become an author to be seen as the ultimate authority. A book screams "authority," "credibility," and "trust-worthiness" like nothing else. People will automatically assume that you must know your stuff very well, and it's so valuable that you collected it all between the pages of a book! The book is a powerful marketing strategy that puts you at an unfair advantage compared to your competitors. Being a published author not only establishes you as the authority, but it opens doors that would have never opened before. If you write a book that becomes a best-selling book, then you've just created the type of marketing machine that you can leverage to further your business in a big way.

Focus On What You Do Best And Outsource The Rest!

I know at the beginning that the 12 strategies I just shared with you seem overwhelming, and you might feel defeated even before taking the first step, but it's like everything else in your business – you have to take it one step at a time.

Too many ambitious business owners who strive to change their income level by becoming the authority feel they need to absolutely be able to master all of these marketing strategies to see any success, but that's simply not true.

Nothing brings me more satisfaction than transforming my clients' businesses and upping their online presences in order to establish themselves as the authority in their respective industries.

Many of my clients have tried to elevate their games on their own, but the reality is that you cannot master every aspect of building a successful business – none of us are that talented.

If you look at successful people like Sir Richard Branson, Oprah Winfrey, Anthony Robbins, Jack Canfield, Guy Kawasaki, and even Mark Zuckerberg, a.k.a. CEO of Facebook, they all focus on what they do best and then either outsource the rest or hire the right person to help them further specific initiatives.

I always love using Facebook as an example because, although Mark Zuckerberg is the brainchild behind the massive empire that is Facebook, he's hired experts like COO Sheryl Sandberg to further his empire and help him better dominate his industry.

I absolutely am a self-confessed research geek. When I dive into a topic or when I have to master an industry in order to help one of my clients, I learn everything there is to learn. Just like the extraordinarily successful business owners I've listed above, I've learned to focus on what I do best and outsource everything else.

Outsourcing can seem scary because it's an extra expense in your business and if you've been the only one running the show, you might feel that there's a sense of losing control, but nothing could be further than the truth if you want to seriously amp-up your profits in the hopes of doubling your business in the coming year.

Your role is to really focus on how you can serve this world best, and you can hire people who can help you establish the type of marketing strategies that will take you from being average to becoming the person everyone wants to work with!

Becoming the authority has its advantages, and a serious boost in notoriety and revenue will definitely change the course of your business and your personal life.

About Krizia (Miss K) de Verdie

Krizia (aka Miss K) is an Online Marketing Consultant, Book Marketing Consultant, Speaker, & Author!

Krizia is known as the "Authority Maker" because she takes her clients from near obscurity to becoming the person everyone talks about.

As an Online Marketing Consultant, Krizia helps her clients create a strong brand presence that acts as a veritable client magnet.

Krizia helps successful business owners become authors and the instant authority in their markets by enabling them to gain the kind of credibility that allows them to attract new clients easier and faster.

She also helps budding authors master book marketing and build a business behind the book to ensure long-term and recurring revenues.

Krizia has been featured in a two-page article in *Forbes* magazine.

She's also been featured in Social Media Examiner, The Globe & Mail, The Huffington Post, and Tech Journal.

She's spoken alongside Guy Kawasaki, Randi Jayne Zuckerberg (sister of Facebook CEO Mark Zuckerberg), and Sheryl Sandberg, COO of Facebook.

You can find out more about Krizia by visiting her websites: http://www.BookPromotionHub.com and http://www.missKrizia.com

You can connect with Krizia on social media: http://about.me/misskrizia

Your Sales Presentations Stink!

By Scott Frothingham

I say, "Your sales presentations stink!" to a lot of new clients... because it is the truth. And there's a good possibility that I would say it to you, too, because, chances are, *your* presentations also need some serious help. I'm not saying that you're not closing business; I'm suggesting that you should be and could be selling a lot more if you would take a hard look at how your presentations position you to the opportunities with your prospects.

The majority of sales presentations are sadly lacking and typically run through three stages:

The Introduction, which usually is not given enough attention because the majority of salespeople can't wait to get into their comfort zone by diving right into talking about their product/service.

The Information Dump, which relies heavily on features and benefits of the product/service being pitched and the shortcomings of the competition (and typically includes wa-a-a-ay too much information).

The End, which is usually too brief and often lacks a strong call to action.

This typical presentation can yield sales, but misses opportunities and leaves dollars on the table.

The Solution? The 5-Point Presentation

My 5-Point Presentation format has been field-tested and proven effective year after year. I have used it successfully myself, and I have trained others who can attest to its ability to keep you moving forward in a logical progression that turns prospects into customers.

The concept is so simple, that, once you have it as part of your sales arsenal, you can use it extemporaneously to make a light pitch in an informal setting; or you can use it along with prepared sales materials in a complex formal presentation in a corporate board room.

The 5-point presentation is a quick, clear, and concise way to communicate with a client and has consistently produced successful sales by:

Keeping your presentation and thoughts organized, as you move through the information that gives the prospect what he/she needs to make a good decision. By staying in the prescribed order of the five points, you never run the risk of bouncing from subject to subject and losing the momentum of the presentation.

Positioning you as a problem-solver, elevating your position from outsider to team member.

Building your credibility. When you demonstrate to a customer that you listened to him/her during the initial information-gathering call(s), and when a customer realizes you've done your homework, your credibility is greatly improved.

Encouraging good preparation, which builds confidence. In the meeting, you face your customer as an equal.

Positioning you to ask for action each and every time.

And, perhaps most importantly, the 5-Point Presentation has been designed to follow the typical buying decision paradigm used by most humans: First, we identify the need and then flesh out the details of what is necessary to answer that need. Then we look for options for filling that need. Finally, we look at those options and select the one that we feel best fills that need as originally identified and detailed. Follow the 5 Points and see how they position you and your products/services as the best option to purchase.

The 5 Points

Setting up a strong call to action, the 5 Points keep you moving in an orderly, logical, step-by-step manner.

1. The Re-statement

Based on your information-gathering efforts with the prospect and from outside research, what does the prospect want/need to change, improve, avoid, or fix? What conditions exist that position the prospect as ready to change his/her current direction. NOTE: the more specific to this prospect's business, the more effective your presentation will be.

2. The Fix

Based on experience, research, and what the client tells you: What is an effective way to efficiently change, improve, or fix what was identified in The Re-statement?

3. The Current Approach

What the customer is currently doing to address that want/need (or what other options they are/might be considering) and why that is not the best choice for addressing that want/need that was identified in The Restatement.

4. Your Product/Service

How your product/service specifically addresses the prospect's want/need (identified in The Restatement) in an effective and efficient manner and is the best choice to address that want/need.

5. The Plan

The best way for the prospect to access your product/service to address the want/need that was identified in The Restatement.

Here is an example of the 5-Point Presentation at its most basic:

Ms. Prospect, based on our discussion of last week, by next year at this time, you need to see your gross revenue pacing at a 17% year-over-year increase. Considering the experience level of your sales team, proper training to increase client acquisition and retention, plus increasing closing ratios, should be the most effective and efficient long-term answer. You are currently considering having your team attend quarterly two-day sales events being offered by a national sales training firm. Although these training sessions can be effective, among other weaknesses, they tend to be so structured and generic that they are difficult to customize to a specific sales team's needs. At www.FastForwardIncome.com, we specialize in team-administered programs that yield impressive measurable results while, at the same time, being incredibly flexible and cost-effective. By investing less than the cost of sending just one of your salespeople to only one of those generic sessions, The 15-Minute Sales Manager™ can give you a whole year of weekly sales training that will be customized to your company's specific needs without taking your team off the streets for two days every quarter. Give me the go-ahead, and I will have The 15-Minute Sales Manager™ in the hands of your sales manager before the end of business today. It will come with fully-detailed implementation instructions so your sales training can start next week. Can we get moving forward on hitting your gross revenue numbers?

Broken down:

The Re-statement: *Ms. Prospect, based on our discussion last week, by next year at this time, you need to see your gross revenue pacing at a 17% year-over-year increase.*

The Fix: *Considering the experience level of your sales team, proper training to increase client acquisition and retention, plus increasing closing ratios, should be* *the most effective and efficient long-term answer.*

The Current Approach: *You are currently considering having your team attend quarterly two-day sales events being offered by a national sales training firm. Although these training sessions can be effective, among other weaknesses, they tend to be so structured and generic that they are difficult to customize to a specific sales team's needs.*

Your Product/Service: *At www.FastForwardIncome.com, we specialize in team-administered programs that yield impressive measurable results while, at the same time, being incredibly flexible and cost-effective.*

The Plan: *By investing less than the cost of sending just one of your salespeople to only one of those generic sessions, The 15-Minute Sales Manager™ can give you a whole year of weekly sales training that will be customized to your company's specific needs without taking your team off the streets for two days every quarter.*

A Strong Close: *Give me the go-ahead, and I will have The 15-Minute Sales Manager™ in the hands of your sales manager before the end of business today. It will come with fully-detailed implementation instructions so your sales training can start next week. Can we get moving forward on hitting your gross revenue numbers?*

That's a simple, off-the-cuff version to help you grasp the concept. Imagine it on a larger scale with more detail and presentation materials to support it. More than just theory, I've seen it work too many times to keep count... not only for me, but for people I have trained through www.ScottFrothingham.com.

When putting together a more formal/complex presentation, group your 5-points into three sections: the Opening, the Body, and the Closing.

In the Opening, in which you set up the presentation, you have two objectives: Get the attention of the decision maker(s) and build rapport. Even if the opening is only a minute, it serves as a pivotal moment and, perhaps, be the most important minute of the presentation. Point 1 kicks off the presentation by hitting the bull's eye of a want or need that is at the top of the prospect's priority list.

In the Body (Points 2, 3, 4), every point must relate the information needed by the decision maker(s) to accomplish your objective(s); detail the plan that you are recommending.

In the Closing (Point 5), summarize the key points and benefits, ask for an action from the decision maker(s).

Let's take a more detailed look at the points and how they work together to move a prospect through the typical buying decision model -- from identifying a want/need, to considering options to address that need, to selecting the best option (you) and making a purchase.

The Opener/Point One: The Re-Statement

The Re-statement is a logical start for your presentation; it is a strong positioning tool to reiterate or restate key facts gleaned from your information-gathering meeting(s) with the prospect. By repeating the information that deals specifically with those areas of the prospect's business that s/he wants/needs to grow, avoid, or solve, you will enter into a unique position with that client as a person who actually listens and understands. This will help to build the credibility you need so s/he will believe you and in your commitment to improve her/his situation.

This step is the affirmation of the commitment you made during your information gathering call(s)... the proof that you are concerned with the client's success and that you are willing to become a member of his/her team.

Various Openers

Based on our discussion, we determined that...

This presentation is designed to show you how to...

According to our last meeting, it was agreed that...

Based on our conversation last week, you suggested that...

There are many other opening lines you can use... whichever one you choose, it will commit the customer to his/her statements and hold him/her to those statements. It also shows that not only were you listening, but also that you *understood* what was said, and that you are focused on helping, not just pushing a product.

The Relationship Between the Points

The Content of Point Two: The Fix

There should be nothing in this section that doesn't relate directly to what the prospect wants/needs to change, improve, avoid, or fix (as offered in Point One).

The Content of Point Three: The Current Approach

Be careful to be informative and helpful in Point Three. You are *not* telling the prospect that s/he has made bad decisions on the current/planned approach...

you are indicating why they might not be the best choice as directly related to Point Two. You are also setting up the idea that your product or service is a *better alternative* (for reasons that you will give in Point Four).

Be brief and to-the-point. In Point Three, you suggest that the competitors being used (or considered) by the client are very good, but perhaps serve another business's needs better than your prospect's, and that they should play a less important role (if any role) in this prospect's situation.

The Content of Point Four: Your Product/Service

This is what the customer needs to know about your company and/or your company's products/services. Point Four relates *exactly* back to Point Two.

Leave out irrelevant facts and features. Just demonstrate how your company matches up with The Fix we pinpointed as the answer to what they want to grow, solve, or avoid. Make sure that each point made directly answers the client's primary concern as stated in Point One.

The Content of Point Five: The Plan

Now the prospect knows that you understand their wants/needs and that your product/service is the first choice for addressing him/er. Also, you have shown him/her the commitment you're willing to make to become a member of his/her team to address those wants and needs.

In Point Five, you show them how to most effectively use your company's resources to specifically address those wants and needs. It's the tactical plan focused on responding to Point One. The plan becomes the logical conclusion to the thought process of identifying a want or need, generating alternatives, and then selecting the best.

Each element of the plan must be detailed with specifics, and if there are multiple levels to solutions you are providing, you need to explain each in totality, including the reasoning behind the selections.

The Close/Call to Action

To this point, more than selling, you have been helping the prospect make a good, informed decision. Now you have to help him/her commit to that good decision with a call to action. Summarize the key points and benefits and ask for the order.

One Quick Tip

When putting together an important presentation, watch out for information overload. The 5-Point Presentation format helps you organize and streamline, but after putting together your first draft, go through every step (especially Point Three and Point Four), testing all of the information with this question: "Does this person need this information in order for me to accomplish my objective(s)?"

If the answer is, "No," excise it from the presentation. Remove it, but don't delete it; save it to a "talking points" sheet to bring with you to the presentation. Even though it didn't pass the tough "Does this person need..." question during editing, you did put it in there for a reason. During the presentation, you might not need your "talking points" sheet, but, then again, you might. It'll be reassuring to have the information at your fingertips.

A Final Thought

As discussed, you want to increase your sales team's closing ratio in order to generate a higher gross income, and to do that, you need the sales team to make more effective presentations. You indicated that the presentations your salespeople are making tend to be overly long and are not tightly focused.

A presentation format that keeps the salesperson focused and helps them follow the typical buying decision paradigm while leading the prospect to see that the best option to select is your product/service is the most logical and effective format to use.

Although they are effective in organizing information and are useful in some situations, the majority of presentation models are designed for telling prospects about products/services, not logically leading the prospect to making a buying decision.

Field-tested and proven effective, the 5-Point Presentation format helps the salesperson guide the prospect through the typical buying decision paradigm, resulting in a higher closing ratio. That higher closing ratio will lead to a greater gross income.

And best of all, the 5-Point Presentation style has been outlined above, so it is available for you to put to use immediately at no charge.

What do you say you start using it right now? How 'bout a commitment to make at least one 5-Point Presentation next week?

See what I did there?

About R. Scott Frothingham

Scott Frothingham is an entrepreneur, consultant, speaker, business coach, and author who is best known for his FastForward Income™ products, including *The 15-minute Sales Workout*™. He helps entrepreneurs, managers, and sales/marketing executives position themselves for success through skills training and personal development -- along with providing tools for effectively and efficiently training and motivating their teams.

Website: www.ScottFrothingham.com
Blog: http://blog.FastForwardIncome.com
Facebook: www.Facebook.com/FastForwardIncome
LinkedIn: http://www.linkedin.com/in/ScottFrothingham
Twitter: @ScottFroth

Get Your Articles Read Using These Awesome Tips

By Douglas W. Guy

In recent months, I have had several of my readers ask me what advice I would offer to a new writer or blogger when it comes to creating content for their blog that will get them noticed. With that goal in mind, I've created a list of awesome tips that will be a valuable guide to use when you first start your new venture, and serve as an article checklist once you really get rolling. Everything I've included in this article, I use in one form or another each time I write a new post, and you should too, if you want to be a serious blogger.

For many people new to the online article marketing arena, they get overwhelmed quite easily, and feel it's an excessive amount of work. Then, before they see any results, they throw in the towel. Many of the folks I've coached have stated they dread having to write online marketing articles because it seems boring and mundane. If you feel that way when you're writing your article, how do you think your reader will feel? When you write something that is fun for you, it will be fun for your fans as well.

For some people, reading articles looks like work, especially when the article content is boring and bland. The main goal is to provide your reader with valuable and informative content that is easy to read. Articles are meant to be read through; that's their intended purpose. If you want to get your message out there, and get the reader to take action when they have a credit card in their hand, your content has to draw them into a strong call to action immediately.

Remember, your time, and the time of your reader, are valuable commodities that should not be taken lightly, so don't waste your time or theirs with weak unfocused material that goes nowhere. A good article marketer should consider themselves as a problem solver and should use imaginative and bold language that leaves the reader wanting more. That's called the hook, and you'll use your call to action to reel them into buying your product or service.

Having said that, your articles should be about something you are familiar with, or on a topic that you have a good working knowledge of, which easily conveys your resident expertise through your words. Good writing should flow like the sound of your voice when you write about your topic and should sound like you were explaining the content to them in person. To make certain that your articles get read and appreciated, you'll find the 20 tips below immensely helpful in achieving that goal. These guidelines will definitely make your online marketing articles or blog posts more valuable presenting informative, entertaining and interesting content.

Tip #1: Make your paragraphs short

Whenever a paragraph is really long, or it fails to get to the point right away, it is very difficult to read. It will force your reader into scanning your content instead of reading it, and they are likely to ignore it entirely. It's advisable to look at your paragraph structure and composition from a reader's point of view, and make the necessary changes that will give it better form and flow. Paragraphs can be a single phrase, or on occasion, a single word! Remember to keep your articles simple and easy on the eyes.

Tip #2: Make use of numbers and bullets

When you want to stress an important thought or concept, consider using numbers and bullet points to highlight that information. You'll want to employ this tactic when you want them to digest what you are conveying more quickly. Structure your bullets or numbers with indentations so your content won't appear like an individual block of square paragraphs. By including a small amount of shape and form to your article, it will add the right kind of polish it needs to pop for your reader.

Tip #3: Use sub-headings to separate thoughts

Utilizing this technique can separate various points into bite-sized snippets that will help your reader find specific information with greater ease. You need to constantly evaluate how you can best help your reader find an answer to solve a problem they've encountered and present them the solution. Breaking down your article into sub-categories will help you better assist their needs and allow your reader to progress from one point to another more fluidly.

Tip #4: Provide a great attention-grabbing title

When the article title peaks someone's attention and interest, you're halfway home. Then, you have only 156 characters to drive your point home in the Meta description just below the title that will get reader to click through to your site. The title, description, and article heading all should utilize your keyword in a concise way that accurately describes your article content. Using titles that evoke an emotion or cause a debate always get attention. Some examples include "Tips On Making The Opposite Sex Want You More," "Some Dogs Get A Raw Deal," or "Support Our Constitutional Rights!" These topics make great article titles, because they connect with a person's thoughts and emotions causing them to take decided action on the spot.

Tip #5: Keep your readers engaged from the start

From your opening statement, try to make use of real-life scenarios that can be adopted by the reader. Apply good depictions and metaphors to drive your point home, but don't overdo it. Driving your examples with graphic metaphors and similes would make it easy so your reader can visualize what exactly you are referring to. Help to make the readers' encounter with your online marketing articles pleasurable and enjoyable for them.

Tip #6: Use statistics to illustrate a point

Working with statistics or published studies may heighten your post by giving it more authority. But, it should not be overly formal and should only be used to illustrate a concept that might not otherwise be understood. Keep it interesting by weaving it into your content in a way that makes sense and is easy to understand. Don't try to look so smart that you cram a ton of information into a small space and lose your reader. "Know-it-alls" are very hard to take seriously in person. So, can you imagine trying to follow someone like that in print? You want to make it fun and captivate the attention of your reader, turning them into an enthusiastic fan.

Tip #7: Keep a diary or a journal with you

I've written several articles on this topic alone and cannot stress enough the importance of utilizing this technique. Your creative ideas can be triggered by anything you may hear, see, smell, touch, or feel. Many of my best articles start with a chance encounter with a perfect stranger I meet somewhere along my daily path or a simple drive through the countryside. There is no grand mystery in finding great ideas; they happen in and around you all of the time. Write down these little events into a journal to use for content as the centerpiece of a featured article on your website. It's really that simple!

Tip #8: Take the time to sort things out

Your experiences are what shape your mindset and your opinions and can be woven into your writing. Try to relax while you think about a past experience or interaction with someone that will be the focal point of your article. Figure out what triggers your emotions, because this will likely do the same for your reader as well. Use these emotions to express your ideas and persuade your reader to interact with your article on a more personal level. When you take the time to evoke an emotion with your readers, your fan base will grow exponentially as a result.

Tip #9: Find a place to inspire your creativeness

In order to create unique and interesting content that can be used as the basis of an effective article marketing campaign, you must make certain that your workplace will make you feel happy and relaxed. Creativity is born when you are in the right state of mind. Give your workspace the same kind of character that makes you who you are. Put up family pictures, favorite quotes, and a dream-board as a reminder of your big why, or anything that can get your creativity cranking. A clean and well-organized workplace also rids of distractions and unwanted hindrances. With a good working place, you can work in peace and never notice the time passing by.

Tip #10: Set the right mood for your success

Setting the mood requires you to just go with the moment or to induce yourself to feeling what makes your mind works best. Finding out what makes you tick can help you find ways to get your creative article marketing juices flowing. Set the pace and tempo for your mood, and everything else will follow. There are many ways to set the mood. Some writers have been known to have a little wine, or a beer to stir up their imagination. Some like some like soft mood music, while others let the lighting of the environment create the mood. Whatever you have found that best facilitates your creativity will certainly transcend into your writing. As they say: "To each, his or her, be it their own!" This could not be truer than in writing.

Tip #11: Get away from it all by doing something fun

Letting yourself go and having fun produces adrenaline that can help your article marketing imagination go wild. For me, I try to commune with nature by taking a hike along one of my favorite trails. When that is not possible, I relax on my back deck, viewing the beautiful scenery right in my backyard. Then, I try to make it out one night a week to socialize with friends, with one scheduled weekend getaway to try something new. Whatever it is that is unusual from your daily routine can take the rut out of your schedule. In no time at all, your creativeness will make use of that experience and get your imagination to go on overdrive.

Tip #12: Take your business blogging very seriously

Aside from creating good relevant content, it is important that you do this on a regular basis. Two or three articles a week is good for a start. However, you do not want to post if you do not have anything worth reading about. You want to engage your reader in whatever topic you are writing about. Learn to develop a level of professionalism with what you are presenting to your audience, and they will think of you as an authority. Blogging solely for the purpose of being discovered will only serve to turn your reader off and do nothing to attain personal branding.

Tip #13: Stick to the basics; write about something you know

Until you have been in the blogging arena for a while, stick with only a few specific genres to talk about. Write about things that you have experienced or are interested in. You do not have to be an authority on a particular subject to write about it. All you need to do is to pick a topic that is pertinent to the audience you are trying to reach, learn about it, and teach them what you have learned. This is a great way for you to put up the appearance that you are a blogging master on a given subject.

Tip #14: Resist the temptation to be a social blogging butterfly

Initially, keep your blog page free of clutter. Resist the temptation to put up the entire "friend me," "subscribe me," and "vote me" links all over the front page. The day will come when you will have a broad enough fan base that you can venture off into the social arena. For now, stay focused on captivating your visitors with your blogging without all of the bells and whistles. Remember, you caught their attention with catchy ad copy, not glitz and glamour. Don't spend your time trying to design a sexy site; there will be time enough for that down the road. You will be better served building relationships, not vanity!

Tip #15: Keep your website clean, simple, and easy on the eyes

Black print on a white page is easy to read and will keep your reader focused on the content. Note that it is fine to highlight text that you would like to emphasize using bold or italicized print. Using a simple border around the page is also a nice touch and will lend a hand in keeping their eye on your article. Before I put any content on my WordPress blog, I use Microsoft Word to write, edit, highlight, and border my subject matter. As you develop your skill level and a unique blogging style, you can experiment with the text style, borders, shading, colors, and images that will give your page more eye-popping appeal. For now, just concentrate on developing your writing skills; the rest will come in due time.

Tip #16: Keep your articles fun and full of energy; happy blogging

This is probably the best tip of all: Enjoy what you are doing. If you keep the blogging fun, it will definitely be noticed. Stay upbeat and positive as you mastermind each article you create. When a person posts a comment to your site, respond in kind with enthusiasm. Visit them back. Pay it forward with a comment on their work. Share ideas, share material, and share your energy. And, before you know it, you will see abundant results that will reward all of your efforts with huge dividends.

Tip #17: 90 brilliant ideas for better business blogging this year

Right about now, you are probably asking yourself: Where is he going with this? Well, my 180 brilliant ideas for better business blogging this year is no great secret when you approach your business by thinking outside of the box. There are 365 days in a year, and here in America most of us celebrate New Year's Day, President's Day, Martin Luther King Day, Easter Sunday, Memorial Day, Independence Day (the 4th of July), Labor Day, Thanksgiving, and Christmas. For those of you in another country, I am quite certain you can come up with your own set of five definitive holidays you would not work on.

Anyway, pick five days that you would absolutely not work on, and divide the remaining 360 days by 2, which will accommodate your vacation time, weekends, and various other cultural holidays. By my count, we have 180 days left that you'll again divide in half, which leaves 90 days, or 90 articles you'll need to write yearly if you want to get any traffic to your blog. Now that I have gotten that out of the way, I've given you a ton of sources up to this point where you can draw your ideas from: Brilliant!

Tip #18: Think one for better article writing and marketing promos

Better article writing for me begins by finding a quiet spot and jotting down some ideas I have for an article. Before I go any further, I am compelled to tell you that I normally do this on a walk along one of the several nature trails that I frequent and will normally depend on the tone I am trying to set for my article that day. For those of you busy raising a family or are working a hectic schedule at your job, you can split this process up by journaling your ideas over your lunch period, at some point after you've gotten the kids settled in for the night, or over the course of several days. Article writing should be a joy, and stressing out over the time factor will kill your creative juices.

Anyway, the entire point of this exercise it to come up with a solid title and overall theme for the article you'll be writing, and that's it! Beyond that, the next steps I will give you will complete the entire process. You should only shoot for one piece of content per week until you settle into your own creative style.

Tip #19: Read one for better article writing and marketing promos

Now that you've got a title, what you may need to change it slightly based on your keyword research. You'll want to do a Google search using the exact title you have designated for the article you will be writing.

On the first page of results Google displays for your article writing content, you'll want to look through all of the organic search results and choose three articles that capture your interest on the topic you'll be writing.

Next, spend one hour reading each article and taking notes on the language structure, body content, writing style, headlines, and subheadings that draw your attention. There are times when I find article content that is so closely matched to the message I want to convey in my writing that I will intermingle some of that content with my own.

Note: In the event that you use another author's article writing as a resource, you need to acknowledge that by linking it back to the source by simply citing the article source with "Read more..." at the end of the paragraph or paragraphs where it was inserted. If you want to be absolutely certain you are not committing plagiarism, you can highlight the text in italics and capture it all in quotes, cite the author's name, or a combination of all three.

Tip #20: Write one for better article writing and marketing promos

Having completed two-thirds of the process to come up with your killer article writing content, you now need to write for an hour to put it all together with your own creative style. You want to avoid using clichés whenever you can and come up with a unique catchphrase of your own instead.

Your goal here is to work on your article writing so that in time, you can get each portion of this process down to only one hour of time. Once you have a solid piece completed, and you think you are ready to publish it to your blog, simply copy and paste it in its entirety from your Word or Notepad file directly to your "Add a Post" page from the dashboard of your WordPress Blog.

About Douglas W. Guy

Douglas W. Guy is the writer, creator and ultimate visionary behind the Empire Wealth Builders Website and network of affiliate websites. The network was founded on the belief that it is the God-given right of every man, woman, and child to enjoy all of the finest health, wellness, and happiness that they so richly deserve in this life. He is passionate about being an entrepreneur, business owner, personal development coach, giving to charities, and being active in his community. He is a proud Veteran of the United States Navy, and father of two.

Every day he wakes up naturally smiling and goes to bed each night reflecting on something positive that happened that day. He's grateful to God for every sunrise, sunset, and feels blessed for each moment he's alive. He always says, "Life is a gift to be treasured, not taken for granted, nor wasted in any way." This profound belief drives him to excel in all that he does, which positively affects others. Ironically, the lives that have touched his throughout the years have, in many ways, helped to create the man that he is today.

His belief in these simple mantras is so strong that a sizable portion of the company proceeds go directly to help various charitable foundations that support these endeavors as his way of "paying it forward." It is his profound wish that his actions inspire others to pick up the torch of hope and illuminate their little corner of the world, making it a better place to live. Douglas recently published his first book, *60 Days To Neverland - A True Motivation Journey Of One Man's Personal Transformation*, which is the first of many in his upcoming Neverland Series of books, and speaks directly to these simple philosophies and beliefs that he holds in such high regard.

For other articles and resources like the one you just read, you may visit my website at:

Websites

Empire Wealth Builders
60 Days To Neverland Blog Page
60 Days To Neverland Book Page
Make The Money Now

Social Sites

Google+
Facebook
Pinterest
Twitter
LinkedIn

Become A Successful Freelance Writer... In Just 7 Days!

By Anna Jones

Author's Note: This book was written for Frank and Anne-Marie.

Do you love writing? Hate your current job? What if I told you that in as little as seven days, you could be on the pathway to success as a freelance writer – would you listen? The chances are that for most people, their dream job, if it's not to become an actress or a musician, is to write for a living. Journalism sounds glamorous and exciting...who wouldn't want to mingle with the celebrities and be the first to uncover breaking news stories?

The trouble is that journalism is tough and, increasingly, the jobs are becoming low-paid, with long hours. And with the current job market becoming ever more competitive, it is fast becoming a fading reality for many graduates, unless they can successfully find work at a newspaper or magazine.

But there is an alternative. The world of freelance writing is quickly becoming a lucrative market, with the attraction for wannabe writers being the lure of setting their own pay rates and working their own hours from the comfort of home. Sounds ideal, right? Yes and no.

As with anything in life, there are pros and cons to being a freelance writer. The above are definite advantages, but it can be daunting for many when they realise they will have to register as self-employed, pay their own taxes, market themselves, and find a constant stream of work. And what if the bills never get paid?! Suddenly, that dream of working from your laptop while lounging in your pyjamas doesn't sound quite so dreamy.

I'm here to tell you to relax. I've been through all of that, so I know how scary it sounds to leave your job or to set yourself up as a freelancer and go it alone. The trick is to stay calm and know that everything is going to be just fine.

My name is Anna Jones, and I started freelancing around October 2010 under the name of A.J. Writing and Editing Services. I have worked with a variety of clients, from writing for local magazines, copywriting, and SEO agencies to large natural health companies. I can assure you that there is a steady stream of work in the freelance writing world – so long as you know how to look for it.

In this ebook, I wanted to show you how it's possible to start off as a complete newbie and get your first paid client – in just seven days. For some, it may be sooner, but if you apply yourself and have a little preparation, you can expect to start attracting paid work within one week. And we're not talking low fees either.

Once you're in the driving seat, remember, you control your rates and set the boundaries of what you are and aren't willing to write for.

Freelance writing has brought me a great deal of pleasure, happiness, fulfilment and, most of all, freedom. It has provided a steady source of income when times have been tough, and it's an amazing feeling to say that you write for a living. Just watch people's faces when you tell them – many just can't believe it!

If you have the passion, love to write, and are determined to make it happen, then this book is for you. I hope it inspires you to live an empowered life because I know that it has certainly done that for me.

To your success,
Anna Jones
8th October 2013

Can I really become a successful freelance writer in just 7 days?

Yes! Why not? You can become one right now if that's what you decide to be. First of all, being a freelance writer means acknowledging that you are one. You know if you were meant to write, as you will get that feeling inside of you; it's known as your gut instinct. Trust it. It's never wrong.

Even if you don't feel that you are a good writer but are passionate about it, that's all that really matters. You can improve your writing through practice, but it's passion that will give you the drive to take you anywhere. This is so important because perseverance and commitment are really the keys to unlocking your success.

You're probably asking yourself what you need to do to launch your freelance writing career, you're wondering what the pay is like, or you are not sure on how you can fit it around your current commitments. This next section is dedicated to helping you attain clarity on this.

What is freelance writing?

Freelance writing is a broad term that encompasses a wide range of services. The following are just some of the areas that many writers concentrate on:

- Article writing
- Blogging
- Copywriting
- Producing ebooks

- Press releases
- SEO writing
- Reviews
- Creative writing
- Ghostwriting
- Reports
- Magazine writing
- Technical writing
- Resume writing
- Web content
- Translation
- Academic writing
- Sales writing

This doesn't even take into account editing and proofreading, which can be in itself a profitable niche if that's what you enjoy doing. As you can see, there are many different types of freelance writing, so you may just want to concentrate on one or two areas.

Is this right for me?

Nobody knows that except for you. But I can tell you that you'll never know unless you try. Freelance writing is suitable for anyone to do if he/she loves to write, but is especially good for students, work-at-home moms, those looking for extra income, people who want to quit their job and work at home, or those looking for a better work/life balance. If you can't stand being bossed around, then freelance writing could be a good fit as you can work at your own pace, and you only have clients to answer to, not the man upstairs.

Which type of writing should I do?

Ask yourself what you like to write. For me, it was always article writing, blogging, SEO writing, press releases (due to my journalism degree) and copywriting. But I have dabbled in resume writing and, like most writers, I enjoy creative writing, producing poetry, fiction, and, now, ebooks. The beauty of freelance writing is that there are no boundaries; you can pick and mix what you want to do or focus on the areas you are strong in.

How much can I earn from freelance writing?

This depends on your levels of experience, how strong your writing is, and what the client is willing to pay. There are many people under the assumption that high paid writing work doesn't exist, which couldn't be further from the truth.
If you want to go for low-paid writing jobs, then you will find plenty on bidding sites such as Elance, oDesk or Guru (don't rule them out completely, however), ready to pay a pittance for hundreds of articles. But if you want to set yourself

apart as a successful and wealthy freelance writer, then you need to focus on finding the places where those higher-paying clients are looking and willing to negotiate better fees.

The good news is that writers have never been in more demand, and copywriting, especially, is known to be a lucrative niche. Exceptional freelance copywriters can earn around five or six figures a year. Bogging is an increasingly popular service, with more and more websites realising the boost that a blog gives to their SEO rankings. This is because a blog offers fresh content that the search engines love as opposed to static content that remains on the rest of the website. So, think about the market, what you enjoy writing, and set yourself a clear goal for what you want to earn. Do you want to make enough money to survive on or do you want to become wealthy? The only limit is yourself!

What should I charge for my writing?

The simple answer is, whatever you feel your writing is worth. This can mean different things to different people. For example, if you are writing to build a portfolio, then perhaps there is no harm in accepting a voluntary position, as you will have samples to show for it at the end. This is what I did, but as soon as I had enough samples to fill my portfolio (about three to four pieces is usually enough to begin with), I moved onto looking for paid positions.

You need to take into account your living conditions. If you have your own place, responsibilities, and bills to pay, then you need to calculate your basic rate of daily pay. Work out how much it costs to be able to live by figuring out your living expenses, rent, electric/heating/water/food bills, health care, work expenses related to equipment, software, and, finally, any extras such as entertainment/lifestyle costs. Then you should consider transportation costs, your self-employment tax, any pay for training and conferences, and the fact that as you're self-employed, you may receive no paid vacation or sick time. Use this office calculator from Freelance Switch to determine what your going rate should be to make a living from freelance writing.

Where can I find clients?

There are two options. The clients find you, or you go find the clients. The latter usually means applying to job adverts looking for writers, but it can mean more competition applying for what is usually a low-paid job. The reason for this is that the client may constantly be on the lookout for new writers, due to the high level of writer turnover, as many realise it's not worth it or that this one gig alone won't pay their bills.

If you have no writing experience at all, then this could be a good option. Sites such as Craigslist or Gumtree don't usually attract well-paid clients, but if you're looking to get that first rung on the ladder into the writing world, then it could be worth it. Just make sure to read any job adverts you apply for carefully and rule out that they aren't phishing scams or money laundering schemes.

Bidding sites are another popular choice with freelancers, who often find themselves desperately looking for work. My only qualm with Elance is the large number of low-paid jobs on there for writers. However, don't dismiss it entirely, as I have found regular work from using the site, and I know many people have benefited from it and found their first paying gigs on there. The trick with bidding sites is to have a complete profile and, once you land one or two jobs (especially if they are respected clients), more clients will find your profile, resulting in more work. It's a bit like the domino effect; once you have proven what you can do, more clients will be attracted to you.

How do I promote my writing?

As mentioned previously, a portfolio is usually best to show potential clients so they can ascertain if they like your writing skills and whether they'd like to work with you. As most of the work will be received from clients online, it makes sense to create your own website to promote your writing and editing services.

Take a look at mine for example. I set up A.J. Writing and Editing Services in 2010 when I started off. Having a place where I can store samples of my portfolio is ideal, and on mine, I have placed clippings from my magazine articles I have written. It's nice to be able to present them in a visual format, as it attracts attention and acts as a 'showcase' for your work.

Alternatively, if you plan to get clients from writing sites such as Elance, then you can create a portfolio of your profile on the site, or even set up your own stand-alone portfolio site at Writers Residence, Clippings.me or Writerfolio, to name just a few. While you can often sign up for free, some sites may require a small fee to create your own portfolio.

Setting up your own website also requires you to purchase a domain name and pay for your own hosting. This is good if you want complete ownership of your site, as you can customise your site name to your own liking, adding a professional touch. But if you don't want to deal with the technical side of things, you can set up a free WordPress or Blogger site and purchase a domain name there. While there are certain limitations with these free blogs, you can do most of the things that you can on a self-hosted platform, except for the addition of plugins (which can enhance the look of your site and provide you with tools to improve its design/SEO ranking).

Where should I promote my writing services?

Once your website has been populated with content, you should do searches for places to promote it. Social media is the number one choice, since that's where most people can be found these days. Facebook, Twitter, Google+, and LinkedIn - I would say these four are mandatory to join if you haven't already.

Set yourself up with a Facebook page to promote your writing services, tweet regularly, and hang out in relevant networks on Google+ and in groups in LinkedIn where the type of clients you want to attract are waiting.

Remember to be consistent with your image and professional branding across the sites; you want to streamline and simplify your services so that potential clients know who you are, what you do, and why you do it.

The "when" can come later in the client consultation stages, and as for the "where," well, that doesn't really matter – as a freelancer, you can work anywhere you want! Though, I do recommend you have a designated office space to work in, and a desktop PC is my preference because I have incurred too many problems with laptops over the years, and, thus, have learned my lessons well.

Turn off the computer and go outside

It may surprise you to learn that there are many writing opportunities outside of the online world. It's not just Web content that needs writing; there are hundreds of local businesses that often require the services of a copywriter or a proofreader to browse through their marketing materials and refresh them if necessary.

You could try printing out business cards and handing them out around town (not to passing strangers, as that will annoy them), but I recommend looking around town at local businesses, such as cafes, restaurants, printers, and checking for any grammatical errors or spelling mistakes on any signs or menus you see, as this is a good opportunity to politely pitch your services. Remember to hand them a business card with all of your contact details on them – primarily your business email address and telephone number.

Another place to look is the Chamber of Commerce. If you can find out where your local Chamber is, attend the meeting, and network with other attendees. Prove to them your value and how a well-written sales pitch, report, or leaflet can entice more customers their way. If you promote yourself in the right way, there's a good chance they will remember your name and be interested in hiring you as a writer.

Cold calling is another option to consider, though be selective and choose what you say carefully. I would recommend doing your research first and emailing/calling graphic design, printing companies, or publishing houses to pitch any article/editing ideas. If you are new to freelancing, I would build up to this and start online first instead, as the latter route is the quickest way to get work in my experience.

Network as much as possible

There is some truth to the saying, 'It's not what you know; it's who you know.' If you want to be known as a top copywriter, blogger, or proofreader, then you need to start writing in those fields and networking regularly with those at the top of the profession.

If you have an idea to pitch a feature article to a magazine, then get in touch with the editor first on Twitter. Don't harass them about how wonderful your idea is - chances are they will just ignore you, as editors are very busy people. But strike up a conversation with them, get to know them a little (professionally), and they will be interested in who you are and what you can do for them.

Success is really about building rapport and trust between your clients and yourself, but always bear in mind that magazine editors/company directors or anyone else you pitch to is human just like you. Know how to market and communicate yourself appropriately, and you will attract the right type of people to do business with.

A great place to network is at corporate events or festivals. When I was trying to break into the field of natural health, I set out with a case of business cards and made conversation with some of the people at the stalls. There is no harm in looking around and, if you're interested in what they do, ask if they ever need any help with their marketing content.

The worst they can do is say "no!" I know it can be difficult if you're not used to selling yourself, but come prepared and try to have a few examples of previous clients you have worked for (if any) and a small summary of what you can do for them – then hand your business card over and see what happens.

Search regularly

Search engines are your friend. Google, Bing, Yahoo! all have their benefits. For Google, I recommend setting up Alerts with the search terms for the niche you want to work in. You can often find writing jobs that you'd miss, or at the very least, you will get some interesting new ideas/angles for articles you can potentially pitch to magazine editors.

On Bing, you can also find more niche job searches that you might otherwise miss on Google. For example, I remember typing 'natural health writers wanted' into Bing, to which it returned a host of sites looking for writers – it is literally a hidden treasure chest of jobs. From there, I applied for a job that was posted by a digital marketing agency, and I have been working on and off for this particular client even to this day.

The pay is very reasonable (about £20 for a 500-word article). I found another digital agency by using this method too, and the rates were even higher (around £90 an article). This proves to me that there are a lot of well-paid writing opportunities available on the Web if you know where to look.

A simple search for 'copywriting jobs' led me to a site called Copify, a site that once you apply and are accepted for provides daily work. The pay is not fantastic, but it has seen me through some difficult times.

There are probably hundreds of sites out there like this – just get searching for them!

Can I find a steady stream of writing clients in just 7 days?

If you're passionate enough, there's no reason why you can't find them today! The key is to find long-term opportunities, as these are the ones that will last. But don't be put off if you don't find something immediately. Some days are better than others when it comes to finding your perfect opportunity, so I would suggest working on your writing skills and doing your own marketing and pitching if you can't find any immediate clients from job ads/posts. Don't be put off – stay positive!

While the title of this book suggests that you can become successful in just one week, it's more the paving stones that I am referring to than a fully-fledged career. This, of course, takes much longer and a lot of hard work and dedication – but it can and does happen if you believe it will!

The important thing to remember is to enjoy every step of the process. We are all learning as we go through life and, like anything, freelance writing is no different. So I suggest you enjoy any bumps or hiccups in the road, learn from them and then rejoice in every mini-triumph along the way. Remember, like life, freelance writing is a journey and not a destination...

Below, I have created a one week plan to kick-start your freelance writing career – please give it a go and let me know how you get on by dropping me a message at: acjones187@gmail.com

YOUR 7-DAY PLAN TO FREELANCE WRITING SUCCESS

Please feel free to follow this plan exactly as shown or adjust the times according to your preference. Remember, achieving the daily goal is more important before you move onto the next step.

MONDAY

MAIN TASK: Getting Started.

MAIN GOAL: Vision, branding, writing sample.

TIME: 09:00-13:00

TASK: Choose your speciality (copywriting, articles, SEO, etc.). What are your strong points? Come up with a name for your business.

GOAL ACHIEVED: A clear vision of what you want to achieve and promote to clients, along with a name to sell your services under.

TIME: 13:30-19:00

TASK: Write a short profile/bio and publish one or more sample writing pieces on a topic of your choice to websites such as InfoBarrel, HubPages or Suite101. Decide whether you want a blog, portfolio, or professional site.

GOAL ACHIEVED: A short bio you can later add to websites/profiles where you promote your services, plus sample piece/s to show clients.

TUESDAY

MAIN TASK: Setting up your portfolio/website.

MAIN GOAL: A fully functional website and viewable portfolio.

TIME: 09:00-13:00

TASK: Set up your website domain/hosting, a free blog at WordPress or Blogger, and then create a portfolio.

GOAL ACHIEVED: Your website is set up, and the content is filled in as much as possible.

TIME: 13:30-19:00

TASK: If you want a professional design for your website, look for a graphic designer on Google or find one cheaply on Elance.

GOAL ACHIEVED: This may be an ongoing job, depending on your preferences. If you choose a free blog, you can get some decent themes in the meantime.

WEDNESDAY

MAIN TASK: Look for writing jobs and order business cards – keep blogging.

MAIN GOAL: Research the writing market – apply for one opportunity.

TIME: 09:00-13:00

TASK: Choose to focus solely on searching for jobs in your chosen niche. Use a variety of keywords to return different results. Write a list of the ones that interest you.

GOAL ACHIEVED: Get an idea of the market, present job opportunities, and what areas you want to consider. In addition, get a list to determine pay/rates available.

TIME: 13:30-19:00

TASK: Sign up for one bidding site or send an email to a digital agency.

GOAL ACHIEVED: Even if you don't use it, there are plenty of clients, including increasingly big clients who are coming onto Elance, PPH, oDesk, and Guru.com to find writers.

THURSDAY

MAIN TASK: Set up social media profiles and make connections.

MAIN GOAL: Social media presence is essential to marketing your services in the 21ˢᵗ century.

TIME: 09:00-13:00

TASK: Set up a Facebook page, Twitter profile, Google+ page and LinkedIn profile.

GOAL ACHIEVED: Completed social media profiles so clients can easily find and connect with you.

TIME: 13:30-19:00

TASK: Make connections with relevant businesses, companies, and/or interests you want to write for.

GOAL ACHIEVED: Communicating with businesses and making them aware of your presence is the first step to informing them about your services.

FRIDAY

MAIN TASK: Reach out for your first client.

MAIN GOAL: Make your job as a freelance writer real.

TIME: 09:00-13:00

TASK: Apply for a job on a bidding site (there is bound to be one), research a blog, and see if you can blog for the owner, or contact a major website to see if they need help with any copywriting.

GOAL ACHIEVED: You are stepping out of your comfort zone and showing the client you are confident in your abilities. Apply to at least one job.

TIME: 13:30-19:00

TASK: Sign up to freelance writing news sites, such as FreelanceWriting.com, Freelance Market News, and Journalism.co.uk.

GOAL ACHIEVED: Sign up to two or three sites so you stay updated with everything in the freelance writing industry.

SATURDAY

MAIN TASK: Market your business offline.

MAIN GOAL: Become confident at selling yourself.

TIME: 09:00-13:00

TASK: Once your business cards arrive, go into your local community and find relevant businesses/markets for your services that you can leave a card for.

GOAL ACHIEVED: If you can, leave three to five business cards in different local venues.

TIME: 13:30-19:00

TASK: Try cold calling, approaching people in person, or researching for any marketing events you can attend.

GOAL ACHIEVED: Make a few cold calls. If business isn't open on Saturday, you might want to try on Friday instead.

SUNDAY

MAIN TASK: Register as self-employed and get yourself set up for tax.

MAIN GOAL: Be registered for tax and ready to start your new career as a freelancer.

TIME: 09:00-13:00

TASK: Do your research and find out what you need to do to be legally set up in your country, including what tax and contributions you may have to pay.

GOAL ACHIEVED: Understand the legalities and tax terminology surrounding life as a self-employed person. You might want to consider hiring an accountant, for example, to deal with your tax return instead.

TIME: 13:30-19:00

TASK: Follow the correct instructions to set yourself up as a self-employed person and understand anything and everything related to self-assessment.

GOAL ACHIEVED: Register as self-employed and be fully set up and legally ready to take on work.

If you follow the above steps, then it's possible to be on the way to building yourself up as a freelance writer in as little as seven days. The more work you do, the more testimonials from your work can be collected and, in turn, this will increase the number of recommendations you receive, resulting in more potential clients coming your way.

If you follow the above steps, then it's possible to be on the way to building yourself up as a freelance writer in as little as seven days. The more work you do, the more testimonials from your work can be collected and, in turn, this will increase the number of recommendations you receive, resulting in more potential clients coming your way.

Congratulations – You are well on the way to freelance writing success!

About Anna Jones

Anna Jones is a freelance writer, blogger, and proofreader. She has her own writing blog, The Finished Copy, and has been working freelance since 2010, before making the leap to full-time freelance writing in February 2013.
She has written for a variety of clients, including Good Health Naturally, easyJet Holidays, LastMinute.com, Staples, and Schwartz, to name just a few. Her main

interests are in natural health, meditation, well-being, lifestyle, and writing.

For more about her writing services or to contact her, please visit

My blog: *The Finished Copy*
My services: A.J. Writing and Editing Services
Email: acjones187@gmail.com

Power Up Your Book Sales With Social Media

By Lynn Jordan

The publishing business is changing more now than at any time since Gutenberg invented the printing press. It's an exciting time, but it's hard to keep up with the ever-shifting changes.

There's good news and bad news for authors today.

The bad news is that publishing houses are doing less and less for their authors and expecting the authors to do most, if not all, of the promotion for their books.

The good news is that it's easier than ever before for writers to reach a huge audience of prospective readers. Technology and the Internet let you build your platform, do your own promotion, and create a worldwide tribe of folks eagerly awaiting your work. You can even bypass traditional publishing methods and publish your own books.

Whichever method of publishing you choose, you need to start your promotion efforts long before your book is published. It's never too soon to start building a relationship with your readers. It takes time to reach readers. You want your name to become familiar because people see it everywhere.

If you publish through a traditional publisher, you can go from unpublished to published with a phone call or email. If you are self-publishing, you want to get your readers in place before your book is ready. Whether it's your first book or not, you want to build anticipation for your publication date.

The technology and the choices can be overwhelming. Most writers become confused and choose to do nothing or else spend their time doing tasks that don't provide the best return for their efforts.

Writers face many challenges. You want to spend your time writing, not marketing. This chapter teaches you how to get started using the technology of social media to help you promote your name and your books.

Social networking allows you to reach more readers without having to go on the road to promote your books. This means that you can make your promotion part of your daily routine and not take weeks out of your writing time to promote.

You'll want a blog or website to be your home on the Internet. All your social networking and promotional efforts should lead folks to your own site. However, most people become overwhelmed at the thought that they have to build a blog or website.

If you start with small steps and build up your Internet presence gradually, it will be less overwhelming.

Maybe you've already started using social media. That's great. You may find some additional tips to make your social networking more effective.

Social media is constantly changing. No matter what you are currently doing, you need to be measuring and testing your results. Find out which sites your audience frequents. Contact your readers who already visit.

Step 1 - First Things to Do

1- Register Your Domain Name

One of the first things you want to do is to register your domain name. For writers, the best domain name is your own name or pen name. You'll want to promote, or brand, yourself more than your book. You'll write many books in your career. If you are publishing traditionally, your publisher may change your title, so don't register a domain for the book until you know for sure what the title will be.

Use the .com extension for any domain you register. People will assume that the domain has that extension. Most web browsers will fill in that extension by default.

You may have to use your middle name or initial if your name.com domain is already taken. If the domain you want is available, register it as soon as possible.

2- Write Your Long Bio

Create a 200-word bio for yourself. Make it interesting and entertaining. This is not the place for the dry facts of your resume. Keep in mind that your bio will be one of the first tools a reader will use to decide if he/she should read your book or not.

3- Create a Short Bio

Edit your bio down to fewer than 160 characters. This is the character limit for bios on Twitter. Make it short and interesting.

4- Have Your Picture Taken

A close-up photo of your smiling face works best. You can use a professional headshot. Just make sure you look friendly and approachable. It's perfectly fine to use an informal snapshot as well.

5- Create a Google Account and Set Up Your Profile

Google provides lots of free tools that will help you build your online presence. Set up a Google account if you don't already have one. Fill in your bio information and upload your photograph.

When anyone searches for your name, your picture will appear. Google Plus is a rapidly growing social networking site. Linking a YouTube channel and holding Google Hangouts lets readers see your face and hear your voice. This is the fastest way to build relationships with your readers. If you don't want to have your face on camera, you can use your book cover for your profile picture. Feel free to start out that way. However, there are lots of advantages to using your face on video and as profile pictures. People want to see a real person, not just a book cover.

Step 2 – Set Up Twitter

Twitter is a very popular social networking site. It's a perfect site for writers because it's all text, and every word counts. Tweets (posts on Twitter) are limited to 140 characters.

Twitter is a great place to start your social networking because creating a short message is less intimidating than longer posts on a blog or other social networking sites. Also, short writing is powerful writing. Using Twitter actually hones your writing skills.

Create an account on Twitter and use your short bio and picture to build your profile. You will want to set up your profile and design before you ask people to come look at it.

Start Tweeting

Twitter messages are restricted to 140 characters. That makes Twitter a simple place to start. Also, there are several weekly chats devoted to writers and different types of writing. Search for #writechat or #storychat to connect with like-minded folks.

Post at least five tweets before you follow anyone. People will check out your profile to see if they want to follow you back. A bare page doesn't give them a reason to follow you.

Build yourself up to be an expert or interesting, then start asking questions and getting into conversations.

You should be only promoting yourself or your books in 10-20% of your tweets. You don't want your followers to think you're just trying to sell them something. No one likes folks who constantly tweet, "Buy my book!"

Twitter is like a cocktail party where you join existing conversations. You wouldn't give out business cards right away at a party. Think of Twitter as one giant social gathering.

Following Others

Start looking for people to follow who have the same interests. Don't just start by adding lots of people to follow. You want to build relationships, not play a numbers game.

Find people to follow by searching for the name of people you know or writers you like. You can also search using keywords such as "writing," "reading," or "novels," or your niche keywords if you write non-fiction.

To find more people to follow, find people in your field and see who they are following. Hold your cursor over the photos to see the names. Click on the images to go to their profiles.

Twitter Tools

Twitter tools come, go, and change names. Pick the most useful ones for you, but don't spend all of your time researching tools. Be careful not to use tools to spam. Spamming can get your account banned.

Hashtags are a way of keeping conversations about the same subject together. A hashtag is the # sign. People use hashtags to label tweets.

Put a hashtag anywhere in the tweet to enable people to search to find it.

Examples: A 30-day blog challenge hashtag is: #blog30
A place to announce your writing goals #writegoal

Chats - Twitter chats are scheduled times when people hold conversations about the same subject using the appropriate hashtag.

Here is a link to Twitter Chat Schedules. Since schedules change and chats come and go, this is an interactive spreadsheet that allows people to update the information:

http://spreadsheets.google.com/ccc?key=ruaz3GZveOsoXUOOt86B3AQ

Tools such as TweetDeck and HootSuite make chats easier to follow.

Step 3 - Set Up Facebook

Facebook is the second most-visited website in the world (second only to Google). Each visitor spends more time on Facebook than they do on Google. Facebook is also the second-largest video site (second only to YouTube, which is owned by Google). It's a very important site to include in your marketing plan for creating your presence on the Internet.

Create a Facebook Account

The Facebook profile should be for family and friends and not promoting anything. Facebook forbids promotion or marketing on your profile page. However, Fan Pages (or Facebook Pages) were created for the purpose of marketing. You actually are encouraged to promote your fan page.

Create a Facebook Fan Page

There are two different categories of Facebook fan pages: Official Pages and Community pages. You want to pick the "Official Page." Then, under Official Page, there are three choices: local business; brand, product or organization; artist, band, or public figure. The information that is displayed will differ depending on the type of page you choose. I recommend the artist choice because you are branding your name.

Advantages to Having a Fan Page:

1. You are limited to 5,000 friends for your profile, but you can have an unlimited number of fans on your fan page.
2. You can also send messages to all of your fans at once.
3. You can brand your business name by qualifying for your own Facebook user name. To qualify, you may need a certain number of fans.
4. Your fan page is indexed by the search engines, which means it will show up in a search.
5. Non-Facebook members can't see your personal page, but they can see your fan page.
6. You can add tabs to your fan page that have customized promotional materials, including an opt-in page for your list.
7. You can create an event with your fan page and promote it to your fans.

When you start a fan page, there are three kinds of pages to choose from: local business; product or organization; and artist, band, or public figure. The information that is displayed will differ depending on the type of page you choose.

Connecting to Facebook Groups

One of the best ways to connect with people, as well as network, is to join Facebook groups, as well as create your own group.

1) Public groups vs. Private groups

- Public groups are for publicity & promotion
- Private groups can be used for private memberships
- Groups are not indexed; Facebook search brings up only public groups
- Searching Facebook brings up only public groups

2) Joining groups

- Once you are really active, you will get invitations to join groups
- Joining a group lets you interact with people who like the same things you like
- Make sure that the group is aligned with your business interests
- Do a search in Facebook for "_____ (keyword) groups" to find groups to join.

3) Create your own group

When you create your own group, you can add connections (or fans) to it, and it becomes a lead-generating list. Now, you can send bulk emails to this growing list, promoting products, services, and events, like teleseminars, Webinars, contests, and virtual book tours.

Connecting to Other Social Media

It's best not to connect your Twitter account to your Facebook account. If you have too many updates to your account, Facebook could ban the account. You want to select what content posts to each social media site.

You do want to connect your blog to Facebook. When you create a blog post, it will also show up on Facebook.

It's best to post on your page three to five times a day. You can schedule posts ahead of time. Pick a time and schedule a week's or a month's worth of posts. You can always post news and other information in real time.

Step 4 - Set Up LinkedIn

LinkedIn is a site that was originally set up mainly for freelancers, contractors, and other professionals who are looking for jobs. Having connections in your field is always helpful. Even having only 25 contacts can put you within reach of over a million potential contacts.

There are over twelve million small-business people on LinkedIn, which is roughly 20 percent of its total user base. As a writer, you are a small business owner, and you can use LinkedIn to promote your business.

Another benefit to being listed in LinkedIn is that your LinkedIn profile page usually comes up on the first page when you Google your own name. This gives you visibility and credibility.

Using a LinkedIn Account

Here are the ways you can use LinkedIn to market yourself:

- Link with people who are related to your business
- Quality counts more than quantity
- Build a relationship with your targeted audience
- When you invite someone into your network, be sure to include a personal note of how you know them or how they know you
- You can ask for testimonials (or blurbs), which LinkedIn calls recommendations

Getting Connected

The beauty of connections in LinkedIn is that you have more connection possibilities because of the tiered structure. You make connections on the first tier by directly contacting people you know. Once you connect with someone, you can export his/her name and email address, unlike Facebook and Twitter.

You can go to your contact's profile and see who he/she is connected to. Then you can ask your first-tier contacts to introduce you to your second-tier contacts, and your second-tier contacts to introduce you to your third-tier contacts. You can go to "Network Statistics" to see how many people are in each tier.

Groups

You can join groups of people in your field of interest. When you join a group, you can link your networks, join in discussions, and see the activity of the members, including how many relationships they have, their recommendations, and their discussions.

One way to use a group is to click on the members to see their profiles and determine if you would like to connect with them or not. You can also find potential joint venture partners in the groups. You can promote your own events, like teleseminars, book tours (virtual or otherwise), and book signings to the entire group.

Recommendations

When you get recommendations, you increase your exposure. Start by recommending other people. They will receive a prompt to send a reciprocal recommendation. If they don't respond, you can ask them to recommend you. You can give them some sentences to get them started on a recommendation.

Step 5 – Video

Why Use Video?

Video is one of the best ways to quickly build a relationship with your readers. Hearing your voice lets them know that you are a real person. You can make videos without appearing on camera yourself. However, if you appear on-screen occasionally, you'll build relationships much faster.

There are a few reasons you might want to use video:

- Simple, short videos can build a relationship with your readers faster than any other method.
- Video lets your personality show. It enables you to relate to your readers on a personal level.
- Most people watch hours of television a day. Even readers watch videos. Take a look at any online writing group to see how many links to videos are being passed around.
- Also, with an enticing video, you encourage non-readers to try your books.

Book trailers are becoming a standard way to promote books. They can be professional productions that cost thousands of dollars, or they can be simple slide presentations. There are several tools that let you create a professional book trailer simply and easily. YouTube is the best place to publish and promote your book trailers and other videos.

Where to Use Video?

- **The "about" page on your blog** - Using a short video on your "about" page is a great way to introduce yourself to your readers

- **Blog posts** - Creating blog posts where you show your writing area or your book setting draw readers into your world

- **YouTube** - YouTube has the potential to put you in front of a large number of viewers, some of whom are readers

Google now includes videos on the first page of searches. If you have a video tagged with your name, it will appear on the first page when anyone searches for you. Putting short videos on sites indexed by the search engines will make sure your video appears with your profile on the first page of Google searches. This can be helpful if others have the same name. Posting videos makes you stand out from others with the same name.

Google gives special love to videos created through their Google Hangout tool. This is an excellent tool for doing video interviews. The videos post directly to YouTube and rank in Google's search engine very quickly.

Getting Started

You don't need a perfect recording to have your readers relate to you. Writers know that readers are drawn to flawed characters. Readers identify with flawed writers as well. They want to know that authors aren't too different from themselves. They do imagine that authors lead more glamorous lives. (If only they knew!). Just reach out with your voice to connect to your readers.

You can use a digital camera to create a video or get a camera specifically for making videos. Once you have the recording, you can use free software to edit it such as Audacity. Both Windows and Mac computers come with recording software.

Another way to create a video is to use your computer and slide presentation software or Google Drive to create videos. You can use your photos or buy photos from any of the photo sites. It's possible to add music or your own voice. Or, if you like, you can hire voice-over talent to record the audio track for you.

Create a YouTube Account

Some people think of YouTube as a place where people put up ridiculous videos of their kids and pets. You may wonder if it's worth your time to use YouTube to promote yourself and your writing.

The answer is a resounding YES. If you don't take advantage of YouTube, you are wasting a golden opportunity.

Here are some benefits of social networking on YouTube:

1. People stay on the site longer, since links to related videos appear when one video finishes.
2. YouTube, the video giant, has become the second-most popular search engine. Only Google (who now owns YouTube) ranks higher.
3. YouTube is a social networking community. Viewers can leave comments and rate videos. The more comments and rating your videos receive, the

higher your videos will rank.

Respond to the comments and build a relationship with your viewers. This is a great way to bond with your readers and potential readers.

You will want to create your own "channel" on the YouTube site. Once you are registered, you can customize your account, upload videos, and set account preferences. Be sure to make proper use of tags (keywords) for your videos so people can find you.

Step 6 – Article Writing

Four reasons you might want to add article marketing to your skills. Some of the more common reasons are:

- Make money
- Share your knowledge
- Promote yourself
- Practice writing non-fiction

Promote Yourself and Your Writing

For authors, the most beneficial reason to write articles is to **promote yourself and your writing**.

Articles can expand your presence on the Internet and bring you new readers and fans. When folks see your name and your articles on many websites, it builds your credibility name recognition.

The most important place to use articles is on your own blog or website. One of the main reasons that search engines rank blogs above websites is that the content of blogs changes more often. (That's the reason you need to post to your blog frequently).

Fiction writers research a variety of subjects. You learn all sorts of strange facts about many different things. Rather than use those pieces of information as cocktail party chatter, why not turn them into articles that bring you and your writing to the attention of new readers?

If you can write fiction, you can write articles. Fiction authors know how to engage readers, use stories to get their point across, and structure pieces with a clear beginning, middle, and end. They know how to write in a voice that draws readers in and keeps them reading.

Non-fiction authors would do well to study the craft of fiction writing in order to improve their articles. Articles can give readers a taste of your expertise and lead them to seek more from your books.

Create Credibility and Authority

When people find your articles all over the Internet, this tells them that you are an authority on the subject. People need to see your name several times before they remember it. Having lots of articles online and in newsletters will make you stand out in the readers' minds.

Step 7 - Set up a Blog

Create Your Blog

You want to create a home on the Web where you can send your readers and prospective readers. This will require a website or blog. A blog is the best way to create a place where you can interact with your readers.

A blog lets you build a relationship with readers in a way that a static website cannot. Readers can interact on a blog by leaving comments. When you reply to people who comment on your blog, you are creating a dialogue.

What Can You Blog About?

If it's a personal blog, you can write about anything that interests you. If you have a business blog, you will want to blog about subjects related to your business that will be interesting to your readers. The idea is to get them to want to return to read more blog posts.

Blog ideas

- Share a resource
- Take a survey
- Have a contest
- Do an interview
- Share a story
- Answer a question
- Make a top five list
- Invite a guest writer
- Preview an article you wrote

There are lots of places where you can create a free blog on a third-party website. This will work to get you started. However, realize that you don't own the site or control the content. If you read the terms of service, you'll see that they can delete your site and your content at any time.

Use the domain name you registered and get hosting from a company you pay. This will give you a site that you control. You'll be able to hook your blog to your social networking accounts to repurpose your content and leverage your online presence.

Free Blog Sites

Blogger.com is a great place to get your feet wet in the online world. It will help you establish your online presence. It is also a great way to gain links to your primary site and to grab readers from other blogs. If you notice, there is a "Next Blog" button on the page. That can take readers away from your site as well as bring readers in.

WordPress is a popular blogging platform. However, there are two different types of WordPress Blogs:

1) **WordPress.com** provides a blogging service in the same manner Blogger does. That means that they provide the hosting and you don't OWN your blog. The domain name includes the word "wordpress."

2) **WordPress.org** is a software program that you upload to your own site. This kind of blog allows you to have your own domain name. WordPress provides program files that you can download and put on your own host. You pay for the hosting and therefore, control what happens to your site. The WordPress software is free, and an easy installation is provided by all good hosting companies. There are developers all over the world working on add-ins (called plug-ins). A lot of the plug-ins and themes are free.

Whatever online service you use, be sure to keep a copy of all of your content.

You can add pages to any type of website. The blogging software makes it easier to add pages. You don't need a webmaster to put up the pages. On a WordPress (self-hosted) blog, every post is on its own page. The home page shows the number of posts you set, but actually, each one is a separate page. Also, you can add "Pages." That's blog-speak for "pages that aren't really posts." The "About" page is an example of a blog page. The "Pages" will show up in the navigation bar, while the posts won't. Of course, there's a way to exclude pages from the navigation bar if you don't want the pages to show up.

You will also need to adjust the blog settings, add widgets, and install plug-ins in order to gain the most use and benefit from your self-hosted WordPress blog.

Connect Your Blog to Other Social Media

1. Connect your blog to Twitter using Twitter Tools
2. Connect your Facebook fan page by using the Facebook application,

Networked Blogs
3. Connect your LinkedIn page by using the LinkedIn application
4. Use FeedBurner to manage your feeds better, track your subscribers, and monitor the health of your feeds (http://Feedburner.com/)

Social Bookmarking

Social bookmarking started as a way to have your bookmarks on the Internet rather than an individual computer, but it evolved into social networking sites where people share their bookmarks.

You want to be careful not to bookmark your own domain/blog all of the time. You will need to bookmark about five other blog posts for every time you bookmark your own post. Bookmark the blogs you comment on as well as other sites. Some social bookmarking sites don't take comment URLs, so just bookmark the post URL.

Here are the top bookmarking sites:

- StumbleUpon
- Technorati
- Digg
- Delicious
- Reddit

Conclusion

This chapter has given you the beginnings of how to use social networking to benefit you as an author. These are some of the top networking sites: Blogs, Twitter, Facebook, LinkedIn, YouTube, and Google Plus. If you were unfamiliar with these, they may seem overwhelming. Start slowly and take small steps.

It's important to find out where your readers hang out and which social media sites yield the best results. If you are selling books on Amazon, you should join their affiliate program and use a different tracking code for each social media campaign. That will allow you to see which of your efforts result in actual book buyers.

Create a system to maximize your efforts while minimizing your social networking time

Most of the time when social networking is discussed, authors say that it is just a "time suck." Some writers spend so much time on these activities that their writing time suffers.

If you spend all of your time promoting, you won't have anything to promote. If you spend all of your time writing, you won't have anyone to read your words. The answer to this dilemma is to set up a system for managing your online activities.

Once everything is in place, having a system for your social networking activities can allow you to maintain a visible online presence while still having time to write. You can create a strong relationship with your readers in just 30 minutes a day.

When you have this system in place, it makes social networking so much easier. For more information about setting up a social networking system and for information about maximizing other social media sites of special interest to authors, visit http://IndiePublishingSuccess.com.

About Lynn Jordan

Lynn Jordan is an author and writing, publishing, and promotion consultant who works with authors to write, publish, and sell more books, reports, and memoirs. Reach more readers and boost your book sales. Drop her a note at Lynn@AuthorsTools.com.

Connect with her and get more writing, publishing, and promoting tips at:

http://twitter.com/lynnjordan

http://www.facebook.com/lynncjordan

http://www.youtube.com/lcjordan

http://plus.google.com/+LynnJordan

http://AuthorsTools.com

http://AuthorsToolsBlog.com

http://RegardingRomance.com

http://IndiePublishingSuccess.com

Do Your Words Sell?

By Judy Kettenhofen

How do you get... well... "you," out there?
How do you get your content out there, realize your dreams, and more?
How do you do it?

Well, the initial fabric of life, the way we interconnect, is through communication...

And, for a major part of our communication, that means using the medium of words....

But, as has been described by MANY linguists, words only constitute 93% of the meaning of our communication....

Right now, though, you are reading my words. You are not seeing my face, nor my posture, nor whether my cheeks are bright with excitement...

Nor a high-pitched staccato voice so you would know I'm excited...

(And, unconsciously, invite you into my excitement....)

Making an impact, an impression, realizing your importance...

These are part of the human experience....

At times, we can feel like a little kid at his/her first recital... timid, fearful, hesitant...

... with a parent nudging us out into the world....

Encouraging, friendly, warm...

Pushing us off into an unknown world, scary, uncertain....

(Is it any wonder that there are some languages where they use the same word for both "stranger"... and "enemy"? Or that many people list public speaking as more fearful than death?)

Our politeness often inhibits our ability to spread our wings....

Our shyness makes us shrink from who or what we can be....

Our fear that our secrets will be known, that we won't measure up...

... that all we know and love will be taken from us...

Keep us from sharing our genius... and keep us from being known and loved by even more....

"Words are more powerful than chains..."

As I write this, I just heard kidnapping victim Elizabeth Smart say these words... she had been held down in chains... but has found words are MORE powerful.... Yes, has found that "words are more powerful than chains"....

So, even though they only constitute 7% of our communication, they can completely construct our world...

... not just build it... but frame it... make it sad, happy, or exciting....

You see... the fearful child on the side of the recital stage is fearful because of the thoughts going through her mind...

... of her anticipation of the WORST possible outcomes...

... of making mistakes, of being shamed and embarrassed....

Words of Wonder...

I make a living from this set of tools of communication known as words...

... at least, most people think that at first....

After all, "writing" makes up part of the name of my craft: Copywriting....

But it really is much, much more than that....

And while I proudly give words to my clients...

... words assiduously chosen, poured over, connected...

... provided to give them "results" (usually, but not always, or always directly, money into their bank accounts)...

words do not live in a "solo" environment....

Few words actually represent an objective reality...

because words contain "baggage"...

(Some might call it "meaning"... but get two people together, and you can quickly see how different understandings of what a word represents can quickly lead to what we call "misunderstandings")...

Unearthing baggage...

... part of my job, then, is to have an understanding of what a particular word means in a particular context....

After all..."pool" means something different...

... in fact, evokes quite different experiences...

... when presented in front of...
+ a 10-year-old child on a hot summer day...
+ someone running a football-betting gambit...
+ someone with a cue stick in hand....

And those are just the more OBVIOUS differences...

... even if the word "pool" evokes a concrete hole in the ground filled with water....

Which pool? What are the associated experiences? And when...

... in fact, it's an amalgam of all of the experiences a person has had with that kind of pool...,

... the experiences not all having a fair share in making the impression....

Primary experiences... the introduction of the term, can have a profound influence...

... as can 'recency'... what was the LAST experience of "pool"....

(The word "shark" -- something unknown and foreign, definitely had a new set of associations after the movie "Jaws" came out)....

And then there is the dramatic... if, for instance, the reader saved someone from drowning in a pool (or was saved himself/herself)...

... or less dramatically, a pool that didn't fit with previous experiences... maybe an odd shape or a different color....

As you can see, the "meaning" of the word "pool" is quite dense....

And, that's just ONE simple four-letter word....

Unearthing baggage takeaways...

So, what's the point of all of this?

Well, first... to dispel the common idea that a word has an "objective" reality....

Second, that word CHOICE isn't merely a matter of selecting a set of impactful words from this or that copywriter's list of "power words"....

It hones in on 'why,' if you've worked with a professional copywriter (or marketer)... you MUST know your market....

And, as well, how your market can be influenced by popular culture...

(which is why I mentioned *Jaws*... but there is a wealth of other possibilities... for Boomers, *Star Trek*, for Gen X, *Star Wars*, for millennials... *Harry Potter*, etc.)....

In fact, I once wrote a tax letter where I mentioned "striped pajamas"... an archetype of prison garb from the cartoons and movies when I was growing up...

... when it was pointed out that it would not connect with many readers... who only know of orange jumpsuits...)

(And yes, I AM showing my age... aren't I?)....

And Just When You Thought It Was Safe to Go Into The Water...

But WAIT... I'm not done!

Because, a sister to understanding your market... the individual people in it, the word baggage they bring...,

(... think about this...now there are schools changing their sports team mascot name "cougar" because of the "new" meanings imbued in the last few years....)

It's also important to tap into the "maturity" of the market....

A brilliant, under-utilized understanding promulgated by the late copywriting Wizard Eugene Schwartz... and which MindValley founder and CEO Vishen Lakhani credits a LARGE degree of their success to...

(... Schwartz's book regularly goes for three figures...when marketers and copywriters can actually FIND it....)

Add In A Few Time-Tested Strategies...

Many years ago (MANY years ago), my (now ex-) brother-in-law was shipped off to Washington D.C. to bring this new found invention to politicians....

It's now FAR more common (you'll find it in Microsoft Word, where it's been for quite some time)... and known by the term "mail merge"....

Another term for it is... "personalization"....

You see... we copywriters are often known for being a word bunch...

... and told (over and over again), apologetically even, by people that they don't read our "long-form" salesletters....

(I'll let you in on a secret: We already know that...)...

In fact, the common retort to those who say, "I would NEVER read a long-form salesletter"... is to challenge them...

(say, if their name was "John Difficult Johanssen"...)

... by asking how much they would read of a letter that was headlined by, "The Secrets Of John Difficult Johanssen"....

Or, if you wanted to make it even more provocative..."The Secrets Of John Difficult Johanssen's Sex Life"....

But, I suspect the first would MORE than get the job done...

And, the one thing that can absolutely ensure that your salesletter will flop is to fail to include what we call a "Call To Action"...

... where we tell the reader to DO something...

(note: we don't ASK, we TELL..."; just go to http://www.nextday-copy.com to find out more")....

And Amazing Capabilities Previously Unknown To Direct Mailers...

I should back up a little...

You see, what I do is not just copywriting, but a very special form of copywriting known as "direct response" copywriting....

The other type of copywriting, FREQUENTLY denounced (quite incorrectly) as "brand" or "image" or "Madison Avenue" or "ad agency" copywriting...

... definitely has a place.

But direct response means... I want the reader to take action NOW....

It may be the one and ONLY opportunity that I have to make a sale....

(And yes, you would be totally correct -- it is, indeed, a "tall order"... requiring electrifying motivators, pulsing persuasion... throughout)....

So... before the Web, before the Internet... direct mailers kept VERY close track on statistics....

(And there's MUCH to be learned from how they found people to mail... as well as "tricks" pulled on them by mailing list providers... including one which helped throw one marketer into jail)....

Profitability in direct mail was (and IS)... very fragile. Many more promotions get sent out than those that succeed. But when one succeeds... the rewards can be HUMONGOUS... and swamp out the pain of the failures....

Remember... direct mail is NOT particularly cheap... and it never was....

(If you want to discover how the most-mailed direct mail piece came to be, written by the late great copywriter Gary Halbert, go check out the "Coat of Arms" Ad breakdown by Gary's sons, Bond and Kevin Halbert, at http://halbertising.com. It's an AWESOME story, full of so much drama and excitement, I've told Bond they should make a movie about it. It's a true story of entrepreneurship, persistence, and, FINALLY, jaw-dropping success)....

... Are Available For MUCH Less Today...

There's no real good reason why any marketer should not be testing...

... well, as long as they've taken care of what I would call the "preliminaries"....

I mean, I had a client who, before moving on to a form of testing that could have actually put money in his pocket...

wanted to TEST a very minor part before putting it into what would become his moneymaking piece....

Oddly enough, he wasn't willing to change certain OTHER things (like the FONT -- granted, it WAS a lovely font)....

So, while testing ABSOLUTELY should be considered... it's not the TOTAL answer....

For instance...,

You MUST know where your traffic is coming from...,

You MUST have enough traffic to come up with sufficient statistical "confidence" levels...,

You MUST be using a robust tracking solution...,

(You would undoubtedly be surprised to know how I once tested three sales pages... two of which were the same, except that one of them had the snippet of software that controlled WHICH version would be displayed...

... and the very well-known tracking solution indicated that ONE of these two versions -- that appeared EXACTLY the same to the reader -- was considered STATISICALLY BETTER than the other)...

... and you really should understand that statistics are based on probability.... They are NOT an absolute..., but are used to generalize a belief based upon a much smaller sample (which is how scientific "facts" are built, by the way)....

So... it's not just enough to say "test".... It's important to understand the strengths, the weaknesses, and, yes, the "gotchas" of testing....

So, while testing "should" be done...,

... it doesn't happen overnight...,

... and while it can very much be cheaper than having to run direct mail campaigns...,

... done wrong, without knowing the idiosyncrasies...

... not only can it be a waste of money... it could send you down the entirely wrong path altogether....

But Be REALLY Careful --

Without going into depth about the reasons why...

... let me ask you about what conclusions you would draw if you ran what we call an "A/B split test"...

... one where every other visitor sees the same page, and the ones in between see the version being "tested."

Results:

Page A: 100 visitors - 2 sales
Page B: 100 visitors - 4 sales

Would you say...

- Page B is better than page A, and start sending everyone to page B?

- Page B is TWICE as good as page A, and get rid of page A right away?

- Page B converts TWICE as well as page A?

Okay... here's where probability comes in....

The answer is...

... there is INSUFFICIENT information to draw a conclusion.

Now, good testing software will figure out the complex mathematics to determine whether there's enough "sampling," with enough results... to "confidently" (hence the name, "confidence levels")...

... draw a conclusion....

Okay?

It's NOT A No-brainer...

Testing comes with a cost...

... not just of the software, the expertise, or the installation....

... It costs TIME...

Meaning, if you have TIME-SENSITIVE material...

(Say, for a product launch)...

... where getting an email (say) out there helps you scoop up more "low-hanging fruit"...

... having a piece of software (as happened with one of my clients) that will split-test your emails and then send out the "better" email to the rest of your list after it has drawn a conclusion...

... can COST you more than the lost opportunity of sending out that email early....

This is why testing is NOT a complete answer...

And why hiring someone like me...

... who has written thousands of words, earned my clients millions of dollars, helped bring them success and fame...

... can be WELL-worth the investment....

And just to entice you further... if you visit this link (http://www.nextday-copy.com/bk1) and sign up within the first month of this book's publication, I have a very special offer for you...

... one you could turn into a LOT of money....

But even if it's LATER... you'll still get a SUPER deal....

I look forward to getting to know you better...

... and help you to get YOUR message, YOUR product, "YOU"... out there....

Oh... just one more thing....

You can pick up my best-selling product on FAST Copywriting here:

http://www.warriorforum.com/warrior-special-offers-forum/710413-warrior-special-offer-day-900-sold-97-off-value-speed-read-copy-speed-prospects-your-buy-button.html

<fin>

Biography: Copywriter Judy Kettenhofen has been plying her trade in Silicon Valley since 2005. Before that, she spent over 20 years at Silicon Valley companies like Apple and Sun doing software development. With many award-winning salesletters to her credit, with conversions of 10% on a tax letter, and over 80% on an up-sell, she takes a few new and very select clients each year.

You can find out more about her and her services here: http://www.NextDay-Copy.com/bk2.html

Copyright 2013, Judy Kettenhofen, Used With Permission.

How Can Mastering "The Operating System of the Universe" Transform Your Life?

(And Why You MUST Master It!)

By Dan Klatt

"Make A Difference Man"
Personal Growth Cafe Head Coach

There's a principle which very few people understand... and far fewer put to use in their daily lives.

However, all individuals who've reached success in whatever their calling is – *without exception* – practiced this principle, whether they realized it or not.

Napoleon Hill, author of *Think and Grow Rich*, tells the story of how Andrew Carnegie, regarded today as the second-richest person in history, taught him everything he knew about making money.

The famed philanthropist told the young cub reporter we each have total control over just one thing, which is all we need to have whatever we decide will be ours. That one thing is the power to control your mind and direct it to "whatever ends you may desire."

Really think about that!

You've heard of 'The Law of Attraction.'

You know, "You reap what you sew."

You may call it 'karma.' And you may live by, "Do unto others as you would have them do unto you."

You may think of it as 'The Golden Rule': "Treat others the way you want to be treated."

You've seen 'The Secret,' the idea that "thoughts are things"... and other representations of the same core concept.

Or you may know it as the 'Law of Cause and Effect,' in all its many subtle ramifications.

The way I get you to understand – *and <u>LIVE</u>* – the fundamental core principle is far more powerful than any other way of conceptualizing this in-born ability you have, which you in fact *NEED* to use... to have everything you're meant to experience!

Think about that point, carefully.

As I mentioned earlier, EVERY person who has enjoyed any significant measure of success has implemented this principle, even though virtually all have done so without knowing it.

The thing is, you're meant to experience something very specific in your life.

You're here for a reason, which is uniquely yours.

In the West, people tend to think of that as their life purpose.

The East has a long, rich tradition of reflection, introspection, and guidance from sages and enlightened masters.

There's not even a word for 'dharma' in the West. Although, that's what you will begin to appreciate and live in harmony with... "the path" that is uniquely yours.

Quite simply, when you do, you enjoy success and happiness. Life just flows.

When you go against what is really your nature or how you're built, you create pain and suffering. It seems life is a constant struggle.

How do you know what your dharma is?

Think about the kind of person you are. (Not "what you've done"... but "who you are.")

Are you more of a teacher, coach, consultant, adviser?

Are you a fighter, warrior, advocate, defender? Or leader or ruler?

Or are you a business person, entrepreneur, merchant, sales person?

Are you the employee or worker who likes the security of a steady paycheck and structure of a nine-to-five job?

Or are you more the artist, the creative person who can't "paint between the lines"?

(Or if you don't fit into one of the primary dharmas, you may be meant to be someone others are meant to serve so their lives have meaning and fulfillment.)

You will understand "The Operating System of the Universe" shortly.

Although, you must first understand your true nature and "how everything works" within that context.

Because if you neglect that step, you may be going against "The Current." If you did that, you could work very hard and become successful. Except, then, you would not be happy, and that success likely would be short-lived.

So, what is your dharma?

How well have you been aligning with it? Or have you been "pushing against it," causing pain and struggle?

Your dharma has been described as "riding the horse in the direction it's going." When you're doing that, you're enjoying the ride. If you don't, you won't.

Think of your dharma as the natural way your life is meant to unfold.

To help you appreciate this better, consider my example.

In college, I wanted to be a disc-jockey because I loved music so much. That was my major and planned career path. Although right after I graduated, the owner of a small-town 24-hour polka station turned me down for the overnight shift, at minimum wage. Right there, I knew it was not "in the cards" for me to be in radio.

I could have tried to "force" it, although even IF I could have found a radio job, I would not have been happy, and probably would not have been able to pay the bills.

Instead, I began pursuing jobs in my minor, journalism, in which I had a straight A grade-point average in college and excelled in. Jobs in newspaper reporting, and later editing, came easily because they aligned with my dharma.

When I quit that profession and became an author and coach, it was easy to see how the journalism career shaped me into a writer, an investigative "reporter" who gets to the heart of whatever issue is holding someone back... and even more importantly, someone who believes in himself enough to have the impact my work is destined to have... on the world.

(Growing up, I had low self-esteem. However, as a reporter, I had to stand shoulder-to-shoulder with governors, senators, and heads of industry.)

Being in newspapers was not my dharma, although it was an important stepping stone that gave me the skills I needed to learn to be an effective teacher and personal growth leader.

Now, it's your turn.

Look back over the major events of your life. See how they fit in with and served "The Master Plan" for your life, the Big Picture.

Be cognizant of examples when you aligned with your dharma and when you resisted or fought against it.

… And what happened as a result?

Share your thoughts and examples in the Personal Growth Cafe Lounge at http://www.PersonalGrowthCafe.com/FacebookLounge/. That way, we all better understand what dharma is and how it's always the undercurrent of our lives.

How aligned are you with your dharma – right now?

What adjustments do you need to make to be in perfect alignment?

Because it is part of my dharma and our shared destiny to help you find that "easy path to success" that comes with perfect alignment, and because my personal mission is answering the question: *"How can I be of greater service to more people?"*

… Allow me to send you the eight-page report I have, "A Rose Is A Rose," which will give you a better grasp on what your personal dharma is and how much you'll benefit from aligning perfectly with it. Get it at http://www.PersonalGrowthCafe.com/dharma/.

(By the way, "dharma" is the one thing missing in virtually ALL personal growth and success trainings, which is why almost everyone gets very little tangible results from the materials they buy to better themselves).

(There is no escaping your dharma. There's only fighting against it, and suffering... or aligning with it, and celebrating!).

Now that you understand dharma, and you're aware of how yours influences and shapes all aspects of your life, you're able to fully appreciate – and benefit from – "The Operating System of the Universe"!

It's called "The First Covenant," and it's... "The Law." It's just how everything works, all the time, without exception. Just as gravity works all the time, whether we know about it or not.

Quite simply, "The First Covenant" is the fact that, "What you give your attention to and empower with strong feelings, you create more of."

I realize you "get it" intellectually. And you resonate with its simplicity. *(And recognize it intuitively as "inner-truth.")*

And, yet, don't underestimate its importance... or how much it will change everything for you once you've taken it to heart... and especially once you've made it automatic!!!

People of all walks of life "get" the first part, that whatever you focus on, you create more of.

For example, even my massage therapist says it eloquently, "You go where you look."

Or my favorite definition of the "Law of Attraction" comes from *The Master Key System* by Charles F. Haanel: "Much gathers more."

Although, even among the people who inherently understand this concept, who do you know who actually lives by it?

Anyone!?

That's because they miss the second part of it, which is where the unlimited, infinite power behind it truly lies!

That's the part of the equation where you "empower what you're focusing on with strong feelings."

It's easy for everyone to "get" this part of it by looking at where a large number of people – FAIL.

We only need to look to the economy to understand this inevitable truth, firsthand.

Think about this: What's the dominant thought you've been having about the economy, or money, more specifically?

What were you giving your attention to before and during the last recession? How were you feeling about that?

For about a year before the housing "bubble" burst and "all hell broke loose" (at least for many people, some of whom lost their homes; for others, their retirements)... it seemed the national media had become what I call "recession cheerleaders."

The headlines and stories everywhere were about the latest threat to your money. Somewhat in jest, I say, the media was all but saying, "Go recession! Go! Go! GO!"

The effect of that "mass fear hysteria" was "The First Covenant" in action!

Think about it: "What you give your attention to and empower with strong feelings, you create more of."

What really happened in that time frame?

People were becoming obsessed with *their fears* about what _MIGHT_ happen. That *focal point* became so concentrated, it became an expectation, or even something "everyone" knew was "going down."

That example helps you appreciate how powerful "The First Covenant" is, right!? And how much you need to be aware of what you're giving your attention to and how you're empowering that focus with strong feelings.... Right?

Obviously, that was a careless use of people's power... (because they didn't know any better – THEN – as you do NOW!).

It also emphasizes the danger of giving your attention to anything you don't want. Because, to the degree you're empowering that focus with strong feelings, such as fear, that becomes the level of power you're sending to what you're focusing on.

Remember that power Andrew Carnegie tells us is the only thing we have total control over?

We have that power because we need it to manifest the life we desire. We have the desire in the first place because we're meant to experience its fulfillment.

The thing is, you were born a Manifestation Master. That's why you have this power.

This insight will help you appreciate even better how your power works:

You know how "The First Covenant" is "The Operating System of the Universe." It's just how everything works, all the time, without exception.

Well, think of your subconscious mind as "The Operating System of Your Body."

It's always there in the background, aware of everything you're focusing on and empowering with feeling.

Because it's taking that focus as a command. And the level of feeling you have about what you're focusing on as the priority level you're assigning to that command.

This is extremely important for you to understand because it determines your level of success, happiness, joy and fulfillment.

Whether you're focusing on something you want or something you don't want, how excited or scared you are about that focus becomes what you're "Creating, Attracting, Manifesting and Allowing" more of.

Because your subconscious mind takes in everything you're thinking, writing, saying, seeing and doing. To the extent you empower that focus with strong feelings, it processes that action as a command: "This is my top priority! This is what I'm instructed to create more of!"

... That's exactly what it filters for and finds everything it can in alignment with the feeling quality of what you're focusing on.

In other words, when you're afraid something might happen, then everything you notice seems to be about that thing that frightens you. For example, when you're worried about money, you suddenly find all kinds of things happening to "justify" those concerns about not having enough money.

And when you're really excited or passionate about something... everything seems to fall into place to support you in living that.

For example, now that you're clear about "The Operating System of the Universe"... you're getting *VERY EXCITED* about all the great things you're going to begin experiencing, starting now.... and you're feeling _WONDERFUL_ about all these great things "happening" *(because you created them!)*.

That's what you're now empowering... and will begin filtering for... and finding!!!

That's just how everything works.

It's just that most people have no clue that this is how they're creating their lives, moment by moment.

(I'm changing that, very quickly, through my training, "Transforming Your Life By Being of Service" at http://www.PersonalGrowthCafe.com/Difference/ - so _EVERYONE_ gets this life-changing truth! If you haven't yet done this training, make sure you accept this heartfelt gift, which actually sells for $2,000 – right now.)

Now that you understand how this works, you recognize how foolish it would be to give ANY of your attention to anything you don't want to experience more of... Right!?

You were born a master of the way you create your life. And your subconscious mind treats you as the master you *ARE*... as though everything you focus on, you want to experience more of. Because that's how you're wired. That's how you're meant to live!

That's part of your dharma, your nature.

Is that clear?

Are you seeing how critical "The First Covenant" is... and how much you need to be aware of it, moment by moment?

The key is to keep your attention on ONLY "what gives you joy, inspires you, and moves you closer to your Goals, Desires and Dreams." Because, when that becomes 100% of your "Empowered Focus," that becomes 100% of your life experience.

To LIVE "The First Covenant," hold "The Focus" as long as you can, feeling it as intensely as you can, and return to it as often as you can.

Do that more tomorrow than you did today. Eventually, once you've done that long enough, consistently enough, it takes root and becomes automatic.

Think of what happens when you boil water.

It doesn't work to turn up the heat really hot for 5 seconds and then turn the heat off. It doesn't work to turn the heat on just a little, either, even if you keep it on lukewarm for a long time.

It's the same with living the fulfillment of your Goals, Desires, and Dreams. Hold "the heat" (your power!) long enough, intensely enough... and soon, you will reach the "Threshold of Manifestation," and the things you want will begin happening very quickly.

... As they're meant to, for you!

You can do this on your own if you're focused and disciplined.

(If you're not, or you allow yourself to be distracted easily, I wouldn't even recommend doing this on your own... I would say begin right away with my "Focused Wealth Build" at http://www.PersonalGrowthCafe.com/focusedwealth.html.)

Or, if you really resonate with this (and you're already pretty successful), then I would especially recommend "The First Covenant 30-Day Immersion" that's part of "Commanding Your Destiny," where you will get my best coaching. We'll jump right in, full force!

If that interests you, carefully empower that... and make it yours!!!

You may apply to join "Commanding Your Destiny" at http://www.PersonalGrowthCafe.com/coaching/.

Either way, make sure you give this issue your full attention... take it to heart... and begin living it!

It _IS_ that important. Begin doing it immediately.

How To Choose Powerfully

By Deb Lange

Mentor, Healer, Nurturer, Mother, Friend
www.deblange.com

Do you go around in circles when you have to make a choice, not knowing what to decide and either choosing the wrong thing and regretting it or not choosing and feeling stuck?

What if you could learn new ways to choose powerfully that are aligned with your inner truth and heart's desire?

What if you knew how to notice choices that...

- Light you up
- Sense and feel right, even though your thinking, rational mind tells you differently
- Create new pathways and new ways to overcome obstacles
- Are tolerable, but are not really for your highest good
- Are connected to a deep sense of your purpose in life and who you are.

Well, yes, you can!

In this chapter, I share a story about one of my clients who has learned to choose powerfully, and I introduce you to three ways to expand your abilities in:

1. Sensing – what your physical sensory body knows is "right" for you
2. Imagining – what your body/spirit imagines when you want to make a choice
3. Feeling – what your body is telling you through your energy and emotional intelligence to activate better ways to choose powerfully what is right for you.

Did you know that when you make choices to "get" others to love you or to please others, it often backfires?

When you choose what is "right" for you, even though you imagine others may not like what you choose, you create your own happiness, and your significant others are happy too!

Jess's Story

I was coaching Jess recently. She is learning how to choose powerfully, and she told me she was so excited because normally her boyfriend would call up and say, "I'd love you to come over, but I have things to do, so I can not spend much time with you."

She would say, "Okay; I'll come over anyway." And she would go. In the meantime, she would be thinking, "I know I want to be with you and if I don't come, maybe you won't like that, so I'd better say 'yes' so you know I love you." Then she'd go over to his place, and just like he told her, he would be busy doing his jobs. She would sit in his house twiddling her thumbs, thinking about all of the things that she would really love to be doing back at her place.

In the meantime, her body was getting really irritated and resentful. Then he started to notice this and asked, "What's going on?' and she said, "Nothing. Nothing's wrong."

You know the story. The next minute, they're having an argument, and it wasn't a good night at all. She ends up leaving after they've had a fight. The next day and the next one after that, they have to recover from the conflict. They had no idea why it arose. The tension leaves residue in their bodies, creating distance rather than connection between them.

You know how that happens, saying "yes" to something that you didn't really want to do or "no" to something you really want to do.

However, Jess has been learning how to focus on her body and how to choose powerfully, so, recently, she said,

"Debbie, I am so excited. My boyfriend asked me over. I asked what we were going to do and what he had to do that night. He told me he had to pack and get organized for his trip. I knew we wouldn't have time for each other, and I said, 'No, you do what you have to do tonight. I have things I want to do and I'm going to stay at my place. You are not going away for a few days. I will see you tomorrow night when we have time to enjoy each other's company."

"It was awesome! I got to organize my room and play my drums and chill out,

which is what I really need. He got to pack and get organized in peace. We went out the next day and it was great. It was fantastic. I didn't say a white lie. I didn't have to pretend. I chose powerfully. I chose what was good for me, and it was good for our relationship at the same time."

Jess has gone on and made powerful choices for her career and her relationship since this time. She has learned to notice what arises in her body. She has learned to imagine new pathways to solve relationship challenges with her boss, family members, and partner. She has also learned to understand the messages that arise from her feelings and what action is the best to take for her best interests.

So here is an invitation for you

Would you like to become an explorer of your innate wisdom just like Jess? Be able to choose powerfully for both the little things and the big choices in life?

In this chapter, we are going to deepen skills in:

1. **Noticing the Physical Sensory Responses in Your Body**
2. **Activating your Imagination and Playing with Options**
3. **Understanding The Messages From Your Feelings**

1 Noticing the Physical Sensory Responses in Your Body

Take the following action today and over the next few weeks.

Today, pay attention to how your physical sensory body responds to invitations and choices. You might not be used to this, as we have been trained to think and consider our thoughts rather than what our body is telling us. So, it may take a little time to notice the messages that you have been overlooking.

Your physical sensory body responds with tingles, tension, ease, expansiveness, tightness, changes in temperature, paralysis, feelings, aches, pains, and more.

Pay attention, and notice how your body responds when asked to make a choice.

While learning to deepen this knowledge, it is good to practice on small choices. Notice your physical sensory responses when you are asked by your partner, friend, or family member what you want for dinner, whether you will go for a walk, what to watch on TV, will I walk this way or that way when I go to work, what flavour ice-cream do I want, etc.

The better you get at connecting with your inner wisdom on the small things, the more powerful you will be with the big choices in life.

There are four things to notice in your exploration:

1: YES

When you say 'YES' to something, and you really know it is right for you.

How does your body respond? Notice. Pay attention. Capture the information.

Does your body tingle with excitement? Where? All over? In your heart? Does your body feel expansive and open? We all feel something different. What does 'YES' feel like for you?

2: NO

When you say 'NO' to something, and you really know that 'No' is right for you.

How does your body respond? Notice. Pay attention. Capture the information.

Does your body feel firm, closed, solid, grounded? Where? All over? In your back? We all feel something different. What does 'NO' feel like for you?

3: MAYBE

When you are unsure, maybe you say 'yes,' but on second thought, really mean 'no,' or you say 'no' and really mean 'yes.'

How does your body respond? Notice. Pay attention. Capture the information.

Does your body feel uneasy, queasy? Where? All over? In your gut? We all feel something different. What does 'MAYBE' feel like for you?

4: PRETENDING

Sometimes, we pretend to want to do something and say 'YES' even though we know we really want to say 'No.'

Sometimes, we pretend we don't want something and say 'NO' even though we know we really want to say 'Yes.'

These are oftentimes when we are pleasing others or doing something as we believe it will make us look good or others will love us, etc.

How does your body respond? Notice. Pay attention. Capture the information.

Does your body feel irritated, like moving? Where? All over? In your legs? We all feel something different. What does it feel like when you are PRETENDING?

You will experience four different physical sensory body and energetic responses.

Learn to notice the difference. You will come to realize this is incredibly valuable body data for learning how to be able to choose powerfully.

Any time you have to make a choice, even if all of the rational reasons in the world would have you say 'YES' because everyone else thinks something is right for you, if you are in touch with your body's response, you can check in and see if it feels good deep in your body.

I invite you to play with this, test it out, learn to connect with the deep sensory, energetic, and spiritual messages that arise through your body/spirit.

So, that is one way of noticing and sensing our physical sensory responses.

Keep noticing, connecting, and practicing every day of your life. Now, we are going to explore different options for the choices you want to make in life.

2 Activating your Imagination and Playing with Options

Did I use the word 'play'? Yes. Just because you are an adult does not mean you have to stop playing.

When you were a child, you learned the most information in the shortest possible time through:

- Playing
- Sensing
- Feeling
- Touching
- Smelling
- Seeing
- Tasting
- Hearing
- Imagining
- Discovering
- Experimenting

So, now, I invite you to play!

Whatever choice you have to make, imagine three options.

Yes, three options.

When you have the three options, I invite you to play with each option as if you have chosen that pathway and see what it feels like with all of your senses activated. Imagine you are in a movie, and you are writing the script of how that choice will play out in your life. Imagine the people you will meet, your physical location, what you hear yourself saying, what you hear others saying. Use all of your senses: Auditory, visual, and kinesthetic, to bring that choice to life.

Here is an example:

Let's imagine you are making a career choice and have been given an opportunity to work for another company.

So, rather than think I can stay or I can go, which are just two options, imagine there are at least three options:

1. You could stay where you are currently working
2. You could work for the new company
3. You could go into business for yourself.

Now, play with how each choice feels in your body. Play with the body sensations that are evoked when you imagine living that choice.

Option 1

Imagine staying with your current company. What is evoked? Is there a feeling of dread because you don't want to really work for that boss? Is there a sense of contentment, as you are happy where you are working?

Just stay with your initial response, and then explore it a little bit longer. Practice staying with the choice as if you are really choosing it and see what else emerges.

Option 2

Imagine working for a new company. Imagine taking that position. Sense how your body feels when you imagine taking that new position or moving to that new company. What's your sensory response? Do you feel energized? Do you feel nervous? Imagine yourself as if you are in a movie, working for that company.

Option 3

Explore another choice. For example: "I'm going to leave the corporate world or employment for good and I'm going to start my own business." Be present to your body's response.

What does your body feel when you imagine yourself leaving your current employment and starting a new business. Do you feel excited, invigorated, enlivened, frightened? Stay with these different emotions, feelings, and body sensations to explore them further to feel what is really a "yes" and what is really a "no" so that you get to know what is a "yes" and what is a "no" in your body.

Summary of Imagining 3 Choices

Your imagination is really important in this process. When you have a choice to make, imagine them all fully. Practice each one. I am going to try on being self-employed. I'm going to imagine what it's like. It's like writing a video script, and you're the character.

Imagine leaving your current employment, having the celebration, packing up your things. Make it as real as possible and imagine it. Imagine setting up your office in your home or finding a new office. Bring it in as if you are making a video, a visual image. What would you be hearing? What would people be saying to you? What would you be hearing in your head? What would you be feeling?

Bring all of this into your imagination and play it out. Live it for a while to see how you actually feel about this choice.

Your imagination, playing, and practicing are important activities to know how to choose powerfully.

Playing is an important part of making new choices and choosing powerfully. Often, we make it such hard, serious work as if our life depended on it. You can play. You can experiment. You can figure out how much time you've got before you need to make the choice. In that amount of time, try it on, experiment, see how each choice feels, which brings us to your feelings.

3 Understanding the Messages from Your Feelings

The Third Way: Our Feelings

When you imagine your three options, you probably noticed different feelings arising. Few of us have learned how to "read and understand" our feelings, so we often take actions and make choices after inaccurately listening to our feelings.

For example, perhaps you felt nervous imagining taking on a new position, so you chose to stay where you are currently employed. You thought the nervousness meant, "do not take a risk and stay with what you know."

However, nervousness means different things for different people in different contexts.

The more you pay attention to your body's responses and notice your feelings, the more you will start to understand what your feelings are telling you in any particular situation.

Here is a brief introduction to understanding a new way to take actions based on the feelings in your body.

This is a guide. It is not prescriptive. Check yourself for what the meaning of your feelings are for you in your current situation. We are all different, but there are some common meanings of our feelings across cultures.

Frustration

Is often related to needing to see new actions, as our old ways no longer work for us. Check that you may have exhausted all current possibilities. Imagine new pathways, new options, new choices. Be creative and imagine totally new ways to understand your situation.

Anxiety, Nervousness, or Fear

Is often related to safety, security, or confidence issues. Check what you need to do to feel safe and secure about a choice. You are responsible for your safety. If you want to choose a new pathway, and you feel anxiety, check in with yourself to see if there are ways to create safety. If there are no ways to create safety, your fear or anxiety may be warning you that it is not a right choice for you.

Joy, Bliss, Expansiveness

Is often related to a right path for us. This usually means the choice, thought, or action is right for you. Check in with yourself. Does this feel true for you? Is your body opening up to what will give you great joy? Will you take it? Are you ready to enjoy the joy, bliss, and expansiveness of this choice?

Anger

Is often related to respect and boundary issues. Where have you let someone walk all over you? Where have you let someone take away your power? What do you need to do to restore your self-respect?

Does this mean you are angry and blaming someone for a choice you have made in the past? If you begin to make choices for yourself, how does that feel in your body? Allow the anger, which is energy, to be released in a safe way. Running, beating a cushion, yelling in the shower, are safe ways to release anger. Taking action for yourself to create respect will release the anger.

Resentment

Is often related to blaming someone or yourself for something that happened in the past. This is also related to living with regret and living in the past rather than knowing you have influence over the present and your future.

Who are you blaming for your current situation? How can you take responsibility for creating your life now? Rather than blame others, see where you can take action to restore your personal power and respect your ability to make choices for yourself. See how you can focus taking action now to create a better future rather than being resentful about something that happened in the past. Learn to accept your regret and take new actions to be happy with your next choices.

Sadness

Is often related to loss. What needs to be honored, cared for, loved? How can you allow yourself to feel sadness at lost opportunities or at the loss of something? What can you do to love and care for yourself to allow the sadness to flow through you? Feel the sadness and let it be released.

This is an introduction to understanding the messages from your feelings. There is much to learn from your feelings.

There are more ways to learn how to access your own inner Guru so you can make powerful choices in your life.

1. Noticing – your multiple 'selves'
2. Connecting – your spiritual guidance
3. Moving – your body to sense what it knows

Check into my website, www.deblange.com, for additional resources.

Summary

Do you have a choice to make?

1: Consider three options.

Imagine each option playing out as if you are an actor in a movie.

2: Notice your physical sensory responses to each choice.

What feels like a 'yes,' a 'no,' a 'maybe,' a pretense.

3: Notice what you feel about each option.

Take the action that the feeling is calling out for you to take to restore your well-being.

Now, choose powerfully what you feel, sense, and imagine to be "right" for you.

In Conclusion

This is a brief introduction to three ways you can add to what you currently do to make powerful choices for yourself, and for your life to be a powerful 'YES' or 'NO' to choices in your life.

Want to deepen these skills?

You can purchase the **"How To Choose Powerfully"** bundle of MP3 audio, slides, eJournal, and eBook for more exercises to practice the deepening of these skills.

Subscribe to my Newsletter at www.deblange.com for additional resources on how you can access your Intuitive Body Wisdom to make powerful choices for your relationships and your life.

There are a few places available for one-on-one Mentoring; apply here. If you have questions, challenges, or comments, come on over to my blog and leave me a comment or drop me a line at hello@deblange.com.

I look forward to hearing how you are now making powerful choices in your life.

See you at www.deblange.com.

About Deb Lange

Author, Mentor, Nurturer, Friend

Are you working on achieving your dreams in life and business, only something is missing? Maybe you are unhappy with your relationship, or you don't believe in yourself or you have had a significant life event throw up a challenge. You have dreams for your business but you feel stuck?

Who do you turn to?

I am a specialist in significant life and business events that leave us wondering, "How on Earth did I get here?" I had a successful management consulting business, fantastic international assignments facilitating leadership programs, I loved my work, had two great kids and a wonderful, successful, supportive husband. But I took my eye off of one part of the big picture: my relationship with my husband. After divorce, I cared for my parents until their passing. Finding myself single, I chose to travel the world to learn from ancient wisdom with people far and wide.

I had my body painted by the Himba people in Namibia; connected with nature with the bush men in the Kalahari; danced with street kids in Soweto to say no to sexual abuse; was inspired by world class violinists and artists in Slovenia; walked a song line in Australia with indigenous people; whispered with horses in Colorado; studied with Thich Nat Hahn, a Buddhist monk in France, and so much more.

I combined this new wisdom with my knowledge from Masters and Business Degrees and my experience in my consultancy business. It is these practices that I now call Intuitive Body Wisdom™ that I share with clients so they can create the success, freedom, peace, soulful businesses and relationships they want to thrive.

In simple terms, I guide you to access the wisdom that is already inside you, only you have forgotten how to listen. Connected to your own "Inner Guru" you have an internal navigation system that guides you to keep track of what is often invisible but is influencing our actions in the world:

- The alignment of our values and principles with our actions
- The consequences and unintended consequences of our actions
- The surfacing of unconscious beliefs that are sabotaging your life, business and relationships
- Deeply connect to the source of our emotional and spiritual wisdom

Subscribe to my newsletter to be the first to hear of the launch of my book, *Be Your Own Guru*, access your intuitive body wisdom and create and sustain the life and business of your heart's desire." You can contact me at my site, www.deblange.com, or email me at hello@deblange.com.

This is what clients say,

"I had a giant life reset, moving countries, ending relationships, changing career direction, it was at the same time I met Deborah Lange, I has amazing, I shared simple and very, very effective tools that are easy to use, and leave you feeling like you've got your own back and all the good feelings and ease (that I have never felt before); the tools are practical ways to apply all the clichés we've heard so often, like "love yourself," "tune in" and "surrender".... I shows you HOW to do it and it feels wonderful."

Candace Loy
Phd Student and Artist, New Zealand

"I highly recommend Deb. I came to my not knowing what my worth is. I have never been happier in my life with my career, relationships, health and well-being.

I can go on and on and on but the bottom line is, Deb is heaven sent to me. I will not be who I am right now without my help. Thank you Deb!"

Vanessa Ilagan
Business Analyst, Hawaii

"Deb helped me to get straight to the core of my issues, and it was really clear to me what I needed to do next. I've already implemented some of the changes and am feeling centered, calm and grounded. So much gratitude."

Linzi Wilson
Entrepreneur, London

How To Grow Your Business By Writing a Book

By Shelley Luzaich

Many entrepreneurs, coaches, and consultants realize that the fastest way to gain credibility in today's marketplace is to write a book. There's just not a better way to gain respect, increase exposure, and build a business. Other platforms are helpful, but often, they serve as an adjunct to the book.

If you own a business that relies on selling expertise, such as a professional service firm (lawyers, accountants, investment advisors, medical practitioners, consultants, or even antique dealers), you will get "instant expert" status by writing a book and becoming the "go-to-person" in your field.

If you're still wondering, "Do I really need a book?," here are several reasons to convince you. Aside from increasing credibility, authoring your own business book will help you:

- Establish authority (author/authority, get it?)
- Gain a competitive edge
- Attract media attention
- Provide value
- Generate referrals
- Capture joint venture partners
- Reach a larger audience (think national, global)
- Leverage online presence (website, social media, blog, etc.)
- Create other marketing opportunities

All of which can help you to increase market share, including accessing difficult-to-reach and affluent clients, command higher prices, and create a passive income stream based solely on your expertise.

The stopping point for most is that, well, quite frankly, it's time-consuming. Another factor is that some people just plain don't like to or want to write. And then there's the whole issue of how to do it well and how to do it right.

But there's no doubt that writing a book will add to your bottom line, so here are some pointers for would-be authors.

First things first: Do I have enough information to write a book?

So many publishers or ghostwriters would tell you to not bother if you don't have anything to say. But a good publisher or ghostwriter is able to fill in the blanks with research and common sense for most typical businesses.

You don't want to be accused of trying to turn what amounts to an article into a book. So begin by writing down a good outline. See what you have. Bring it to an expert for advice. People expect details, facts, figures, case studies, testimonials, etc. If you just hung out your shingle yesterday, you may have a tough time coming up with enough information to produce a solid book. You may want to wait until you have a little more experience under your belt.

Should I write my book myself or hire someone to write it for me?

If you're an experienced writer or plan to hire a good editor, you can definitely write it yourself. In fact, much of the flavor of your own voice will come through in the book if you write it yourself. That said, you have to devote a lot of time and energy into its creation. A book isn't something you sit down in one evening in your spare time and crank out just for the fun of it.

On the other hand, even if you do hire a ghostwriter, you have to ensure that he or she does capture your essence. And when it comes right down to it, you're the expert, so you will be significantly involved through the interview process and the editing process.

Whatever you have to share, whether it's a unique style or a new twist, will have to be conveyed as if it's coming directly from you. That's possible, but it takes a writer with a specific expertise. Experienced and amazing writers will most often charge a premium price. However, like anything valuable, the cost is worth the result.

Where do I start?

Most first-time authors don't know where to start or what to do first. So know that you're not alone! They're simply overwhelmed with the thought of writing and end up with too much information and not enough action-taking.

On the emotional front, feelings like fear and doubt may seep in. Other times, confusion or lack of clarity can stop an author in his or her tracks before the first step. Another big challenge for authors is thinking, or even knowing, that their book has already been written by somebody else. I'll let you in on a little secret: The more competition, the better. Here's the caveat: You must stand out from the crowd with your unique spin.

The simplest advice is to just start writing about what you know. For example, if you consult with chiropractors on how they can increase their practices, you can easily write a book on that topic, assuming that most chiropractors are too busy to do the work themselves and will hire you and your done-for-them services. Or, you could write a book on how to become a consultant to chiropractors. This, too, could develop into a done-for-them service, membership, or other product line.

Everyone leads busy lives. Carve out some time in the morning, the evening, or use your lunch hour to write. Try to write at the same time each day so it becomes part of your routine. Set a goal – whether it's 15 minutes a day or five pages a day – then stick to it.

If you're truly going to write it yourself, the best thing to do is to just get started. Jump right in. No need to scratch your head trying to create the catchiest title right now. You'll have plenty of time to work on that later. Just give it a working title if you feel the need for a title. If you work with an editor, it will probably change anyways.

Do people really judge a book by its cover?

There's only one honest answer to this: YES! They judge it by its cover, and they judge it by the fonts, and they judge it by the grammatical and spelling errors. If you don't believe me, go read some negative reviews.

Only words of advice here are to hire a professional graphic designer for the cover and any artwork you plan on using and have it properly formatted by a pro as well. Do not scrimp, or you'll regret it. You are a professional, and this entire book is a direct reflection of your image and brand.

How do I get my book published?

I'm going to tell it to you straight: By far, the easiest method is to self-publish your book. No, I'm not talking about the vanity presses that charge you hundreds of dollars to print your book. I'm talking about using Amazon to publish your work. CreateSpace for print-on-demand books and Kindle for ebooks are fantastic publishing platforms.

They're beginner-friendly, and Amazon does some of the promotion for you if you learn the insider tips and tricks. However, don't be fooled into thinking you can just sit back and collect your royalty checks. You will have to hustle or hire someone to do it for you if you're writing this book to make money. Now, if your primary goal is to use it as a business-builder, then anything you make on book sales is just gravy.

If you think you have a really incredible story to tell and want to pitch your idea to the major publishing houses, that's another deal altogether. They want you to send them a query letter that outlines your book proposal, as well as sample chapters. Some will only accept manuscripts exclusively from literary agents, who then also get a piece of the pie. Often, you won't hear from anyone for months, and then, in most cases, it's in the form of a rejection letter.

All in all, I'm still a firm believer that if you really want to use a traditional publisher, you should go for it. For sticklers, a traditional publishing house adds even more credibility. However, don't discount Amazon... especially if you're doing a straightforward how-to type book. On the plus side, if you do get a contract with a publisher, they already have established sales distribution channels in place. Not to say that you don't also have to promote your own book, but their system certainly gives you a leg up.

Really, no matter which route you take, there's never been a better time to become a published author. Yet, the majority of entrepreneurs are still talking about it instead of doing it.

Once it's written, how do I distribute, market, and publicize it?

Assuming you wrote your book as a business-builder first and foremost, and you produced a CreateSpace version, the easiest thing to do is to go buy copies of your own book. It may sound crazy, but using your own book is the best business card you could ever dream of using. Just don't hand them out indiscriminately because they're expensive business cards.

Here are just a few ideas to get you started:

- Use them in your personal office
- Place them in the waiting room
- Mail them to prospects with a personal note
- Bring them to trade shows
- Hand them to select individuals at networking events

People unfamiliar with the publishing world wrongfully assume that marketing and publicity always come at the tail-end of the process when in fact most smart publishers and authors start their campaign long before a word is even written!

Getting the word out ahead of time generates buzz and excitement. After all, even a basic business book can have a cult following.

Marketing your book to get the most exposure and publicity is the subject of entire books and courses, but here are a few ideas to spur your creativity:

- Join KDP and use the free promotion days
- Start an author website or blog
- Offer to guest blog for others
- Write a press release
- Design a Facebook fan page
- Post it on your social media sites
- Buy Google or Facebook ads

- Start a group on LinkedIn or Facebook
- Get involved in networking events
- List yourself on HARO (Help a Reporter Out)
- Talk to your local Chamber of Commerce
- Participate in an online book tour
- Host a book release party
- Get on BlogTalk radio
- Ask to do a book signing at the library
- Invite people to a Google Hangout
- Create a Meetup group
- Get reviews
- Offer to speak at trade shows
- Optimize all of your online marketing
- Shoot for local TV and radio shows
- Join Goodreads
- Create a YouTube book trailer or Q&A
- Host a webinar or teleseminar
- Become a bestseller in your category

That list gives you a small taste of the variety of marketing tactics available to promote your book. Marketing and public relations experts can create an entire plan to get the most bang for your buck.

If you got this far, you're an ideal candidate to write a book to help build your business. The question remains whether you think you want to put forth the effort to write it yourself or if you prefer to leave it in the hands of a professional writer and publisher.

So, if you're ready to take the next step by becoming an author and instant expert authority in your field, contact us for more details, risk-free. We'll help you decide which path is the right one for you to take.

As experts in writing, proofreading, editing, and publishing for more than 20 years, you can rest assured you're in good hands. We can do all the research, interviewing, and writing so you can concentrate on what you do best.

We can also contract with designers to create your cover, purchase graphics for inside your book, and format your book properly for both CreateSpace and Kindle.

You can find out more information by clicking on http://www.bookwormpublishers.com and requesting our free information or contacting us to set up a free, 30-minute phone consultation to determine your needs.

Just imagine how good it's going to feel when you can tell your business associates, friends, and family that you're a published author!

Your Blessed Marriage – By Design

By Jay W. Maresh

The Principle and Promise

The idea that we can implement principles into our marriage that sets us on a path to lasting love and allows us to recognize that the way our marriage looks in the future is a result of a conscious design process that we start today.

There are a series of steps that we can incorporate into a bad marriage, and they will position it to become better. That, all by itself, should really provide you hope that things in your marriage can improve. But wait, there's more; these steps can take a good marriage and position it for something more than you may have ever imagined. So, let's see how we can take a better marriage and make it great.

This process begins with understanding that in order for a bad marriage to become better and for a better marriage to become great, we have to envision the future of our respective marriage. It starts with implementing four steps. I like to remember these four steps using a little acronym, "AWWA." The acronym goes like this – Ask, Wait, Write, and Activate.

Let's begin this vision thing with the first step of asking questions. Let's ask the right questions. Ask questions that point us in the right direction, the specific direction that we want our marriage to go. Let's try out a few questions:

- What does your vision for marriage look like?
- What can we do to set our marriage on a path for lasting love?
- How can we rekindle, reignite, or rebuild our marriage?

Before we begin to answer these questions, let's understand the context on how this principle was put into use. We find this principle in a story dating way back to about a thousand years ago during the times of the Old Testament found in the Bible. I realize the idea of something dating back to the seventh century may not seem very relevant for today, but stick with me here.

In the story, we find a prophet of God named Habakkuk. I know that's a mouthful. I always remember how to pronounce it because, if you say it kind of fast, it rhymes with that big hairy creature from *Star Wars*, Chewbacca. So, Habakkuk kind of rhymes with Chewbacca, the 'k' in Habakkuk kind of disappears when you say it fast…. Habakkuk! Okay, so, back to the story. This prophet has regular dialogue with God. Yeah, they talk to each other- pretty awesome!

Habakkuk finds himself ministering to the nation of Judah, trying to help them through a difficult time. At this time in history, we see the nation of Judah is unwilling to turn away from their sinful ways and is heading down a path of self-destruction.

Habakkuk comes before the Lord with a question. His question had to do with how long God was willing to let these people flagrantly ignore and violate the Laws of God. Habakkuk felt like God was just allowing this sinful nation to get worse and worse without any apparent (Godly) justice at hand.

So, the point is that this mighty man of God had a need, he had a question, and he brought it before the Lord (the principle). In chapter 1, verse 17 in the book of Habakkuk, we see where he asked the Lord his question, and then he followed it in chapter 2, verse 1 with something that can be a little difficult for us; he watched and waited to 'see what the Lord would say.' I don't know about you, but for me, waiting isn't a fun thing to do. It's not a natural thing for most of us, but if you're going to ask the Lord a question, it's best to wait for Him to give you an answer. The answer might be immediate or it might take a while. When it comes, you will know it because it will be Truth. It will resonate with your soul.

Once you get the vision, the picture, of what you see for **your** marriage, now it's time to 'write it down.' The story with Habakkuk continues in chapter 2, verse 2 when the Lord tells Habakkuk to do just that. He says,' write my answer in clear, large, easy-to-understand language.'

Now that you have the vision for your marriage in place, understand that it's not going to manifest itself overnight. There is some more 'waiting' involved. God continues in verse 3: 'It won't happen right away, but slowly, surely, and *Steadily, the vision will be fulfilled'* (there's the promise). God then reminds Habakkuk one more time when He says, 'If it seems slow, wait patiently for it; it will surely take place, it will not be delayed.' What do you think God is trying to tell us here? I think He's trying to tell us that I've made you this promise. If you bring your request to Me, I will give you an answer, and I will see it through. Stand true in faith, believe Me for it, and it will come to pass.

Know that God wants His absolute best for your marriage. He wants you to have a blessed marriage. He wants your vision to come to pass and to give you the desires of your heart. It starts with putting your marriage in His hands.

Move forward, press through, not in your own strength, but by His power.

In your marriage, he is waiting for you to call on Him. He knows 'the time of our deep need' (Hab 3:2), and He is there to help us.

It's time to put it to work. It's time to activate your great marriage.

Moving Forward in Your Marriage

Let's continue the journey as we look at Moving Forward in Your Marriage. To move forward in your marriage, it means we have to take our good intentions and transform them into intentional actions.

We established the idea that you need to have a vision for your marriage. If you're single, set an expectation for yourself (based on Hab 2:2-3) of what is important to you in a marriage. If you are married or engaged to be married, the two of you can sit down and create this vision (based on Hab 2:2-3) together. Discuss it; only the two of you know what you want it to look like, how it should feel, and where you want it to take you. This is your (as a couple) vision for your marriage. As you create this vision for your marriage, anchor it in love, not just a momentary state of emotion, but an everlasting love that takes you from where you are today to where you want your marriage to end up.

Let me back up just a moment to make sure we don't miss out on a huge opportunity. The opportunity is the *process* of creating the vision, the vision for your marriage. If you haven't done this before, it provides for a great opportunity for couples to come together. This exercise allows the two of you to be in one accord in the design of your marriage.

When I counsel with couples prior to a wedding, I like to have an understanding of what to expect at their particular wedding. With any wedding, whether it's a big or a small affair, there are several pieces that are brought together to create that special day. Each bride and groom has their own formula, their own design of how they want their wedding to play out. Ultimately, they are looking to create a wonderful wedding day; a day that they will never forget.

Orchestrating this special day can be quite an effort for these couples, and it requires a tremendous amount of planning and expense.

A wonderful wedding day has components to it that make it special, memorable, and intimate. These are components the couple has decided on that makes that special day just right for them. As you know, there are lots of pieces to a wedding that need to be put into place to allow it to meet whatever kind of expectation it is you are trying to create. Let's have a little fun with it.

First off, you have the venue and the Minister, which really set the mood and the tone of the ceremony. Then you bring in some flowers, some catered foods and drinks. Let's not forget about the decorations and props to make sure we create a welcoming and comfortable atmosphere for the guests. As with any special occasion, you gotta have some cake.... might as well make it two; one for the bride, and one for the groom.

Bring it all together with some music of your choice; as a result, you bring in a band or DJ to entertain your guests. Creating some type of 'keepsake' or goody bag to leave for your guests will ensure they remember your special day. With this being such a special day and all, you want to make sure you catch those special moments on camera. So make sure you have a photographer or two, and don't forget about the videographer. They can create that special video piece that is sure to capture the essence of the day.

Finally, as you wrap up the night and you're saying goodbye to all of your friends and family for sharing in such a wonderful wedding celebration, the newlyweds hop into their limo and are whisked away to their 'pre'-honeymoon retreat, where they will spend the first night together as Mr. & Mrs. 'Married Couple.'

I guess we could go into the design, coordination, and expense that is involved in the respective bachelor & bachelorette parties and the vacation of all vacations, the honeymoon, but for time's sake, let's just keep it to the events that make up the wedding day itself.

As you can see (and if you are already married, you might be flashing back to your own wedding day), designing your wedding day is a big deal. In many cases, it takes lots of people coming together adding in their respective talents. It takes a significant investment of time and effort from the bride and groom as well as many others. There is a lot of planning and coordinating that goes into the big day, and at the end of it all, you truly have a 'day to remember.' You end up with a wedding day that is designed by you, for you, just the way you always envisioned it would be. Now I realize that not every wedding will have these exact components to it. There will be some common components, but there are pieces to it that only the two of you can decide on. It's your vision; as a couple, it's your design; it should have your desired outcome attached to it.

Okay, so you just designed and experienced a magical wedding day, and now it's time to start your new life together as husband and wife. So, where do you go from here? What is your vision for your marriage? What's your plan? Where do you see your marriage in 5, 10, 20, 50 years? Here's the idea behind the wedding day story. Let's take the idea of designing your wedding and putting some of those concepts into place to design your marriage. The two of you have likely discussed some of these items before. This is a natural part of the 'getting to know you,' or courting, process. In fact, it's likely during these intimate conversations or special moments that you found yourself thinking or saying, 'This is the kind of person I could spend the rest of my life with.'

Let's get back to some of those moments, whether they were just recently or even if they took place many years ago. Let's break them down, create a plan, and set you off on a path that leads to a specific and intentional destination. I want you to understand the power of those special moments we are talking about that will be the starting point for this marriage design. Take yourself back to the time and place where you knew that the person you are now married to or are going to marry was undoubtedly the person God has put into your life to be your mate. Reflect back on the qualities of your spouse that caused you to fall in love in the first place. Go back to the time when you think about your spouse and know you can't see yourself being married and not being with this person.

What are those thoughts that come to mind? I've had some wives tell me that in their husband, she knew he would always be there for her, she could trust him, and he would never abandon her. I've had husbands tell me that their wife brought out the best in them. I've had grooms and husbands alike gone as far to say that, the woman of his life has brought light and peace to a place in his heart that gave him a renewed hope and love for God and life itself. I know this is some deep stuff, and let me tell you, we need to look to designing a marriage that is anchored in deep stuff; in deep-rooted, emotion-evoking, heart-tugging…. love. This is the kind of love that endures, the kind of love that lasts, the kind of love that stands for something so important that we will not allow anything to come between us and that love. So, tell me, what are those qualities that cause you to think that this man or this woman is the person God has put in your life to be your spouse?

Your Flight Plan

In my days prior to the Ministry, I can reflect back on the time when I used to work for the airlines. Working for the airlines was a wonderful experience, and it was one that embodied almost 17 years of my life. I have to say that my favorite area to work was the area we referred to as the 'Gates.' The Gates is where all of the airplanes arrived and departed from. For me, the Gates is where all of the action was. It was exciting, it was invigorating, and it was intense. There were a lot of moving parts that came into play at the Gates. Each part was working together; every step was connected, all with the same agenda, to prepare the airplane to get to its intended destination.

Have you ever been on an airplane before and wondered what was involved from the time the pilots of that plane pulled away from the departure gate all the way until you arrived at the gate of your destination city? It's a rather interesting process. As you can imagine, the attention to detail for the preparation of this trip is very specific. It's intentional, it's calculating, and it's literally dialed into a specific set of coordinates. This path is established by something known in the airline business as a "Flight Plan."

Once a Flight Plan was generated from Flight Control, it would be sent to the gate agent in charge of that flight. We would then review the plan and advise the Captain of the aircraft if there were any ground security issues he needed to be made aware of. The Captain and his co-pilot would then begin to review the Flight Plan. This Flight Plan would act as a map to get them to their destination. It told them what runway to use and it told them what channel they could dial into to find both ground and air traffic control. It advised them of what coordinates to set, it told them how high to fly, what kind of weather they could expect along the way, where to land, what gate to pull the aircraft into once they arrived at the destination…….. this Flight Plan thing had it all.

Bringing It All Together

As we looked at earlier, putting together a wedding day requires a lot of planning. As you took a walk with me down memory lane at the airport, the steps that go into the departure and arrival of a commercial aircraft require a Flight Plan to get it to its intended destination, and this too requires a specific and intentional amount of planning.

The journey of your marriage is made up of many steps that are all connected. Individually, those steps may not look like they have any real momentum behind them. Individually, these steps don't really look like they're too big of a deal. The fact is, each step we take along the path of our marriage is going somewhere. Having a vision, establishing a design, and implementing a plan will help you to stay on course. In married life, sometimes, the proverbial rains and winds can get us off course, but with a plan, we can make the necessary adjustments to stay on course. Proverbs 16:3 reminds us to 'commit our works unto the Lord, and our plans will be established.' On the journey of marriage over the next 5, 10, 20, or 50 years from now, at each point, we need to be consciously aware if we are still on the intended path. Have we got off course? Do we need to redial the coordinates of our destination? These types of questions require that we discuss potential speed bumps with our spouse. I realize having this kind of conversation with our spouse can be a little uncomfortable, but if spoken in love and truth without blame or condemnation, it can be a little more comfortable. After all, this conversation is based on the design that the two of you created together. This design is something that you both want - it's something you have both committed to.

Make those necessary adjustments upfront. Don't let them brew and fester into something bigger and more difficult to work through. If, however, you find yourself at the place where the proverbial speed bump in the road is more like a blockade, preventing you from going forward, it's time to check in with the ultimate marriage designer for some direction, and ultimately, to get you to a point where you can make some changes. The ultimate marriage designer is, after all, the one who instituted the union of marriage from the very beginning. He knows what you need in your marriage. He knows what will be a blessing to your marriage. In the third chapter of Proverbs, King Solomon shared God's desire for us as it relates to knowing exactly what we need. In verses 5 & 6, he instructs us to "trust in the Lord with all your heart." This point becomes so important because, many times, we (in our flesh) will not necessarily want to do what we know (in our spirit) we need to do. The types of changes you are looking to make are heart changes. They are changes that have to be made from the inside-out. Your spirit has to be convinced to do it because your rational mind will likely try to talk yourself out of doing it.

Here's the order: Let God lead you in the spirit, bring the thoughts of your mind alongside, and then allow your body to follow. If you are looking to make changes and you initiate it in a different order, it's likely the changes you make will not be in line with your ultimate desire and vision for your marriage. These types of decisions become distractions that get you farther off course. Sometimes, these distractions, at least in the moment, might even make you *feel* like you're being productive. Don't allow negative distractions to deceive you and take you off course.

So, with our trust firmly planted in the Lord, he reminds us "not to lean on our own understanding." He knows that our mind will try to rationalize things. He knows that our mind and its limited understanding wants to lead the way, but he warns us right upfront about it. He's basically saying to us, "Take your focus off of your limited understanding and put it on Me; 'acknowledge' my ways for your marriage.' When you do this, He makes us a promise. He assures us that He will "make our paths straight." This is huge. We already know that the steps we take in our marriage establish a path and, sometimes, we may find ourselves off course. Now we know that when our focus for our marriage is on His ways, it will get us back on track. It will make our path straight once again.

It's my hope that this time we have spent together will bless you and set you on a path to a loving and lasting marriage. This, however, is just the beginning. If you would like more information on putting together and establishing a path that leads to God's best for your marriage, please visit us at the link below.
http://www.YourBlessedMarriage.org

About Jay W. Maresh

JAY W. MARESH is a pastor, author, publishing consultant, and real estate entrepreneur. In his marriage ministry, he regularly counsels with brides, grooms, and married couples alike to set them on a path for a marriage blessed by God.

YourBlessedMarriage.org is about bringing an understanding of God's love and wisdom to the union of marriage. The idea behind Jay's teaching is to position a marriage for God's best. Where bad marriages become good, good marriages become better, and better marriages become great.

"Scripture confirms that it's God's desire to set our marriages on a path that positions us for His blessing. It's my desire to help you bring that realization to life in your marriage."

In 2010, Jay co-founded Four Winds Bible Church, a non-denominational Christian Church located in San Antonio, Texas.

Jay and his wife Dana live in San Antonio with their two sons, Jay Wesley and Brady. Dana has also brought her vocation and ministry together as a full-time career as a teacher at a local Christian school.

Jay is available for speaking engagements, marriage counseling, and publishing consultations. Contact him through www.YourBlessedMarriage.org.

How To Produce, Publish, Promote & Profit From Your Own Book (Like A Pro)

By David Lee Martin

Are you aware that we are right now in the midst of a radical revolution that is changing the landscape of information publishing forever? I hope so!

The most amazing thing about this revolution is that it has placed technology in the hands of ordinary people like you and me that several decades ago even NASA could not dream of. Today, with the right know-how, you can have your own TV or radio station, your own publishing empire. You can have a global online shop shipping products to the ends of the Earth. Moreover, you can do this from the comfort of your own home!

The Limits Have Been Lifted

The limitations have been lifted, restricted only by your own passion and imagination. In this short manual, I will show you how to harness your passion and provide and distribute knowledge and value to people who are hungry for what you have to share with them.

So you want to know how to publish your own book and make money from it? But you don't know how.

Yet.

I was in exactly the same place several years ago. Now, I can say that I enjoy a good income (one of several streams) from my self-published books and information products on the Internet.

I sell digital books, video-based training, printed manuals, and books. Every week, my bank account gets fatter as a result of just quitting my excuses 'why not' and going for it!

For each one of us, there comes a point in time where we stop dwelling on 'why not,' and instead concentrate our energies on 'how.' 'How can I do this?'

I am very pleased to tell you that you no longer need some big publishing company to pick you up in order to be a successful author. You can encourage, inform, and influence countless lives, and you can begin the process right now.

I promise you, if you have not already discovered this, you will be amazed and delighted how EASY it is, how QUICKLY you can progress, and how INEXPENSIVE self-publishing can really be.

You can piggyback on the massive market share of some of the biggest online marketplaces, and all are begging for you to place your unique and valuable content on their digital shelves, ready for them to send qualified buyers to invest in your books. Let me tell you - this works! And it works well.

PRODUCE

Quick & Easy Keys To Create Great Books That People Will Love To Read...

Sometimes, we have the false notion that creating a book has to be a hard and arduous journey. Nothing can be further from the truth. If you will apply some of the keys I share on the following pages, you will be amazed at how quickly you go from idea to pressing the 'publish' button and unleashing your work of genius on the world. Take 10 minutes now to read through these key principles of content creation, and then take 7 days to apply them. By the end of the week, you can have your first book polished and ready to publish.

What Is Your Passion?

Please let me encourage you. You know some things that others will gladly and thankfully pay to find out.

We live in an exciting time in history, where an information revolution is taking place all around us. It is no longer an industrial age. We live in the information age. Information is valuable currency. What you know has real value, and it is just waiting to be shared.

A media explosion is happening all around us, and ordinary people just like you have embraced it to share their passions with the world. In doing so, many have also opened up significant income streams. They make a living doing and sharing what they love!

There are many kinds of books we can write. Just a few...

- Educational books
- Historical books
- Entertainment books
- Fictional books
- Children's books
- Biographical books

Different books will take differing amounts of time and research to complete, but each one will require the same principle to be put into action: The 'Eating an Elephant' principle.

How do we 'eat an elephant'?

One bite at a time.

So let's dig in....

3 Simple Keys To Writing Your Book

1. Choose Your Subject

In doing this, consider what you know that can help someone else, educate someone else, inform someone else, entertain someone else. You have knowledge that can easily help others. Why do you think that the 'Dummies' series of books are so successful? Because they solve a problem for people. What problem can you solve?

An example from my own experience recently would be that I have had to prepare my accounts for the tax man. Are you an accountant who could produce a short manual helping people organise and prepare their accounts with as little pain as possible?

Or how about my friend who produces really simple, easy-to-implement cookbooks and publishes them to Kindle? Are you a good cook? Maybe you could share your favourite recipes with others.

Or another friend of mine who writes simple rhyming children's stories?

Are you a singer? How about a book about how to sing better?

There is always something you can pull together. I have two passions. I love Jesus Christ, so I write many books helping people to follow Him more closely, especially in prayer, and I love children, so I write and produce children's books, from toddlers through to teens!

Recently, I produced two joke books. I simply pulled hundreds of jokes together from across the Internet, carefully chose and edited the ones that were appropriate for my book, and then threw some illustrations I purchased from a stock photography site to make it more interesting and enjoyable to read. In all honesty, anyone could have done this, even if they could not write one line! Don't limit yourself; jump over to Amazon and have a look around for books that are selling in areas that you have some expertise.

2. Write The Headlines

This has always helped me to bite into the elephant without too much trepidation. Instead of tackling a whole book, I tackle one chapter (or one idea, one point) at a time.

Write down chapter headings for each section or point you want to make. This is how I pull together my teaching books in particular. I pull the subject apart into clear, easy-to-grasp points, one idea or point per chapter.

Once I have chapter headlines, it is then easy to take one chapter at a time and fill in the details.

My son is presently writing a book about a game he loves to play called *Minecraft*. He had the idea of creating a book called *50 Tips For Minecraft*. We sat down in Starbucks together and brainstormed what the 50 headlines would be, then it was just a matter of writing a few paragraphs under each headline explaining the tip and dropping in a screenshot or two to illustrate his book, one bite at a time. 50 bites for the headlines, 50 bites for the 50 or so illustrating screen shots, and 50 bites to complete the short paragraphs of text under each tip.

If you are writing fiction, take it character by character, scene by scene, plot line by plot line. Maybe start with short stories rather than a *Lord of the Rings* style epic (just a thought).

Make it your goal to take at least one or two bites each and every day, and you will be amazed at how quickly you progress. It is always motivating to see yourself move forward with a project, and this approach gives you clear, progressive steps.

Once you have the individual elements in place, it is simply a matter of organising them into a cohesive structure.

Every step will increase your confidence and conviction that your writing dream can indeed become a living reality!

3. Illustrate

Do you require illustrations for your book? It is possible to source and purchase royalty-free images for just a few dollars or pounds from the many stock photography sites on the Internet. This is how I illustrated a number of my kids' books. There are also some great places to get illustrations done specifically for your book by professional artists (and it does not need to cost you the Earth!). Try oDesk.com, for example, and post your job description outlining clearly what you are looking for. People will then bid to fulfil your brief.

Certainly, you will want to create (or get created for you) a fabulous cover. Again, you can pull this together yourself or pay a small amount to have someone else do a great job for you. Try Fiverr.com and look for Kindle book cover creators. You will be able to get your cover created for as little as five dollars!

Publish

Where And How To Publish Your Masterpiece

In all honesty, the real game changer for writers and publishers has been the vast opportunity that has opened through the megalithic retail giants like Google, Amazon and Apple. For ordinary guys and gals like you and me, we can piggyback on their massive market reach and their tremendous ability to reach the farthest corners of the Earth with our ideas through online Search Engine Optimisation.

I have books and products that sell because I created sites that appear on the first pages of Google for my desired search terms. My wife's dance books at www.praisedancetoday.com are examples of this. Thanks Google for your help with this one!

I then have several books I publish exclusively to Amazon, leveraging their KDP program (more about this later).

I also have books that I publish physical editions of using Lulu.com and Amazon's print-on-demand service, CreateSpace.com.

The amazing thing to grasp is that it cost me zero, nada, nil to do all of this, other than the time it takes to create the book, and then leverage the promotional tools (which are already in place, waiting to be used by you) to get the products in front of as many eyeballs as I can.

Here are my suggested routes to publish your finished work.

DIGITAL PUBLISHING

Amazon Kindle
kdp.amazon.com

The Kindle platform is exploding right now. Believe me when I say, there is room for your book on the digital bookshelves. With the right know-how, you will most certainly see sales if your book really does speak to the passion or problem of others.

I have found the Kindle platform to be by far the easiest and most profitable to publish to. Formatting for Kindle can be a little tricky at times, but a small investment in KD Publishing Pro (http://davidleemartin.net/kdpublishpro) or my personal favourite, Scrivener, can ease the pain significantly!

Apple iBookstore

The iBookstore is a little more complicated to create and publish to. Nevertheless, because of this, the marketplace is not so saturated, meaning that you can position yourself much more easily and be seen by those who are searching the iBookstore, even for highly competitive search terms.

There is also a small cost involved to publish to the iBookstore if you want to sell your books in their marketplace.

Apple does provide software for free that aids the process of book creation, but nevertheless, it is still more complex than producing a book for Kindle. I recommend that you take a look and give it a go, however, as, undoubtedly, the iBookstore will grow, and now is an opportune time to position yourself ahead of the curve.

PRINT-ON-DEMAND OPTIONS

Presently, Lulu.com and CreateSpace.com are the two popular options for printed versions of your books. Both have a wide distribution network and provide free ISBNs if you want them. Again, there is no upfront cost; there is just the time it takes to prepare and upload your files.

These services require only Word or PDF files and will convert them to the right format once uploaded.

PROMOTE

OK, we've got the book out there, but how will people find it in the sea of other titles? Thankfully, there are some great ways to get your title out there where people are looking.

Possible promotional avenues include the awesome Amazon KDP program (this comes with a few provisos), social media such as Facebook and Twitter, several websites that are dedicated to book promotion that you can post to, setting up your own website or blog to promote the book, and even sending emails to friends and family.

Sometimes, the viral potential of social media snowballs your efforts, and many people whom you have never met will end up on the book page, downloading your book.

Another important key to getting noticed is how you present your book cover (this needs to look great!), your book title, description, keywords, categories, and tags. All of these elements will affect how and where your book appears in the various online stores. Pay close attention to the fact that your cover must be readable even at the small thumbnail size in which they appear in the Amazon listings. Make your cover clear, bold, and eye-catching for the best conversions.

There are also ways to orchestrate your efforts through working together with others who are in the writing and publishing arena, sharing tips, promotions, and reviews. All of this can help tremendously to push your books through the ranks so eager buyers can part with their cash to taste your work of genius!

The Amazon KDP Program

I have personally found that the Amazon KDP program is by far the most effective way to promote your new book. It allows you to give the book away in their marketplace for 5 days out of every 90. Combined with a little external promotional advertising your free days (and this can be done for under $10), you might see upwards of 1000 downloads in just a few days (sometimes, many more!).

The downside is that to make the most of their KDP program, you hand over exclusive digital rights to Amazon. The copyright on your creative works remains your own, but you agree to publish the digital version only to Amazon's Kindle store. You can publish to the Kindle store and other digital platforms if you want to, but this means you cannot enrol the book in the KDP program.

Weighing up the pros and cons of this may differ book by book. I have some books that make more money through direct website sales, so although I have published to the Kindle store, I have chosen to not enrol these particular publications in the KDP program. Other books I sell were languishing out in the wilds of online search and sell many more copies through the Kindle program, so I have pulled them from other platforms and thrown my all-in with Amazon for those titles.

If this is your first digital publishing adventure, I would definitely recommend trying the KDP avenue as part of your initial launch, and then possibly pulling out of the program later in order to publish to other marketplaces.

My Story So Far

The Publishing Dream Unfolds

My own publishing dream began with a bookmark that my wife gave to me when we were courting.

It reads...

"You are a Lover of Words... One day, You Will Write a Book. People turn to you because You give voice to dreams, notice the little things, and make otherwise impossible imaginings appear real. You are a rare bird who thinks the world is beautiful enough to try to figure it out, who has the courage to dive into your wild mind and go swimming there.

You are someone who still believes in cloud watching, people watching, daydreaming, tomorrow, favourite colours, Silver clouds, Dandelion's, and sorrow. Be sacred. Be cool. Be wild. Go far. Words do more than plant miracle seeds. With you writing them, they can change the world. – Ashley Rice"

These few short words inspired my heart and touched something inside of me that I knew had been planted by God himself.

It was just the encouragement that I needed to begin writing. My first book, entitled 'Speaking God's Language,' was a book about prayer. At that time, we did not have the wonderful avenues of publishing that are open to us today. I designed the book in a way that allowed me to photocopy the pages, print a full-colour cover, and then staple it down the spine. It was pretty home spun, but nevertheless, every great journey begins with the first step, right?

During this time, I was also employed to write, edit, and publish a newspaper on behalf of a group of churches. Having worked in the newspaper business prior to this time, I had some great contacts and was able to strike a good deal to use their presses for this short run full-colour publication.

Since these early beginnings, I have written several other short books to encourage people in their walk with God. Like I said earlier, writing and flowing with what you are passionate about will always work better than publishing on subjects that mean little or nothing to you.

I was then asked, several years ago, to write a Bible School curriculum and place it online to encourage, strengthen, and train people in the truth of God's Word. This vast project became the Spirit Life Bible School (www.studythebiblenow.com). In order to complete this brief, I also had to learn many new skills. I had some experience in Web design, but developing an entire membership site with multimedia delivery of an entire school of information was a technical challenge. Nevertheless, it taught me a great deal, and those skills have proved massively useful, not only in the continued development of the school, but in other arenas as well.

Step-by-step, I learned about self-publishing and ways to deliver information to people both digitally and in printed form that did not require me to personally print, ship, or fulfil the orders that were being made. All of this was done automatically utilising some of the fantastic systems that are now available to us online. Today, in addition to running the online Bible school, I have digital and physical books published across several platforms. I have affiliates who sell some of my books, to whom I give a significant commission (again, all this takes place automatically without requiring my intervention). I have many books published to the Amazon Kindle platform (several of them bestsellers), and have learned streamlined ways to produce great books quickly and with excellence.

One of my passions now is to share this information with others who are presently where I once was. They have a wealth of value and information, stories and poems, keys and principles, to share with the world. They have stopped dwelling on why it is not possible, and have realised that the only question they need to answer is "how." It is surprisingly simple and very satisfying when that one question is answered!

I would like to encourage you: You have everything it takes, and the resources are right at your fingertips.

Go for it!

For more hints and tips to publish and promote your own books, or to contact David Lee Martin, head over to David's blog...

www.davidleemartin.net

Meet David Lee Martin (yep, that's me)

David Lee Martin teaches ordinary people to know and walk with an extraordinary God! He is a passionate and anointed Bible teacher who hates dead religion, and brings the Words of the Scripture alive with fresh significance.

As an ordained minister and the author and developer of the Spirit Life Bible School (www.studythebiblenow.com) and the popular Christian website www.jesuschrist.co.uk, his books and free teaching materials are helping to strengthen and encourage believers in many nations across the world.

David is also passionate about young people and has written several children's books with life lessons to sow seeds of faith and courage into young hearts and minds.

David is married, with four great kids.

You can connect with David & Larna through their websites:

http://www.jesuschrist.co.uk
http://www.studythebiblenow.com
http://www.praisedancetoday.com
http://www.davidleemartin.net
http://www.tabernacleprayer.net
http://www.Facebook.com/TotallyJC

You can also connect with David through his Amazon author page:
https://www.amazon.com/author/davidleemartin

Keystone to Optimum Health

By Dr. James Martin

Hello, this is Dr. James Martin with the Nutrition Wellness Center in Sarasota, Florida. We're going to be addressing one of the most significant changes that has occurred and what I believe to be one of the most important pieces of information in the field of nutrition. After 37 years of experience in the field of nutrition and detoxification, the one constant that always exists in chronic disease and ill health and aging is, **oxidative stress**!

Most of you are saying, "OK, what's oxidative stress?" People think they know working onwhat oxidative stress is because they take antioxidants. They also may have the notion that because they take antioxidants, this will address oxidative stress. I take antioxidants. I've been taking antioxidants for years and, you know when you talk about nutrition, most of the world that takes supplements or vitamins has heard the word "antioxidants." Here's my point: 99 percent of the antioxidants we've all been taking, and I personally know, they haven't worked. I've been challenging myself to find the answer to reducing this oxidative stress with all of these different products from the multitude of companies out there, and I failed. I haven't found anybody who has successfully resolved this issue until now!

First, we're going to just cover what oxidative stress is. It's rusting. You know when metal rusts? That's oxidative stress. When you cut an apple open and it starts turning brown, that's oxidation or oxidative stress. Oxidative stress is the aging or accelerated aging of anything. In this case, it could be your heart, which we're going to go into. Skin's a good one because it's the obvious example. You know, everybody knows when someone's getting older. You can look at his/her picture when he/she was 30, and you can look at his/her picture when he's/she's 45, and I bet you the one thing you say is, "Oh, my gosh! This person's really aging!" Of course, that is the majority of us. Aging is associated with oxidative stress, which thousands of studies validate, as found in PubMed.gov, the National Library of Medicine's website.

If you go to PubMed and you type in oxidative stress, how many studies will you expect to find? There are over 101,000 published medical studies associating oxidative stress with more than 250 diseases. This is why correcting oxidative stress is so critical! We have to find the cause of oxidative stress because, if you don't fix it, you're still trying to run and jump on the tail end of the train to catch it because it stays out in front of you.

A large number of medical studies (1,500 to be exact) say oxidative stress is associated with causing Parkinson's disease. How about obesity? Now, we're not talking about being overweight; we're talking about being obese. There are almost 2,000 medical published studies showing oxidative stress being a causal relationship in causing obesity. There are over 4,000 studies showing oxidative stress is associated with the hardening of the arteries or causing plaque in the arteries. Do you know that most type 2 diabetes is associated with oxidative stress? There are over 8,000 medical studies saying diabetes is associated, or that oxidative stress has a causal relationship. There is also evidence that oxidative stress plays a role in causing cataracts and macular degeneration as well.

A lot of people spend a lot of money on cosmetics and nutritional products in order to try to prevent the aging process and/or not looking as though they're aging. I'll repeat it again: If you're not fixing oxidative stress, you're not stopping the aging process. Over 8,400 studies show the relationship of oxidative stress causing and accelerating the aging process. A lot of people are becoming more aware of family and friends who have Alzheimer's. You want to help yourself prevent it? Address this issue of oxidative stress, as over 2,000 studies show that oxidative stress plays a role in Alzheimer's.

Several years ago on the cover of *Time* magazine, it focused on chronic inflammation, which is associated with cancer and all chronic disease. Well, you know what? That's true, and there are approximately 13,427 studies showing oxidative stress as being associated with causing inflammation. This is virtually any type of inflammation in your body:

- In the joints
- Associated with brain conditions and brain diseases
- In your heart
- In your kidney
- In your prostate
- In your ovaries
- In your adrenals
- In your eyes
- Elsewhere

The phrase "oxidative stress" is almost synonymous with inflammation.

Until recently, heart disease was the number one cause of death. If you have high blood pressure, if you have heart disease, you have oxidative stress. If you have any of these things on this list, I can just about guarantee that you have oxidative stress affecting that part of the body, system, or organs.

More and more people have thyroid disease. A lot of people don't know they have it; they are just tired and lethargic. Their hair is starting to fall out; they're getting a little depressed; their cholesterol is going up a bit; they might be a little on the constipated side. A lot of these are thyroid symptoms, but a lot of those symptoms can also indicate a hypothyroid, or an underactive thyroid. In 90 percent of hypothyroid cases, it's due to an autoimmune disease known as "Hashimoto's disease," which is associated with inflammation and oxidative stress.

Other conditions that have a connection with oxidative stress include allergies, liver disease, Immune-related diseases, and osteoporosis. Most people probably don't think there would be an association between osteoporosis and oxidative stress, but there is.

It is imperative for you to understand the impact that one entity, in this case, oxidative stress, has on so many different types of health issues and, more importantly, on a cellular level. Everything happens at the cellular level. We live or die at the cellular level. The number one factor of damaging the cells is oxidative stress.

First of all, you see the phrase, "receptor site damage." Receptor sites are something that occurs on the outside of the cell membrane, so it doesn't matter what type of cell we're talking about: Thyroid cell, heart cell, kidney cell. Any cell in the body has these little landing sites on the outside. Picture a cell, a round cell, and on the outside of this cell membrane is all of these little landing sites. That's where hormones and other chemicals go to; once they lock into their little landing site, that's what makes a specific chemical reaction in the body. Receptor site damage is a big problem that is associated with hormones. Oxidative stress damages these receptor sites and causes hormone issues.

The issue with oxidative stress and cellular metabolism is its role in damaging many components of the cell. Oxidative stress causes DNA damage (17,000 studies) and mitochondria damage (your source of cellular energy), as well as produces havoc on the internal metabolism of any type of cell (i.e. heart, thyroid, brain, glands, etc.).

What causes oxidative stress?

Environmental toxins (heavy metals, pesticides, solvents, artificial sweeteners), **Sugars** (high fructose corn syrup), **Bad Fats,** and **Emotional Stress**. These are your primary causes of oxidative stress. The big myth is that antioxidants will take care of oxidative stress – they don't. You must understand the difference between primary antioxidants and secondary antioxidants, which consumers do not have sufficient knowledge about.

Why have your antioxidants failed to correct oxidative stress?

There are two types of antioxidants. The difference between the two makes all of the difference in the world. If you know the difference between secondary and primary antioxidants, you probably are ahead of 98 percent of the population on antioxidants. Primary antioxidants are the ones your body is supposed to make. There are only three of them:

Glutathione (this is the antioxidant people are most familiar with)
SOD (Superoxide Dismutase)
Catalase

These are the natural antioxidants your body is supposed to make to address oxidative stress and environmental toxins.

Now, here's where the big, big, light bulb comes on once you get this piece of the puzzle. One molecule of primary antioxidants quenches over one million molecules of free radicals in seconds. Let me repeat that. One molecule of primary antioxidants (glutathione, SOD, or catalase) quenches one million molecules of free radicals in seconds. Now, what's the comparison there, folks? Secondary antioxidants are 1:1, while primary are 1:1+ million. Keep in mind that your body's supposed to make the primaries. So, the real key to optimal health and longevity is pumping up the primaries. I will tell you, the most dramatic challenge with that has been pumping up those primaries.

So, the point here is, if you have oxidative stress, you have a deficiency of either one of the three or a combination of the three primary antioxidants. Most of the time if you're deficient in one, you're usually deficient in the others. Saying this the other way around, having a deficiency of your primary antioxidants equals oxidative stress. Know that primary antioxidants, not secondary antioxidants, are the real key for addressing oxidative stress.

Now, are secondary antioxidants good? Sure they are. They have a lot of other biochemical functions, but are secondary antioxidants really handling and addressing the issues of oxidative stress in our lives today? They have not, as I have been testing this. We do two or three different types of oxidative stress tests in our office, and they're not getting the job done. And I'm not saying that based on a few weeks or a few months. I'm saying that based on 30+ years of expertise.

There is another point that I would like to make about primary antioxidants. Most people who are aware of any of these three, mostly all they've heard about is glutathione. Glutathione is probably the master antioxidant, but I will tell you, SOD and catalase play very, very powerful roles as well. You can't have optimal health with just glutathione.

Now, here's the real dilemma, at least for me. This has been my quest for the last, I'd say, 10 years, trying to find and resolve this issue with no luck up until several months ago. Most people's source of primary antioxidants has been supplements. You can take a supplement of any of the three primary antioxidants. The problem with this is that the absorption rate is very, very low.

The next option is to do an IV, which a lot of people do. They do IV glutathione. Generally, when they do this, they're just doing glutathione; they're not doing SOD or catalase. They just do glutathione, and I don't know about you, but are you going to go in and get an IV once a week for the rest of your life? I seriously doubt it, especially when there's a less invasive way of doing it via a nebulizer. Here, you inhale glutathione. It is still an expensive procedure, but it is less invasive than an IV.

Again, though, my question is: Are you going to go in once or twice a week to do your nebulizer for glutathione? And really, if you ask the question, wouldn't it be much, much better if we got our own bodies to just make more of our own glutathione? Again, remember my point here: Most of these products are either a glutathione product or an SOD product or a catalase. Therefore, you're still not getting all of the pieces of the puzzle. When you do it piecemeal like that, it's not a holistic approach. The holistic approach is raising your body's own production of glutathione, SOD, and catalase naturally.

The new science that has changed everything!

Nutrigenomics is the study of the effects of food and nutrition on our genes (genetics). We know now that there are certain natural substances in food and herbs that can turn on the good genes and turn off the bad genes. Nutrigenomics is the future of nutrition and optimal health.

Through nutrigenomics, we can not only expand our longevity, but our optimal health as well. With the advent of nutrigenomics, we can decrease our chances of contracting many chronic diseases, including the following:

- Alzheimer's
- Cancer
- Cardiovascular diseases
- Diabetes
- Many more

In addition, we can also slow down the aging process itself.

What is the role of genes on your primary antioxidant production and oxidative stress?

Nrf2 is protein in the body that turns on the genes that promote primary antioxidant production. Nrf2 also turns on the anti-inflammatory genes as well. Nrf2 has been considered by scientists as 'the guardian of the health span and the gatekeeper of longevity.'

The Nrf2 pathway may indeed be the master regulator of the aging process. What is so exciting about this is that there are specific herbs and phytonutrients that are considered Nrf2 activators. Several studies at the National Library of Medicine have documented the Nrf2 activation properties. We researched several natural Nrf2 activators and found a product that has demonstrated to significantly decrease oxidative stress in one dose. That's right, in one dose!

We've used a urine oxidative stress test that has consistently demonstrated this over and over. In some cases, it has reduced oxidative stress levels by 600%. The manufacturer of this product has created a unique synergistic formulation that has changed the game when it comes to all chronic disease processes. I find this to be very exciting. Unfortunately, I am not the manufacturer or developer of this product, but we do sell it to our members. I am so excited about the results we are seeing that I have been teaching other doctors about this nutrigenomics product.

Our testing results have been amazing, and members have also been excited about the results they are receiving. If you would like to get the home test kit to check your oxidative stress levels, call our office at 1-800-222-3610. If you take antioxidants, do the test to see how well they are working. Find out if the money you're spending is producing the anticipated results. I challenge you! My website is www.howtoxicareyou.com. Watch the full video on "Your Keystone to Optimal Health."

Dr. James Martin ND, DCCN, DACBN, BCIM, FAAIM

Oxidative Stress is Associated with at Least 250 Diseases

Studies Published on Diseases Associated with Oxidative Stress

PubMed.com is the government resource for the National Library of Medicine.
PubMed.com has **101,646** published medical studies on the role of oxidative stress in many diseases.

Parkinson's disease ----1,512
Metabolic Syndrome----1,223
Alzheimer's disease ----2,266
Atherosclerosis--------- 4,300
Stroke------------------1,802
Autism------------------131
MS----------------------343
Cancer------------------10,414
Depression--------------673
Inflammation------------11,520
Diabetes----------------8,065
Liver disease------------4,515
Immune function-------2,362
Thyroid disease---------442
Obesity-----------------1,983
Cataracts---------------628
COPD-------------------820
Heart Disease----------6,061
Kidney disease--------4,304
Pulmonary disease----3,661
Osteoporosis-----------229
Allergies----------------964
Mitochondria disease—9,023
Cell Membrane--------8,045
DNA damage----------16,728
Aging-------------------8,426

The above is a small list of the Oxidative Stress articles published on the National Library Medicine website, PubMed.com.

Getting Organised So You Can Get On With The Business Of Business

By Nick McCloud

Most of us in the business world have heard the saying, "Failing to plan is planning to fail," and I wholeheartedly agree with this sentiment, however hard it is for us to get around to doing. But, there is something equally important to do, if not more important, that is a combination of a one-off activity & setting routines:

"Get your ducks in a row"

This means getting organised so you can get on with the business of business and not being constantly sidetracked or sideswiped by stupid mundane minutia that just keeps popping up over and over again, draining our time, our pocket books, and our will to live. Automate, delegate, & script all of the recurring stuff that provides a solid platform for success so that you can concentrate on the tricky bit that makes you unique in delivering your product or service to your customer base.

When I say "get organised," I'm not talking about getting focus or having a goal: big, hairy, audacious, or otherwise, nor am I talking about objectives, however SMART they may be. I'm just talking about the day-to-day stuff:

- Which quotes to follow up on
- Does that client take sugar in his coffee
- Where the paperclips are
- Why the service light is still on in the car
- What to do if the printer goes kaput
- How to feed the family
- Still get the accounts done on time

There are so many things to do and so little time to do them that every effective efficiency is vitally important to the running of 'things' so that you can deliver the goods, get the job done, and bill. How small an amount of time? Well, most of my clients are single-handed entrepreneurs, a staff of one, and that's it. As a result, I found the following time split to work well:

Sales & Marketing: Everything from new product creation, quotations, blogging, outbound phone calls to SEO - 33% of your time. With a healthy stream of new businesses, you can call the shots. Keep the production department in work and you'll never go hungry.

Production/Delivery: Be it packing widgets for distribution, writing the most beautiful copy, or crunching the numbers, you've got around 50% of your time available to do actual billable work.

Other stuff: This is where your time disappears to, all of those urgent but not very important things that take you away from success, a healthy bank balance, a two-week holiday, and enough sleep. This should be 17% of your working time, and absolutely no more!

Now, if your domestic ducks are in a row, then you may be able to squeak 60 hours of work out of your frail frame a week - this is almost doable if, and ONLY if, domestics run like a finely-tuned machine. Which means, **kids are out**. If you have kids, you either subcontract out their care or you scale back your business to fewer hours. Sorry, but that's the honest truth; your kids won't thank you for building a business of any size at the expense of hugs and quality time.

As we've just mentioned the domestic angle, let's do a quick review of that before we move on:

Food: Stop buying food - your supermarket most likely delivers, so get them to do the shopping, buy the same things on a regular basis, sort out a fortnightly-rotating (i.e. two weeks) menu plan, buy in bulk, cook in bulk, and freeze it, and have a secret cupboard with emergency dinner and treats for when you or someone in the house has a bad day.

Cleaning: Stop doing this too. If you are running anything like a reasonable business, your hourly rate is higher than the cleaners.

Washing & Ironing: The cleaner you just hired? Get him/her to do this as well.

Bill Payments: Again, assuming you aren't quite destitute and have a budget (please tell me you have a budget), put everything on automatic. You do not have time to want to worry about sitting down to write cheques for cable, mortgage, utilities, etc.

The next few are all joined together. Each one of these is absolutely essential to your sanity and productivity, as they really are an interlinked jigsaw puzzle:

Recreation: Maintain at least one "you-time" hobby. Even if you are appallingly bad on the golf course or only revisit your crochet once a fortnight, do something just for you for a couple of hours each week.

Friends & Family: Put away your smartphone, turn off the TV, cook some pasta and sauce, open a bottle of wine, and spend some time with your nearest & dearest. Ask them how things are, listen to them, tell them the truth when asked about work, but don't overdramatise.

Your Love Life: If you have a significant other, make time to keep him/her in the loop on work and make time to do something together that is just you, the couple. If you are single, you may want to consider the comments about kids, as well as the fact that the whole dating thing is a huge drain. Being committedly single whilst you get your business started (or on an even keel if it's not) is pretty sexy, and you'll be surprised what not being on a partner hunt turns up.

Holidays (a.k.a. "Vacations" in the States): Several of these are needed throughout the year - maybe not a full two weeks off in the summer - but take full advantage of the seasonal holidays to have a couple of days off. If you can, add a day at the beginning and end of those holidays just to stretch them out a little longer. Most people have low expectations of service availability the day before and after a holiday, so don't worry about the clients. Just take a break.

Health: This is the biggest must-do of all of the domestics. Your business is YOU: If you are un-well, tired, run down, depressed, or worse, you won't have a business for long. You might be the boss, which means the team needs direction, or you are the production department, which means nothing gets done if you are sick and not working. So, look after your health. A 20-minute brisk walk 3 times a week is a good start on exercise, watch what you eat and drink, and above all, get plenty of sleep.

Now that you have got your domestic ducks in a row, you've got a reasonable chance of doing up to 60 hours a week. By that, I'm assuming 10 hours a day for 6 days a week so that you have one full clear day off a week. I'd also recommend you don't try to plan the 60 hours to the max; shoot for 45-50 hours. Being pleasantly surprised you've got more done during the week is a good strategy. The 10 hours I'm thinking of is also spread out between 8 am and 10 pm - so you are taking an hour for lunch and an hour & a bit for an early supper (so you then can do two, possibly three, hours afterwards, then go to bed early).

The first area to address is all of the time-sapping other stuff mentioned above, the miscellaneous tasks that are part & parcel of running a business, but are neither promoting it nor earning actual money.

This other stuff usually looks like this:

Invoicing & Collection: Of all of these things, this is an essential task, one you should be personally involved in to ensure that the invoices are accurate and that they are paid on time. Feel free to delegate some of this activity, but insist on written weekly reports so that you know that the money is coming in.

Accounts: Stick everything in a big envelope, give it to your accountant, who will produce the outputs you've already agreed upon (such as monthly reports, etc.), and move on.

Government Paperwork: You need to stay on top of this, as it can get messy very quickly when things get missed or are late. Ensure that anyone working on your submissions is on the case and gives you a timetable. Insist on regular reports and that deadlines are met a week early.

The Office: This includes all of the paperclips, reams of paper, toner cartridges, and so forth. Just keep a few months' supply in so you don't end up without an essential item at 8 pm the night before a big presentation.

Maintenance of Equipment: This can be the car you absolutely have to have to get around, your computer, the alarm system, or the air conditioning. Have these maintained regularly so that you aren't faced with the aforementioned, unpleasant 8 pm surprise.

There will be other stuff that may be specific to your work or that I've just glossed over; the takeaway here is that you get it looked after, you have a routine in place, and you try not to do it all yourself.

Onto the next area that needs organising and automating as much as possible: the sales & marketing. It's so very important to get this area into a routine, not just because it takes up a large chunk of your time, but because a full pipeline of prospects is essential to your comfort. If you are known, in-demand, and have choices about which clients & what sort of work you do, you have control. If you don't have choices, you end up not doing your best work for less money - a death spiral for the heart & soul.

There will be patterns in your sales & marketing cycle that occur on a daily, weekly, fortnightly, monthly, & quarterly basis. Anything longer than a quarter is too long; you need to steer the marketing juggernaut with small course corrections and not have to try to implement a wholesale change of strategy, which is pretty much the same as starting from scratch.

The main part of your sales & marketing routine is keeping in touch with clients personally, whether you are working on a current project with them or they have been dormant for a few months. The old adage that we all know but don't act on is so true: It is far cheaper/easier/less stressful to keep a client & win business from him/her than it is to find a potential new client, map out possible projects, win over the business, learn their ways, train them in your ways, and get the job delivered, invoiced, and paid.

You don't have to turn your clients into your BFF ("Best Friend Forever"), although for a microbusiness, one principle I adhere to is that if I couldn't stand an evening dinner in a restaurant with them, they are the wrong fit for me (same goes for team members too). So, you don't have to date them, you don't have to know everything about them, but you should be able to call them, have them take your call, have a brief catchup, exchange news, and have some sort of forward plans, even if it's that you will call them again in a couple of months.

To this end, you should have a contact plan, a log, and a reminder system. It doesn't have to be fancy; a spreadsheet will do just fine.

Keeping clients happy is remarkably easy with only a small amount of effort. Pay attention to the information they tell you, including the personal details, make notes, and use that information when you see them next. One typical example is the "kid status check-in." Keep track of what their kids are up to; you can casually ask how X got on with Y and see their face light up, as you remembered a personal detail; you are a nice human being. The other favourite is the sports fan. I don't follow sports, but the Internet will give me results and the latest news. When you are doing the small talk, you can casually mention that you noticed that W had beaten Z in the league, then keep quiet to leave them to fill in the details. This, again, provides a warm fuzzy feeling within them.

Therefore, keep notes of important details such as the ones mentioned above to keep your customers happy. Get into a habit of doing this.

The other routines you need to get into when meeting with clients are the following:

1. Bring snacks/cookies/donuts to every meeting.
2. Check in every so often when the work is on an upbeat note about any new business contacts that they can refer to you.
3. Overdeliver a little bit in a demonstrable way.

By #3, I don't mean give away the farm on each and every job. I mean add a little percentage of effort to the work here and there that you can clearly identify as being above and beyond what is called for so that you can ensure they notice that you are doing more than the minimum. Practice this: Most people think that overdeliver is a love bomb of 'stuff' or that it's quietly putting in a huge hidden effort that never gets noticed. Neither of these will do you any good at all.

Try and arrange some sort of checklist & log for the above. It may seem a bit sneaky and artificial, but having a reminder of what to talk about, when it happened last, what the last referral was, when you last asked, what your over-deliveries have been and so forth is just good sales management. In the old days, BI & BL ("Before Internet" & "Before laptops": Yes, I am that old!), sales representatives had filing systems with pre-printed cards that had this and far more on them to help them keep track. The need to keep track hasn't gone away; how we keep track of them now has changed.

The next part of your sales & marketing routine is the follow-up of your proposals. This should be done regularly; if it doesn't happen (you did call and were told that they were not available or that they needed a few more days, right?) you move that entry into your diary, either manually or electronically. This will keep the reminder front and center so that it's in your face. At the end of every day, check what you need to follow up the next day.

The last part of your essential routines is your actual marketing efforts. For many of us, this is our website. Therefore, to wrap this up, let's look at what it takes to maintain an effective Internet marketing presence.

Your website needs regular (i.e. weekly) updates to give your visitors something new to look at and to give the search engines the hint that this is an active website that people want to come and visit. It may take a few people writing blog posts for you in the way that you are satisfied with, but getting someone to do it for you means that this regular item can be left on automatic.

If social media is part of your marketing, this should be regularly maintained. This isn't quite the same as frequently - you don't have to update your Facebook Page status every day, but do it regularly. At worst, just post a link to your website update! For Twitter fans, the point of Twitter is to tweet a few times a day. Not 20 times a day, not once every three months. If you can't maintain the tweet rate, don't do Twitter.

If you have an email list, then you need to plan and implement a contact strategy. If you do it much less often than fortnightly, it will get lost in the inbox of your recipients, who will probably have forgotten who you are and why they subscribed. Your newsletter doesn't have to be long or complicated, just useful. It doesn't take much to pay someone to come up with some top tips, find a picture on Pinterest, or hunt out some YouTube videos. Once a fortnight email means two links to your blog entries, plus a top tip and your current offer/campaign. Trivial effort that is regularly done will result in high impact.

Getting your ducks in a row means being organised about all aspects of the personal and routine parts of your business life. Have timetables and reminders, delegate and sub-contract out as much as possible, streamline, and if you can't, let it go. By doing this, you substantially increase the chances you'll be in top form when an opportunity arises, be in a position to take advantage of it, and maximise your energies for your best work.

Want more? For a free copy of my *Small Business Owners' Productivity Cookbook*, go to http://thepurplepod.co.uk/free-cookbook/.

7 Important Tips For How YOU Can Help YOUR Business

By Sue Messruther

It comes with the territory: Everyone slows down at some point. The economy can make or break small businesses every day of the year, and depending on how you are operating your business, you could be closing your doors next week! Oh, you don't want to close your doors? Well, that is great news! Let me give you a few tips that you can put into place rather quickly and successfully that will keep your business on track regardless of what is happening around you!

A lot of small business owners become the same as everyone else; they start up because it seemed like a good idea at the time, or it was just something you always wanted to do, so you look around at your competitors and begin to do what they are doing. After all, they look successful, right?

Don't do the "monkey see, monkey do" syndrome!

You need to stand out from your competitors and be unique. Give your customers a reason to come to you! So, start by asking yourself, "What makes your business better or more unique than your competitor?"

Is it your solution to a problem? Is it something you actually do that nobody else does? Is it the way you treat your customers, or the particular service you're providing?

This seems to be a lot of questions I know, but I want you to ask them of yourself so you can really look at your business. After all, it is these types of questions your customers will be asking that will determine what they think of you when they hear about your business. Come up with something that will be uniquely yours, like, "Lift the lid of your thirst with..." or "Quick as a flash to your front door...," and so forth. I am sure you can come up with some catchy phrases that you can then build upon.

Customer Demographic

Where are your customers? You see, when we are asked to do SEO for small businesses, we realize that they have been trying to market to everyone! But not every business is right for everyone; you need to specify your exact market in order to become successful

Think of it from this point of view: "Can you really afford to market to everyone?"

I certainly can't!

Now, if you did have the budget, the other problem is that customers probably won't find anything in your marketing that they need or want! The smart way is to work out who your market is, make them feel that you understand what they are going through, that you have the answers to help them, that you understand them, and that your product or service was created just for them.

Let me give you an example. We asked ourselves:

- Who are our potential customers?
- What was the common need amongst our clients?
- What was already available and how can we make it better?

We realized after designing websites for clients that there was a need for booking software that could be "plugged" into any website to take bookings online, so we went about creating a software that could do this, take payments and details, etc. for the customer (so it was easy for them to use). Then, for our clients, we made a backend so they could control it by adding editing and deleting their items/products (so it was easy for them to use).

Now, for our guest houses and hotels, we set up the software so it targeted these businesses. Then, we set up the same software on another site, but we targeted car hire, utility car hire, and truck hire businesses. On another site, we set it up for baby hire, then exercise hire on another site, then targeted those specific businesses. We made it an annual license with no other fees to make it easier to budget for!

We did three things here:

1. We created an answer for a need and made it UNIVERSAL.
2. Then we set them up to target our intended customers!
3. We created a flat annual fee yearly rather than taking a percentage, *which they all pointed out to us they didn't want.*

Had we set the software up as a universal software, then when clients looked at the software, they didn't know if it would suit them and would look elsewhere! You have to target your clients, provide a solution to their problem, and then price it within their budgets! We listened to the remarks of "they take 20%!" or "we lose 15% per booking!"

So, you need to be focused on who your potential customer is so that you can find them and get them to be an actual customer who will do business with you over and over again for years to come!

This brings me to another very interesting point....

Your customers' value!

What on Earth is a "customer's value"?

1. The value every customer brings to your business
2. The impact that losing a customer will have on your business
3. The amount of money you can afford to spend to get a new customer (*This is also important to know because it will help you to understand how to increase that number.*).

So, how do you calculate your customer's value?

Well, you take your total dollar amount of a sale, then times this with the total number of purchases your customer makes in a year, and then multiply this by the total number of years a customer has been with you. (Some of ours have been with us for over 18 years!).

Okay, most of our customers start with a website, then add hosting and a domain name in the beginning, so let's give this a figure of say, $700. Now, most customers want a minimum of 1 hour of work per month on their site at $30/hour. Now, we multiply that by the number of years, and you have your customer value.

So, let's say "Country Style" asked us to design their site, work on it during the year, and they stay with us for 10 years. This customer value is now $700 + 30×12 = $1060 after the first year. He has his hosting, domain costs, and work on the site. Therefore, work on their site each year at one hour per month, the yearly costs are now $440, multiplied by nine years and added to the first year = $1060 + $3960 = $5020.

Now, of course, no client has ever wanted just one hour of work done, and he/she certainly has never had the same site for 10 years, but I wanted to show you the value of just one client at a bare minimum.

So, how would we treat our clients so that they don't ever want to leave? And, what could we do to encourage him/her to stay longer, and how will this affect our bottom line?

Well, we would offer him/her VIP status. This status would apply to clients who stay with us for five or more years. They would be offered great discounts, and they can see the value in what we offer (like discounted hosting, graphic work, backlinking, setting up social pages put together great packages, etc). This then encourages the client to stay with us and spend a little more money, which results in our bottom line growing!

So, what can you do to help increase your business?

How about Cross-Promoting!

We encourage all of our clients to do this simply because it works so well! So, what does it involve? Simply, mix with other businesses! Networking!

Look, other businesses are not your competition. They can possibly leverage the benefits of all businesses involved. Many companies fear other businesses and play cards close to their chest because they are afraid they will give the "golden secret away." This is why we tell our clients to reach out and grow. Let me give you an example of what cross-promoting is and how it works

This is a method where two or more businesses get to know what each other offers in products or services. This can benefit each of them with the added exposure and personal recommendation or endorsement from other local, trusted businesses.

For example: Let's take Rosendale Guest House. John, the owner, knows there are lots of activities in his local area that his guests could enjoy and wonderful places to dine, so John heads off to a couple of the local activities and introduces himself over a cup of coffee. He exchanges details with them and keeps in contact with them. While he is out, he gets hungry and heads off to a local restaurant. While there, he thinks that his guests might like to come there and eat, so he speaks to the owner and gets their details. John has just cross-promoted his business with other businesses in his area that will COMPLIMENT his own business!

When done right, cross-promotions can help you:

1. get added exposure
2. get new customers
3. reactivate previous customers
4. bring in quality leads
5. and much more

So, head out like John and look for "complimentary businesses." Keep in mind that the businesses you should be cross-promoting are businesses that are not direct competitors to yours. These businesses just share similar types of customers!

Another wonderful free tool we use in our business that can help you with yours is....

Using Testimonials

What is the world's single best and most used recommendation? Word of mouth! Testimonials are word of mouth! I mean, selling is difficult enough, but mix in testimonials, and suddenly things, are moving a lot better. Just like people judge a book by its cover, they also judge your business by the testimonials they read about you. Testimonials are a perfect way to tell your potential customers all of the benefits they will gain by dealing with you or purchasing your products. They are far more likely to believe those testimonials because they came from someone else. They want to know how others have been helped by you, what your service is like, were you supportive or friendly, were there any difficulties, etc. Testimonials must be part of your online and offline marketing efforts- no doubt about it!

Put testimonials on:

- Postcards
- Websites
- Brochures
- Flyers
- Online and offline ads
- Phone on-hold messages
- Walls of your business
- So forth

You see that I mentioned postcards above. Postcards?! Aren't these the cards you send to family and friends at holiday events?!

Postcards opening doors to potential new customers!

I love postcards! I didn't start using these until about 2010 - I know, a bit slow on the uptake! But, one day, I got one through my door and, "click," it hit me – why wasn't I sending out postcards!

If you're a business owner like me who hasn't been using postcards, then you're missing a very real and very large opportunity to get more clients and expand that bottom line of yours!

Postcards are now the most effective marketing strategy we use today, and for the price of them, you can get great value for your money and budget. When I say postcards, I don't mean in the local newspapers, but heading to www.vistaprint.com, or if you're in the UK, www.vistaprint.co.uk. You just can't beat their prices, plus they deliver to your door! We usually order 500 or so at a time and have several different types of postcards, which I will tell you more about later. I am paying about 15 cents per postcard! Now, that is extremely cost-effective advertising – let me tell you how we get our postcards back!

When we design our postcards, we put in a discounted offer, but only if they hand the postcard in at the time of their order! This means we get back a very good percentage of our postcards, so we can then post them out to another and another and another! Now, we don't get them all back, which is why we order more, but we do get back a lot of them. We get their details and have permission to contact them and sell our services to them. Remember that they are getting a discount, so, to them, they are winning. However, we are too!

The point I want to get across is that postcards are so cheap and are a very beautiful way of marketing your brand, your business, and your services.

I mentioned that we send out several different types of postcards; that is because we use postcards to do the following jobs:

1. Effective marketing & branding
2. Part of a lead generation system
3. To follow up with potential customers (we have a second- and third-contact follow-up)
4. Marketing to current clients (with bundles and specials exclusive to them)
5. Offer our coupons (again to get leads and branding purposes)

I mentioned referrals above, so I will share with you how we get referrals in the next section.

Referrals: Why you should and how to get them

After doing business for over 10 years, we sat down and decided to talk about where to go from here. How can we improve things even more? How could we use our current clients to help us? The answer was clear – referrals!

Referrals actually became the very lifeblood of our business because we valued our clients and looked after them, trying to wow them at each turn, that these quickly became the simplest ways to get new customers.

You see, new clients came to us either through postcards that I mentioned above, organic search engines, or by word of mouth from our customers' referrals! If someone has recommended your business, this is valued highly because they have used your services, and they trust their friend or acquaintance opinion's over any sales letter or pitch!

Referrals are great because:

- Low costs (can be free to get – see our tip below)
- Customers referred to you are ready to do business with you
- Those customers who refer others to you become loyal customers to your business
- Referrals result in a new customer

Where can you find people who will refer business to you?

Your best referrers are your happy customers, but let's not forget about other influential people in your area.

- Influential people directly related to your industry
- Influential people not related to your industry, but come into contact with lots of people
- Your happy customers who you have treated so well

Anyone can refer your business; it is a great way to build your reputation as well. Just remember to be reachable, and that includes the sociable online arenas. There will be more on this in the next section, but, first, I want to pass on our favorite tip from that meeting where we developed and grew our referrals instantly!

For every referral that resulted in a sale large or small, we gave our referrers 10% of whatever the total sales amount was to be credited to their accounts (not redeemable as cash). This was an instant and huge hit with our clients! For the rest of that year, we did NO advertising, yet we had a six-week waiting list! Many of our clients paid for their hosting and SEO work with their referrals - it was great! While the economy around us was closing doors, we were busier than ever, all because of referrals!

You need to be the queen or king of social behavior

Okay, here is my last and final tip for you; it is just as important as all of the above to help your bottom line expand along with your dreams. That tip is social behavior. By this, I mean Facebook, Twitter, Google+, LinkedIn, and YouTube, as these are the top social media platforms on the Internet today. Yes, there are many others, but hey, we are running a business here – your valuable time is limited here!

When you set these up, make sure you keep your branding in check; use the same logo, same colors, same themes, and same information. This is how you brand yourself by being consistent in everything that is online about your business. Now, yes, like I once said myself, I hear you saying, "But I don't have enough time to be doing all of this! How can I get this done?" Well, of, course you can pay someone to do it all for you, as that is a great time saver, but you still have to give them all of the details, etc. to post each week for you. This includes any sales you're having, changes people need to be aware of, new staff, new products, etc., so it only saves a certain amount of time. Now, I do this for many of my clients because they don't have the time to do this, and that is fine. Their time is better spent where they are needed for their businesses; what I do is compliment their businesses. (They send special events as and when they happen; I do the other posts by collecting information from their site, their professions, and their fields of interest.)

What we did was link as much as we could together so that when we posted on Facebook, it would tweet that post to Twitter. We did this by clicking apps in the client's Facebook account, and then selected Twitter. Shortly thereafter, however, I found another great timesaver via a free online service called www.hootsuite.com. Now we sit for an hour and put up posts that will automatically go out twice per week to Facebook, Twitter, Google+, LinkedIn, for YouTube we upload manually.

We set it up for a month of posting, which has been pre-organized according to our event diary. Our event diary has all of the holidays marked in, so we can advertise and jump on the back of holiday advertising, including Valentine's Day, Easter, Halloween, Christmas, etc., you get the idea. Therefore, one calendar has all of this marked, with each one in a different color so we can see it at a glance on the wall. We then know to begin advertising in mid January with Valentine-themed posts, videos, and packages, etc.

Now that Google looks to see who is talking about us and who links to us, it helps our websites and online business reputation by being active, involved, and reachable. Therefore, never let an opportunity slip by you; wherever your customers are, this is where you want to be!

Sue Messruther
Scarborough Web Design Ltd
www.scarboroughwebdesign.co.uk

"Fixed Income" or "Expanding Income"
Which Retirement Option Will You Choose?

By Fred Raley

The Retirement Loophole Nobody's Talking About

Financial gurus want you to believe you can save for retirement and make it work. This has been a staple of their advice for decades. But is it still true in today's economy and work environment? Signs are that it is not.

Is a "Fixed-Income" Retirement strategy still good?

Fixed-income retirement strategies may have worked for the majority in the early to mid-1990s. But much has changed since then that affects most workers. I'm sure not everyone is affected, but I do believe that a vast majority of the workforce **is affected**. If you believe you will have enough cash to live out the rest of your life, then you don't need to read the rest of this article. On the other hand, if you don't or are not sure you have enough cash for retirement, keep reading for an alternate solution.

MSN Money has an article, "*Why 1 in 5 US workers won't retire*" (http://money.msn.com/now/post—why-1-in-5-us-workers-wont-retire). There are plenty of scapegoats to blame: The economy, the severe lack of available jobs, the meager retirement savings... I could go on and on. I am sure you likely see yourself in some of these situations. And I am also sure that that number cited in "Money" will be far higher than 1 in 5. More like 3 or 4 out of 5 will not be able to retire. There does not seem to be a comprehensive solution in place to prevent these negative factors from ruining your chances to retire in comfort.

Here's another national article from the *Today Show*,"*I'll be working 'til I die*" (http://www.today.com/money/treading-water-why-its-gotten-harder-save-retirement-8C11319975). Saving for retirement just does NOT work for most folks. There are too many things that eat up your money too fast these days (can I have a "*Hell Yeah*" here?), and none of them are likely to stop any time soon. Examples:

- Mortgage
- Taxes

- Insurance
- Education
- Taking care of others (parents, drop-back-in kids)
- Transportation
- Food

The list goes on and on.

I mean, do you really think you can work for 40 years and then retire on less than 40% of what you were making that only barely got you by? And that's if you get a "pension" from the company you worked for. This might have been possible for folks born in the first half of the 1900s. But not today. Not by a long shot.

Many folks, who have very optimistic thoughts, keep thinking that an inheritance or lottery win will set them free. Those odds are astronomical if you have not checked them out in a while.

Others are thinking of moving to Panama or Nicaragua for the lower cost of living upon retirement. I guess that would be okay… if you like leaving your friends and family and living in a new culture. Is that really something you want to take on in your 60's or 70's?

What about this "Fixed Income Retirement" idea?

Many reputable financial analysts and firms make a living teaching retirees and soon-to-be-retirees how to budget to live on a "Fixed Income." This can be based on any number of factors. Income can be from one or both individuals' SSA (Social Security accounts). Also, potentially included can be Individual Retirement Accounts (IRAs) or 401K Savings accounts and other assets the couple or individual might have accumulated during their or his/her earning years.

The analyst basically constructs an income vs. expenses balance sheet for the person or couple and projects how much of their (his/her) savings and SSA will contribute, based on assumptions about the market and government actions on funding SSA.

If the assets will provide enough income to cover the expenses, you will be in good shape. This is, of course, dependent on whether all of the assumptions about the economy and government come true or not. It stands to reason that there is a fair to good chance that those assumptions will not come true.

- And do you understand all the ins and outs of investing your portfolio?
- Are you really an expert on bond trading?
- Are you an expert on the stock market?
- Are you an expert of the right mix of investments to protect your portfolio? Is anyone?
- What about forex trading?
- Day trading?
- Investing and holding?

The choices go on and on. Frankly, how can anyone know enough about you and your specifics and be able to accurately predict the future to make the right choices for you (assuming you are not an expert in all of these areas?)

Here is a recent ad I saw on this subject: "*Create A Fixed Income Strategy In Five Simple Steps*"

You have got to be kidding me!

There are more (way more) than five steps to achieving this. Even then, you still might not get it right.

Some of the pros and cons of a fixed income are:

Pros:

- You know how much should be coming in on a monthly basis, so you know how much (or little) you have to work with for extras.

Cons:

- Prices may rise faster than your assumptions.
- The government could default on SSA. (It's more likely than not... or, at least, will cut back your benefits substantially.)
- The investments in your IRA/401K might not perform as well as your assumptions predict.
- You might have unexpected expenses during the fixed income time that were not planned for.
- You might not have saved enough during your working years due to job loss, divorce, caring for aging parents, college costs, etc.
- There is little chance you can get a loan to "tide you over" or cover emergency expenses because you no longer have a "job."

A huge issue is the unexpected expenses that might rise up. In my instance, I was out of a job for over four months, living off of my meager 401K savings and, thus, depleted about 40% of it in four months. That will take a LONG time to make up... and that assumes the employment market stays level and I don't lose out too early... i.e. before my projected savings/SSA/etc. can match my expenses.

- What if your house needs a new roof?
- What if your car breaks down and needs major repair?
- What if a kid moves back in due to loss of a job or divorce?

The list goes on and on with "life experiences" that can drain your meager resources.

There is too much uncertainty in a "Fixed Income Retirement" scenario on which to base your retirement decision.

One of the key solutions you should consider putting into place to fund your retirement is to have **your own business** that continues to bring in **ever-increasing income** for you that can keep rising through your retirement years. That way, you don't have to depend on savings, 401Ks, the stock or bond market ups/downs, Social Security, or any of the other shaky parts of your failing fixed-income retirement strategy.

Investing in your own business does not cost much.

Many people start their own businesses with little to no investment. It's not like you have to buy into a brick & mortar storefront and incur rent, insurance, hiring/firing employees, etc. That's "old school" thinking about business. Today's home businesses require little more than a computer, a fax, a phone, and some hard but fun work on your part to make it a big success. Some of the things you can do from home to bring in income are:

- **Public Speaking:** Perhaps you have a favorite hobby or an interesting and unique career or life experience you could talk about. If you are good, you can charge really exorbitant fees and get them paid to you on a routine basis. Public speaking is a very lucrative career... but most folks would rather jump off a cliff than get up in public to speak. So, although this might be a viable option for some, it's not for the masses.

- **Hobby to Profits:** Some folks have hobbies that might easily be turned into viable, profitable businesses: Painting pictures, creating graphics, sewing, etc. Make sure you can ramp up your hobby efforts to bring in the type of income you are seeking. You could easily get into a situation where you no longer enjoy your hobby now that it has become work.

- **Virtual Assistant:** A "VA" is an entrepreneur who works from a home office providing administrative, secretarial, and clerical support or creative and/or technical services for a client. If you have these skills, bring it on! The main issue with this type of work is that your income is limited by the hours in a day and the rate you can charge. Unless you hire a team to work with you, you cannot scale easily to reach higher incomes.

- **Building an MLM team:** Most folks are thinking "I'm trashing this!" at this point. But it's because they don't know how to build an MLM team or have a bad opinion of MLM (scam, pyramid, etc.). But you also know that it can build some huge incomes for people who stay with it. I am still receiving income in my MLM that I built back in the late 1990s! Don't tell me that MLMs don't make money! They sure do.

There are tons of ways to make money from home, but there is one (MLM) that everyone can do and be a big success with. The reason you might not have had success in MLM in the past is that you failed to learn new skills to make it work!

MLM is legal: Back in 1979, Amway paved the way for MLM (Multi-Level-Marketing) as a legal and legitimate home business. See http://www.mlmlegal.com/landmark.html for details. Amway is now a $12B per year business, still using the MLM model worldwide. (No, I am not in Amway.)

Since then, many companies have come and gone for many reasons, but a few have weathered the years and made it through thanks to good products, good compensation, and fair pricing.

You will have to learn new skills to make an MLM business successful. The main reason people fail in MLM is that they are given a pitch, making it sound like overnight riches are achievable, so they get the idea that "if I join, I will make money," which is not true. It's more like, "If I join and learn how to market, I will make money."

Let me repeat that: *"You have to learn new skills to be successful in your own business."*

Are these skills hard? **NO!** But you have to learn them.

People love the idea of doing work once and getting paid over and over and over and over. It just makes sense! This is the huge benefit of having your own MLM business.

And, with our company, you don't buy products you don't use; you just buy ones that you already use. Just "Switch Stores." The products cost a bit more, but are WAY higher-quality than you get at your local stores. That's your "cost of doing business" if you want to look at it that way.

Millions of individuals and couples are doing this quite successfully. In my case, I started another small business ($10/month) that I worked during the evening hours in the early 2000's after the kids went to sleep. Over the years, it has brought in over $100,000; these checks keep coming in every month like clockwork. That's money we could not have done without. Kids' schooling and sports expenses, car repairs, wife and/or I out of work periods, etc. Work that I put in to build it over ten years ago is still sending me checks monthly.

Many people grab onto this business idea, but fail to learn the skills needed to make it work.

Let me repeat that: *"But you have to learn new skills to be successful in your own business."*

Why this will work for you

So what I have done is to create super simple, easy-to-use, effective tools that my team uses to build a solid 15-year-old MLM fast and at low cost. I provide these to you at no cost so you can start using them immediately to pull in success quickly and to see your checks grow quickly in your own business.

I also hold routine conference calls and have recorded calls that you can use to build your business.

These tools work great, don't cost anything, and work to build your entire team.

The other neat thing is, I don't expect you to learn how to market online with blogs, websites, autoresponders, graphics development, etc. I give you everything you need to bring in new customers on a routine basis so this will work for you too. I see about a dozen or so "big personality" people who seem to be having all of the success in building online MLM businesses. But there are thousands of others who don't have this "big personality" persona who are quietly and discretely pulling in hundreds and thousands of dollars monthly from their MLM companies.

And the good part is, this MLM has products that you use every day in your home, so it's just like "switching stores" to your MLM to buy your products. You don't have to buy products that sit in your garage or that you will not use. You just buy what you use each month.

For me, I buy their great tasting energy bars and weight management bars and use them for breakfasts and snacks during the day. So, I eat better (no fast-food breakfasts and no candy bars in the afternoon that just end up sitting on my thighs!), and I save money at the same time.

It just makes sense.

And, our easy-to-use tools bring in more customers to "switch stores" all of the time. You get these for free; they are customized just for you.

People love the idea of doing work once and getting paid over and over and over and over. It just makes sense! You will love seeing those residual income checks arrive like clockwork. Use them to pay off bills, cover unexpected expenses, save for vacation, or any of your other needs. These REALLY come in handy. And, the nice part is, you can keep building with your team to make those monthly residual checks go up to a substantial income over a short period of time.

Having your own business makes sense even before retirement. Read the article, *"On the brink: Many working moms falling apart, author says,"* at http://www.today.com/moms/brink-many-working-moms-falling-apart-author-says-4B11184706.

Her final statement in this article:

Q. How are you doing today?

A: I'm self-employed now, so I'm a fantastic boss. I'm the best boss I've ever had.

Building your own MLM business and getting those monthly residual income checks is not hard. It's not like the old days of going door to door, pitching products, stocking your garage and delivering products to customers, or any of that yucky stuff. Today's MLM is all about online ordering, shipping direct to customers' doors, not ordering more than you need, etc. The company keeps track of your team and your commissions and sends you a residual income check each month. It's easier than ever!

Summary

I know you were not thinking of starting an MLM business. And you are probably really going to blow me off no matter what I say here. But do you really have a retirement plan that is working to provide you retirement income that is working? Or do you have a plan to retire early? Think about this. Talk to your spouse. Talk to your parents. Talk to your friends. See how many are happy with their retirement plans and income. Most of them, if they're honest, will not have much in place for a comfortable retirement. You will be able to help them too.

Putting your own business in place to provide retirement income is just smart business. It's VERY smart business. It's easy, it's low cost, and it works, but not until you take action. Don't put it off any longer. Get yours going today.

Action

Grab my free info at http://www.JoinFredsBiz.com where you can find out how to easily and quickly put your retirement income plan into place. Grab our free report here and make your own evaluation. http://www.JoinFredsBiz.com

Michael Jordan: *I can accept failure; but I can't accept not trying.*

Interviews - If I Can, You Can!

By Jean Shaw

I'm guessing if you've been online for any length of time, you'll have both listened to interviews and been encouraged to do them yourself. That's because they're easy to do and provide an element of trust to your potential business partners, customers, or clients.

I was first encouraged to do them at an event in Las Vegas, so, during a break after his presentation, I immediately asked the speaker when I could chat with him.

Well, why not?

Actually, at the time, I could think of lots of reasons, but the one that sprang to mind when he agreed was, *I've never interviewed anyone before. How on Earth do I do it*?

Then I reasoned that it couldn't be that difficult. After all, it's only talking to someone, and what's the worst that could happen? Apart from making a bit of a fool of myself and facing a few of those technical challenges I hate so much, it wasn't likely to kill me.

Also, as the interview would just be between me and the person on the other end of questions, if it all went horribly wrong, I could just bury the whole thing and no one would ever need to know. The only thing I would lose would be time, which admittedly, I could never get back. However, it would be a learning experience, and a beneficial one at that, provided I learned from the experience.

We all know we tend to buy or be influenced by people we Know, Like and Trust, but since the Internet has a global reach, it's clearly not possible to meet everyone face to face.

Seasoned marketers will tell you there's nothing like live workshops and encouraging everyone to get to these belly-to-belly events where possible because that's where you meet like-minded people. Not everyone can do that though, so the next best thing to put a face to a name is to create videos. They're great mediums to use, BUT not everyone feels comfortable in front of the camera, certainly not me. That's why for most people, audio is the next best thing.

Admittedly, people can't see your face, but they can hear your voice and form an opinion of whether you sound trustworthy, genuine, and know what you're talking about. We are fickle creatures, though, and depending on the sound of your voice, it may be harder to convince people to listen to your message.

In the past, I confess to having bought a course just so I could listen to the product creator's voice, but equally, I've bought a course even though the sound of the product creator made me cringe.

In both cases, the content was excellent, though, so I had no complaints.

I've interviewed several people now, although I prefer to think of them as being friendly conversations. Apart from the introduction and ending, my interviews tend to be unscripted. I hate those contrived question and answer types, but if you only have a limited amount of time and specific details to cover, they're probably the safest bet.

At least, that way, you know you've covered everything you wanted, but product creators or service providers have confided they really get fed up answering the same things over and over again, so if you can make your interview stand out a bit in some way, it could make it more memorable.

Obviously, the most important thing you can do before the chat is to do some research and take a few notes. After all, if you ask someone for an interview, you must have a reason to do so, and you don't want the conversation to dry up.

Preparation, as they say, is everything. It's just common courtesy, and it makes the person you're talking to aware you've looked into their background and products and are genuinely interested in their views and opinions.

Speaking of preparation, you'll need to ensure you have the recording equipment in place, the room is quiet, the dogs and kids are happily occupied, you've got a note on your door not to be disturbed, you've removed that noisy clock from the wall, and you've turned off the phone(s) and anything that might bleep on the computer.

Of course, it would be Sod's Law (a.k.a. Murphy's Law) that a noisy motorbike or airplane would go past your property or someone would ring the door bell halfway through the conversation, but if that happens, you can just pause, wait, and resume the chat when it's quiet again.

That's provided it doesn't inconvenience your guest too much. Failing that, you can always make a note of where it happened and cut out the offending piece when you edit the interview later.

Oh, most important, you'll want to have a glass of water or a drink on hand in case your throat dries up or you suddenly get a coughing fit.

Believe me, it happens!

I've done most of my interviews using Skype, which is free to download on computers or smartphones, but have held interviews over the normal land line, had the 'phone on loud speaker and just recorded the conversation using Audacity - more about that later though.

It's not as good a method, but if you only need the content for transcription or for reference, it's okay. I tend to use this method when I'm chatting to clients who want a website, and I want to get a feel of who they are and what they're hoping to achieve. In those cases, the question and answer-type interviews are invaluable.

When I use Skype, I never turn the video option on. As I said, I hate being on camera, but that's not the only reason I keep it turned off. You see, when you have to edit an interview and cut bits out, it's much easier to do when there's just audio.

I have a good microphone, but usually wear an inexpensive Logitech headset microphone when doing the interviews. It doesn't have to be expensive to set yourself up, but I would advise against using one of those built-in microphones on laptops, as they aren't usually very effective.

I record the conversations using a program called Pamela. It's a free download by Scendix Software, which you can use with Skype. The basic version only allows you up to 15 minutes recording though, so if you're planning on making lengthier recordings, which most people do, you'll want to opt for the Professional edition. It's a nominal one-time fee, but well worth the investment.

I also cover myself by recording the conversation with Audacity because I have had some great calls in the past only to discover Pamela had stopped recording halfway through the conversation. Not only was it embarrassing, but frustrating because the people I interviewed were hard to pin down. They were extremely busy, and I'd felt very lucky they'd graciously spared me some of their precious time.

It was hard asking for a repeat performance, but I did, and they all agreed, so I must have done something right. Most people are very understanding though. We're only human after all.

Audacity is free, and like just about everyone else I know, is the program of choice to edit conversations and cut out all the 'Ums,' 'Ahs,' and background noises. It's surprising what you hear when you play your interviews back.

Audacity is actually a free audio-editing application, which works on all platforms - Windows, Mac, OS, and Linux. It can be downloaded from Sourceforge.net. You also need to download LAME, which enables you to save your edited files as MP3s, making them accessible to all.

LAME is a codec and will come in a zipped folder, so you'll have to extract it and then save the file somewhere on your computer. It doesn't matter where you put it as long as you remember where you put it because, the first time you try to save your recording as an MP3, Audacity will want to know where the lame_enc.dll file is located.

Once you've installed Audacity, you'll need to check to see that your recording and playback settings are correct. You can do this by clicking the Edit - Preferences-Audio I/O tabs and then selecting the correct microphone and speakers from the list of devices.

Click OK.

Once you're happy with the set-up, you can do a test call to Skype and record it on both Pamela and Audacity. Listen to the playbacks on both to make sure your volume levels are correct. You want to do this every time you have an interview, and you should also do a quick test with the person you're interviewing because, even if you have your system set up correctly, it's quite possible they don't.

You want to make sure the recording comes out as clear as possible. There's nothing worse than having two different volume levels where one person is speaking loudly and the other is speaking softly. If people struggle to hear, they'll most likely switch it off regardless of how good your content is.

Recording with Audacity is really simple. You just press the red circle record button. When you want to pause, you press the pause button with the two vertical stripes. To stop the recording, you press the stop button with the square on it.

If you need to take a break in the middle of a recording, you should press the pause button and then press it again to resume. That way, you'll continue on the same track. However, if you press the stop button and then continue again, you'll be taken to the very start of a different track. The problem with that is when you play the recording back, you'll hear both tracks at the same time, which will certainly be confusing.

You can do a bit of cutting and pasting to get everything back on one track, but it's a bit of a hassle, and you must remember to close or delete everything off of the second track before you export the file.

It's much easier if you do it right the first time, so remember, 'Pause,' don't 'Stop,' unless you've finished of course!

If you've done everything correctly, it's wise to immediately save your work as an Audacity file as soon as you've finished recording, just in case your computer crashes or something. That would be a blow, wouldn't it?

Once saved, you can play it back, edit if necessary, and save it as an MP3 file.

To play your recording, you press the little button with the green arrow on it. When you find a bit that needs editing, you can highlight it and cut it out using the scissors, or you can just press 'Delete' from the 'Edit' menu.

Of course, if you're anything like me, you'll get a bit overzealous and delete too much, but if you make a mistake about what you've deleted you can either go to edit and select 'Undo Delete' or press the little arrow button that curves backwards. Either will restore your deletion, and you can have another go at it.

I find it helps to use the magnifying glass, which increases the size of the audio waves and makes editing much easier and more accurate.

Make sure to keep saving your work as you make your changes, just in case you get called away and something happens. You won't be able to actually tell from looking at the sound waves if you've edited correctly, so you'll need to play it through from the beginning again to make sure.

If you want to get really professional, you can play around with the effect settings, but apart from removing some background noise occasionally, I tend to just add some music to the beginning and end of my recording, save the file, and then export it as an MP3 file.

I decide where I want to save the file on my computer, enter an artist name, the date, and maybe a title or brief description. That makes it easier to remember what the recording was about, and it will also be required if you want to submit it as a podcast somewhere.

I then either upload it to my hosting account or to Amazon S3, grab the link, and tell people where it can be found, either on my blog, websites, or social media accounts. Obviously, I also forward a copy of the completed MP3 to the interviewee and thank him/her again for his/her time.

You can also have your recordings transcribed. Unless you want to do it yourself, probably the best place to go for that is Fiverr.com. Have you heard of it? You can get just about anything done there for multiples of five dollars.

As a purchaser, Fiverr is free to join, and you'll be amazed at the services offered. I recommend you take a look. Each service is called a "gig."

For transcriptions, you'll want to look under the writing section. There will probably be a lot, and it's best to look at the ratings and reviews first before deciding who would best suit your requirements. Most of them charge five dollars for a set amount of minutes, and as you'll already know how many minutes your recording is, you'll know how many "gigs" to buy.

Most people recommend you try to keep your recordings to around 20 minutes, but mine never are. I do tend to ramble on a bit.

One thing you can do though if you know you're having your interview transcribed is to submit your MP3 without the intro and conclusion music as, sometimes, that can be the difference between needing to order an extra gig or not.

Then, you just add the music later.

Simple!

So, as you can see, interviewing someone isn't that difficult or expensive. If I can do it, you certainly can.

Good Luck!

Jean Shaw
www.JeanShawInterviews.com
http://www.amazon.com/Jean-Shaw/e/B001K8A1A0

Film Podium Talent

By Teo Smoot

Thanks to the digital age, a Hollywood professional look and level of independent and guerilla film production has become not only possible, but cheaper and more prevalent than in years past. More and more "Auteurs" are popping up every minute, grabbing a camera, and expressing themselves thematically. Equal amounts of film schools are cropping up online and offline. How-to forums and lighting and lens lessons footage constantly flood the Web. In fact, film wunderkind, Robert Rodriguez, has a popular '10 Minute Film School' YouTube video that professes to teach all you need to know to make a film. Everything -- in ten minutes right here:

http://www.youtube.com/watch?v=W-YpfievjSk.

Yet, with all of that information and products out there, studios and production houses are shuttering their doors at an alarming rate. And, while the quantity of stories told has quadrupled, the quality of storytelling has faltered to near non-existence, with the only compensation being 3-D and special effects -- the filmic equivalent of sweeping the character dirt under the rug.

So, what has happened to film teachings between *Citizen Kane* and *Catwoman*? How can you, as a young film explorer, call "action" on future time-honored masterpieces? Read on.

Probably the greatest pairing of the digital age and films is the computer. The ability to storyboard, pre-vis, color-correct, edit, and so much more on a single, portable device is truly the end-all, be-all. Though there are still some old-schoolers that balk about the death of celluloid, the fact is that digital video has given new life to the industry and the gift of wondrous possibilities that is unparalleled by any other time in movie history. Some are able to use this to their advantage, but many are using it to their detriment.

I, myself, was fortunate that I came up before computers and the Internet. In childhood, movies were mostly entertainment. From a pre-teen age on, they became more like friends really. When I was sad or upset about something or other, I would take my problems to the local theatre. Movies didn't punish or judge me. Instead, they took my mind to other worlds and made me feel great for hours. Long enough to reposition my thinking on whatever the problem initially was.

I've felt forever indebted to my motion picture buddies, though I never thought I'd ever grow up to become a filmmaker. Actually, it was all kind of by accident -

In the short version, I was a young musician who relocated from the East Coast to the West to pursue a career in 1988. I met a photographer who needed a subject for his project. I enjoyed it so much that I signed up with a model agency. This led to print and commercial work that I enjoyed so much, I decided to try acting. After observing some of the name directors, like David Lynch, Paul Verhoeven, and David Fincher, who hired me, I knew directing was next. In 2004, I became an award-winning filmmaker with my first project, a comedy short that I also wrote and co-produced. There you have it. A 15-year journey to the director's chair. Simple.

Because of my pre-established love and respect for movies, the pressure was on early in to do or create something great with my first effort. There was no time nor money for film school. Besides, my education had already come from actual Hollywood film sets. I just needed to fill in a few holes and close the gap on how to pull it all off on a MUCH smaller scale. What I learned then is what I am going to teach you in this chapter. Afterwards, you will understand how to do the same... without the 15-year adventure.

To be clear, however, this book portion is NOT a "How-to" on shooting a film. There will be no discussion about cameras, lenses, blocking, and/or editing. As I mentioned earlier, this information is available pretty much everywhere. What is not as available is training for what I call, "Film Podium Talent."

"What is that?", you ask? Quite simply, it describes those primed for or who already have a film career. That is the goal. Sort of the "teaching one to fish" scenario. If you know how to put together a career, it answers, or at least, helps to determine so many other questions of an aspiring filmmaker. Such as, "What do I pick for my first film?" "How do I survive as a filmmaker starting out?" And so many other questions not as readily available as camera and audio selections.

Film Podium Talents are there to receive awards for career work, give lectures regarding the craft, are often quoted, consulted, or referred to in their field, et cetera. That is the reason I created my blog, www.filmpodium.com, and the upcoming talent-training series and books for directors, writers, actors, and producers, www.filmtalentacademy.com.

The chapters below are to help you prepare for a career and not just a project.

LESSON ONE: VOCATION, VOCATION, VOCATION

You do not have to attend film school to be a great director, writer, producer, or actor. But you MUST respect that they are all technical skill sets that need to be learned. Now, lets take this a step further:

Martin Scorsese, Alfred Hitchcock, Steven Spielberg, Stanley Kubrick, Quentin Tarantino, Francis Ford Coppola, Orson Welles, Akira Kurosawa, Woody Allen, Christopher Nolan, James Cameron, Clint Eastwood, Billy Wilder, Ridley Scott, David Lynch, Federico Fellini, David Fincher, Charlie Chaplin, John Ford, Ingmar Bergman.

I'm confident that most every filmmaker or filmgoer will agree that the twenty names listed above represent some of, if not, THE finest directors the film community has ever bred or honored, past and present. They are all clearly film podium talents (FPT). Though different eras, schooling, and genres, each of them has a single common denominator. It is this similarity that is the first and, perhaps, most important step in achieving Film Podium Talent (aka career) status.

They are all... wait for it... more than directors. Each of them is also a writer. Most are also producers. Twenty of the best directors ever?! This is not a coincidence, folks. How could it be?

In fact, we can keep adding exceptional FPTs to the group:

Nancy Myers, The Cohen Brothers, Spike Lee, Callie Khouri, Peter Jackson, Nora Ephron, Tim Burton, Kathryn Bigelow, Michael Mann, David O. Russell....

The list goes on. Film Podium Talent(ed) directors are, by and large, writers and/or producers. Now, the thing to note here is that not all are recognized or remembered as writers. Some, like Spielberg and Hitchcock, wrote earlier in their careers. So, the point I'm trying to make here is not that you have to go out and become a known or skilled writer if you want to direct. In fact, you never have to direct anything you'd write or produce, and vice-versa. However, as a career-oriented filmmaker, you should have, at minimum, a STRONG knowledge or base of at least one other skill set than just directing. Other than just writing. Other than just acting and/or producing.

Notice that I used the term SKILL SET. The basic difference between a skill set and a talent is that one is learned, while the other is a natural gift. Though they can/should be expanded with learned technique, rules, and structure, any of these four abilities can start out as natural.

You can't really be a natural gaffer or natural script supervisor or natural DP or makeup artist. These are learned skill sets. You can, however, see natural images in your head that you're recreating as a director (camera placement is learned). Or, naturally hear character dialogue and think of stories (scriptwriting is learned). Even to naturally cry on cue or emote (hitting your mark and character creation is learned). But I digress....

The point is that the more diverse you are, your main focus has more to draw from for the overall task, whether completing it yourself or requiring it from or recognizing it in another. I am a better writer because I direct. I am a better director because I write, because I act, and so on (they all make me a better editor!). Or I can better communicate to another writer, director, actor, or editor that's been hired.

As we continue on, you'll see how this can be used over and over again in full FPT mode.

LESSON TWO: KNOW YOUR INNER PLACE

There is only one you.... Don't you dare change just because you're outnumbered! --- Charles Swindoll

Another thing that the 25+ directors listed above share is knowing what they bring to the table as talents and individuals. A Hitchcock movie would never be mistaken for a Woody Allen movie. A Tarantino movie will never be mistaken for a Cameron nor Burton movie. Similarly, a Chris Nolan film stands no chance of being confused with a Spike Lee joint!

Film Podium Talent is individual, from vision to execution. This goes for writers, actors, and producers. You must know what you uniquely bring to the table and use it to stand out, to "trademark," if you will. Don't misunderstand: Influence is expected and understood, but keep it respectful. It should be muse, not overused.

Your technique will show itself when you tap into your individual truth. This is a process I cover in my upcoming book, *The Talent of Truth* (www.FilmTalentAcademy.com), but it mostly deals with tapping into who you are, no holds barred, seeing it as a talent, and using it to set yourself apart.

The bottom line is that your true, harnessed uniqueness is what is used to build your career because it helps put and keep you in demand. Studios would rather hire Scorsese than someone like Scorsese. This also gives them something more to sell. Picture how you've seen films promoted. They all say something like, "From the director that brought you..." or "From the writer of...," right? They are hoping to cash in on your unique/individual take on the said material.

The talent of truth puts your "you" on display and, properly developed and exploited, on your chosen career path. Understand that your truth only plays out on your path. That is to say that, despite all of the stories of how another talent was discovered or established, that has nothing to do with how you will be. That was his/her path and experience based on who he/she is in truth and how he/she used or didn't use that ability. You will not and should not expect to duplicate their successes. Even if he/she "opened doors" that had been previously closed, you must lay the groundwork for you own successes.

LESSON THREE: THE MAJOR MINIMALIST

Quality films can tend to be pricey, whether they are Indie or Hollywood brand. Filmmaking is like a Vegas slot machine investment. You finance your project and pull the lever, not knowing what will hit the jackpot at the box office and DVD receipts, and what will come up as 'no match.'

This all boils down to knowing how to do more with less. Tarantino used to only use old soul records on his earlier film soundtracks as opposed to a new score. He said that this was because he hated the idea of paying a musician to compose a score only to not like the submitted music. He felt that it was a wasted risk he didn't need to take and would use that budget on something else in the film.

Robert Rodriguez is known for scaling a crew down to the very bare essentials, but constantly turning the movie into a premium project. He still writes, directs, produces, and runs his own camera, but in recent years, has added scoring his own films as well. Michael Bay's first film was *Bad Boys*. When he found himself at budget's end, but wanted additional filming that would put him over budget, he returned $25,000 of the $50,000 director's fee to complete his film. The gamble payed off, and his career took off.

Knowing when and where to put your budget, again indie or Hollywood, is a task that varies from film to film, but an obstacle you will definitely encounter on every project. Therefore, this is a developed skill set that will serve you well.

I go deeper into these and the other methods of FPT practices in my book, *FILM PODIUM TALENT: The 7 Career-Building Principles*. www.FilmTalentAcademy.com.

QUESTIONS ASKED & ANSWERED

There are a number of questions I am often asked by new filmmakers looking to get established. I will address the most common ones here:

Q: Where should I start?

A: Start by preparing for a career and not just a project. Decide what type of filmmaker you want to be and what project you want to start with, then go make it happen. As far as the first film, make the kind that you want to see and that will speak your voice, but with an audience in mind.

Q: There are so many options. How do I decide what film to do first?

A: Well, if you haven't made anything, I'd say start off with a short as opposed to a feature. Either way, start with the showcase in mind. In other words, know what specific festivals and/or venues you want to submit to at the beginning of the project. This can help to establish a schedule and timeline for completion.

(www.withoutabox.com - This site will tell you of every festival in the world, its qualifications and submission rules. You can also use festivalfocus.org).

Q: How do I find cast and crew members?

A: Craigslist. You can also find local film groups on Facebook. Or, start your own if necessary. Also, attending film festivals is a great way to find like-minded people who are already interested in making a film.

Q: How do I find or raise money to make my film?

A: Well, the less money you have, the longer your pre-production should be. Spend time like money. Start off by making a list of all of the house locations, wardrobe, props, and the like that you have access to through friends and family. Start with quantity, then narrow down to quality. This is part of your budget.

We have only scratched the surface in these pages. There are so many more project details, do's and don'ts, and information to share, including how to fund your survival and projects without a day job.

If you like what you read and want to learn more, please visit my blog, www.filmpodium.com, or my website, www.coolrooment.com.

About Teo Smoot

Teo is a multi-award winning filmmaker whose diverse entertainment career as an actor, writer, director, producer, editor, and musician has spanned the last 30 years. He is a proud father and husband and currently resides in Washington, DC.

How to Focus Your Marketing With the Right Questions

By Brenda Trott

My Curse Became My Talent

When I was a student, my teachers always knew my name before lunchtime. It wasn't because I was a big behavioral problem; it was because I always asked so many questions! When I was younger, this was really a sort of curse because I drove people crazy all of the time with all of my questions. Yet, by being true to who I was, and becoming more mature, my curse became my talent.

Coworkers started to approach me to ask questions in meetings when they were too shy or when they were afraid they would make management upset. As a teacher, I learned how to ask questions of my students to encourage learning. As more people discovered my talent for asking questions, I was invited to participate in some pretty cool things. I took part in selection committees and other types of government events specifically because they wanted to hear the types of questions I could ask. More and more often I heard and embraced, "You ask some really good questions."

If you've ever tried to write down the events right after an emotional event, you may understand how difficult it can be to get information across when you are close to the situation. When you wait for some time to pass and you are not still wrapped up in the emotion of it, you are able to tell the story more clearly. When I was a teacher, I found I would get much better recall from the students when a different teacher asked them about a lab experiment we had done or a field trip we had taken than when I asked the questions myself. This is because the student knew that teacher wasn't there and the questions were truly authentic.

Now I help small business owners get their message across to others through social media, authorship, and other publications, and I always start by asking them questions. It's really difficult to do this on your own because you are too close to what you do. In other words, you already know everything about your business, and it is difficult to imagine what someone else won't understand. So I step in and ask the questions that you need to answer in order to get found by your best potential customers.

The First Step

Before I help anyone write their own book, design an elevator speech, get copy for a website, or do ANY kind of marketing, I always start in the same place: I help them create their avatar. Maybe you've heard of the avatar. I'm not talking about the giant blue creatures in the feature film; I'm talking about the one person you are talking to when you are writing, creating videos, or creating any type of information product for people.

Maybe your English teacher told you that you need to know your audience before your write. I'm not arguing with your English teacher; I'm just defining the word "audience." No matter what you are doing, your audience should only be ONE person at a time. Yes, even when you are speaking from the stage, you should really be speaking to one person. The most talented speakers make you feel as though they are speaking directly with you.

When you set up an avatar and speak or write directly to him/her, you don't get caught up in the semantics of how your sentences are formed. You are not trying to be a writer; you are just trying inform him/her, and you are doing it in a much more personal way.

If you look around at the people we do business with today, including doctors, insurance agents, and attorneys, fashion has changed. There are less suits and ties, and people are removing the barriers between themselves and their clients. You see more of them as a person rather than three layers of clothing between them. That is because today's clientele want to do business with people. They don't want to do business with suits.

Having this avatar created helps you define the way you speak to someone. It reforms the way you speak and removes the barriers that language can sometimes create when you are marketing. When you speak directly to a real person, magic happens.

Many people are resistant to creating an avatar because they don't want to leave anyone out, but when you are speaking to your one person, your message comes across far more personally, and you end up attracting even more people to your message. I didn't make this up, by the way. Have you ever heard of Warren Buffett? He writes his own letter to his stockholders every year. When he writes this letter, he writes it as though he is writing to his sister. If Warren Buffett can think of one person to write to, I think you can too!

When we create your avatar, we are deciding who it is that you are speaking to when you are on stage, writing a book, or informing people in any other way. The creation of an avatar is pretty detailed. You need to know everything there is to know about that one person to whom you are talking. Just some of the details might include:

- Are they male or female?
- What kind of car do they drive?
- Do they have kids living at home?

- Do they wear jeans or suits more often?
- Which social media platforms do they use?
- What are their passions?
- What types of food do they eat?

The list can really go on forever, and the creation of an avatar can totally consume you, but I have a pretty unique way of helping people to create their avatars that makes it both easy and more effective.

Creating Your Avatar

Actually, by using this method, you are not creating your avatar at all; you are just selecting one. Here is how we do it: Close your eyes and promise yourself you won't lie. You have to pay very close attention because you might get multiple pictures, but really, we want to know which one shows up FIRST. Ready? Now grab onto the one image you get into your head when you read this: "Favorite Customer or Favorite Client."

Did you see one person pop into your head? People who have trouble with this and say that no one popped into their head at all are lying to themselves, and it is usually for one of two reasons. Either they don't believe they should have a favorite, or they think that they will make the wrong choice. As human beings, we often try to overcomplicate things, and simply going with the first person who enters into your head seems far too easy a task. We think there has to be more to it.

I had one client who sat with his eyes closed for a very long time and finally said, "I'm having trouble choosing." The thing is, I never asked him to choose anything! I asked him to discover who popped into his head first. This is your subconscious telling you that it is your favorite.

Why Your Favorite?

Your next question might be, "Why does it have to be your favorite?" There are really two reasons for this. As entrepreneurs, we try to make everyone happy. When someone is unhappy, we find ourselves focusing on the complainer, and thereby, spend lots of time and energy trying to fix the problem. What ends up happening is that we end up attracting even more customers who make our lives miserable! It's a lot easier to wake up every day and do business with our favorite customer than it is to do business with the complainer, so we should concentrate our energy and our marketing efforts on our favorite customer.

The second reason I tell people to use their favorite customer is that by nature, humans (myself included) are lazy. I'm not saying that I don't have a good work ethic, but if I can find a way to do something faster and easier, then I am going to do it that way. When we use a real person (our favorite customer), we can easily answer all of the questions we need to about our avatar to get a very clear picture on who he/she is, what his/her likes and dislikes are, and where he/she "hangs out" in media.

Making the decision to use an avatar can be troublesome for some, but once you get over the hump and understand that speaking directly to one person makes all sorts of good marketing sense, you can move into a marketing campaign that attracts more of your favorite kinds of customers.

When You Don't Have Customers

If you are just starting out in business and you don't have any customers yet, you might be tempted to make one up. That can take a lot of time and really does not ever become a real person, so it is difficult to really be focused on him/her. Instead, think about the people you already know who might become customers, or try bartering. Anyone who exchanges something of value for your product or service can be considered a client, and he/she is fair game for becoming your avatar. Of course, as soon as someone hands over real cash, your avatar might suddenly change!

Your Avatar Will Change

If you are still really shaky about focusing your marketing attention on just one person, this might help you out. Nothing is permanent. As your business grows and you become more confident in your skills as a business owner, you will discover new favorite customers which you can use as your new avatar. Your new avatar will make more money and become a higher-paying client. When you start focusing on them, you will attract even bigger clients, and your business will grow even bigger.

Another really cool thing that can change the dynamics of your avatar is when your avatar's business grows because of you. I love when this happens to my customers! This makes a major change because even though you are writing to the same person, they have different needs that you can address now that they are better at what they do.

The Three Reasons Someone Won't Buy From You

Once you understand who your avatar is, you can move on to marketing in a way that is tailored toward marketing directly to them. There really are only three reasons why someone doesn't buy from you:

- They don't trust you
- They don't understand your offer

- They don't believe they need it now

If you think back to the last thing you didn't buy, it fits into one or more of these reasons. One way to get past these reasons is to be interviewed by someone who knows your avatar.

When someone else interviews you, the first reason gets canceled out. If you hear someone on the radio, for example, you are more likely to believe him/her than if someone mailed you a postcard. When someone else interviews you, that means you know more than the person who is interviewing you, hence you are an expert, and people are more likely to trust you.

In my world, anyone who knows more about a subject than I do is an expert. The same is true in the business world. When you are seen as an expert in a field, you are opening the doors to fulfilling a need for those who know less about it than you do.

By understanding your avatar, the person interviewing you can really step inside of their shoes and ask you the questions that your avatar needs answered in order to trust you, understand your offer, and believe they need it now. It is important that the interviewer is skilled enough to do this because if your avatar is an insurance agent, the questions they have and the way they are worded would be far different than if your avatar was a homeschooling mother.

Even though much of the information in the interview would be the same and both of them could learn from it, the way the questions are asked, the pacing of the interview, and the verbiage would be starkly different in order to attract each of those potential clients.

What To Do With An Interview

You can use interviews to showcase your expertise both online and offline; here are some examples of what my clients have done with interviews:

- Use a QR code to put your message on your business card

Imagine the look on people's faces when you hand them a card with your expertise attached! They might be so impressed that they will share the interview with their friends and associates.

- Add a slideshow to it and create a video (for your website, YouTube, and more)

We are definitely in the era of video. You can break up your interview into the main points and create several videos that invite people back to your website or to a lead capture page that allows you to follow up with them later.

- Create a CD to sell or give away

Of course, you could give your book away, but if you really want people to HEAR your message, you should hand them a CD. They are more likely to listen to it in the car than they are to read the book you've written.

Summary

Asking the right questions is imperative to getting your message out to the RIGHT customer. You need to start by finding out who the right customer is and writing or speaking directly to him/her. Once you have your avatar in place, you will be able to get past the three main objections to buying from you. It is far easier to overcome all three objections by being interviewed by an expert who knows your avatar.

If you found value here, be sure to join my Group E-list at BrendaTrott.com, where I share exclusive marketing tips. If you need additional help discovering your avatar or would like to take advantage of a highly discounted offer, head over to BrendaTrott.com/skillshare.

Offline Marketing Soldier Secrets

By Matt Woityra

What I'm about to show you is something that most people never get a chance to do in their lifetimes. But, something has to do with this success: Taking a company from zero to making over one million a year. It wasn't easy; it was through hard work, dedication, and long work-nights. But if you listen to what I'm about to show you, you will have success beyond your wildest dreams.

Hi, my name is Matt Woityra. I am a person you've probably never heard of before because I'm the guy always behind the scenes. What I'm about to tell you and share with you will change your life forever. I won't be sugarcoating anything, as I am going to share my biggest secrets with you.

Who am I? I'm an average person who took advantage of every opportunity. Nothing has ever been given to me. Everything that I have has been achieved through blood, sweat, and tears. My childhood is just like every child around. I had one goal, and that goal was to become a United States Marine. In the years growing up, I realize I had to work twice as hard to become good at anything. The moment that I found out that I was good, I then wanted to become great.

When I hit 18 years old, I achieved my goal of becoming a United States Marine. I never stopped dreaming after that. I just focused on new goals and went after them. Some people say they don't have any talents, but I do not believe that. We are all born into this world as "winners." You just have to work twice as hard to achieve whatever you want in life.

When I became a marine, I just did not want to be any average marine; I wanted to be the best marine that the Marine Corps ever had. I went up the ranks fast because I worked diligently on whatever it took to rise to the top of the ranks. My peers around me had the same opportunity. But I was not like the average marine. The average marine would drink, play cards, play video games, or go out to the bars. I would work day and night on becoming a better marine. I made sure I kept myself physically fit by working out in the gym every other day. I would work on my uniforms and make sure that they were in perfectly great condition. I studied all of the rules and regulations of the Marine Corps Code of Ethics. This driving force led me to who I am today.

After getting out of the Marines, I then became a firefighter. It was an easy job because all you do is save people's lives and preserve property. But I knew I needed more out of my life. I knew that I could not be financially set for the future by living off of what the fire department paid me.

After leaving the fire department, I took on some new ventures. Those ventures led me to the skills, abilities, and the marketing blueprints for success. I did not only acquire this knowledge on my own. I went out and looked for people to mentor me. I did not want to just settle for being an average person. I went after people who are already multimillionaires. And what I'm about to share with you now are the secrets that I learned from these millionaires. Plus, I want to share with you my best marketing promotion that led me to make $168,000 in just four days. It is not all about the money. It is about what the money can do for you and your lifestyle, as well as how it can impact the future for your family and leave a legacy. I worked so hard to achieve what I have today. In the past 10 years, I have made in excess of $12 million. That number might sound big, but it's not. I had to make so many sacrifices, lose so much sleep, had so much stress, spend time away from the family.

Most of all, I never quit. That, is the secret to success. If something doesn't work, tweak it, test it, and then find success and duplicate that over and over again. Let me share with you my most successful marketing campaign so far. I do not believe in conventional marketing. I believe that if you have competition, you just don't compete with them. You have to put that competition out of business. In business, especially, when it comes to your competitors, they are not your partners; they are your competition. So, you have to do guerrilla warfare marketing to compete with them.

I had an advantage over my competitors in business. That advantage had to do with utilizing the online marketing world and merging it with the offline marketing world. The advantage was that I had a list of buyers. A list of current and past customers. I had their mailing address, telephone number, and e-mail address. I went after their family and friends too. I called this campaign a "fire sale."

Whatever type of business you're in, any business can use this to make a lot of cash. We all know it costs money to make money. Each customer costs us money just to get into the store. That customer has a lifetime value to you once they become a client.

The basics of a fire sale is stacking the deck with offers that are hard to resist. Your competitors will think, "How can they do that, survive, and make money off of the business?" I knew I had to get them into my business. But the best part wasn't just getting the money upfront; it was on the back-end sales that I made off of the sales funnels I had in place. All businesses work off of this strategy. It costs money to get you into the door through the marketing channels that they use. An average car dealership knows this via their metrics. For every person who walks into a car dealership, it has cost them over $100 just to get them through the front door. This is why they know that they can give away free toaster ovens, free movie tickets, and other freebies because they know the value of a customer who walks into their business.

This fire sale was about stacking the deck with a bunch of offers and giving it away at an affordable price. The affordable price did not matter. That's because it is the cost of a new lead. The money was made on the back-end of the sales funnel. This is the way I have the system set up. I set up a special page on my own website domain. That page subdomain was called a "fire sale." It had a real countdown timer on the page. You had 96 hours to make a purchase or you would forever lose the deal. Then what I did was that I sent out a four-day email campaign to my targeted list of prior and present customers. The subject line always read something about the business being on fire. That got a great open rate. After they opened the email, I had to convince them to visit the new page on the site. Once on the site, their computer was logged in, so their computer's IP address would be linked to the countdown timer. That was phase one of that marketing promotion.

Phase two was utilizing all of the present and past customers' telephone numbers and sending them messages. These customers received text messages that were just shortened condensed versions of the email notifying them that there was a fire sale going on at the place of business. This went on for four days. Mobile text marketing has an 80% chance of having the message read within the first 60 seconds of a person receiving a text message.

Phase three of the marketing promotion was still involved with mobile marketing. I sent out a promotion that called on my past and present customers with an automated message coming directly from my voice. This message had a *Spy Hunter* theme and directed them to either calling the place of establishment or going directly to the website.

Phase four of the marketing promotion was direct mail advertising. All current and past customers received a direct mail postcard that was 5" x 11" big. This drove all of the traffic to the website or in-house sales team.

Now, I want to share with you some marketing methods that you can use to make a boatload of money, even if you have little to no experience. Some of the phrases that I share with you, you might not be familiar with. But go online, "Google" them, and you'll be better acquainted with the terminology.

One of the easiest ways to make money online is selling offline business websites. The concept is quite simple. Find a business and sell them a website. But what most people do is find a business and sell them a $1,000, $2,000, even up to a $10,000 website. That does work, but most the time, it is the hardest job to close that sale.

This new trick that I am going to show you is very ninja-like. First, what you have to do is to find a niche. In this example, we are going to choose a dentist. Now, there are two ways that you could go about getting the website designed. The first one is for you to design it yourself or to find some template and have it designed through your own time and labor. The second way is to hire someone to design the website for you.

Once you have the website designed, I would go out to find dentist offices throughout the whole United States of America who don't have a website or have a poorly-designed website. Then, what I would do is to clone the website and have it deployed on the person's new domain. I would give the website to the new client free of charge. I would charge them a monthly hosting and maintenance fee, anywhere from $25-$100 per month. This can build you quite a big continuity income for yourself each month.

The next "Golden Nugget" that I'm going to share with you has to do with reputation management. Basically, this is about you finding businesses online through Google, Bing, or Yahoo. Look for businesses with negative reviews. Then, approach that business with the negative reviews and show them the good reviews that their competitors have over them. Explain to them how those negative reviews are impacting their business and how they are potentially losing thousands of dollars every month. Then, you help the business build a reputation program to reward happy customers who leave positive reviews. This business concept can make you anywhere from $500-$2000 per month based on the type of business that you're going after. One type of business that you should consider going after are hotels and motels.

The third business model that you could go after is SEO. That stands for search engine optimization, which basically means that you rank websites, videos, articles, press releases, and so forth higher in the search engines. This can be add-on services to what you are currently offering. We all know that when you do a search within the search engines that you normally only look on the first page of that search. This can be detrimental to some businesses that only appear after page one. This service can bring you anywhere from $500-$2000 per month. The best part of this SEO is that you can have all of this done through an outsourcer. This outsourcer will normally cost you half of what you'd charge to that current customer. The great part is that you won't have to do any of the work; you just explain to the customer on how his/her website is ranking. The proof is in the results.

About Matt Woityra

I am glad I was able to share with you some marketing ideas and concepts. If you would like more information and get some free additional training, then go to my blog at http://www.MattWoityra.com or connect with me on Facebook at https://www.facebook.com/matt.woityra.

Using Digital Marketing To Promote Your Business On The Internet

By Jeff Yoe and Dustin Yoe

Let's talk about business and the need to generate more revenues. The lifeblood of all for-profit businesses is revenue. While there are many factors that go into a successful business without sales and customers, clients, or patients, the business ceases to exist. Many smaller business owners are a one-person show when it comes to doing all the tasks within a business. As a seasoned entrepreneur of several businesses, the area where my efforts were focused never seemed to be the one that I wanted to spend most of my time. Most business owners went into business and want to focus on what they are good at within that business. Business owners need to either hire or have a great support team to handle the actions that they are not good at by themselves. These areas can include strategic planning, legal, accounting, supply channels, marketing, transportation and/or sales. Generating new revenues or customers is not normally one of those areas a business owner is completely comfortable with actions needed to be successful.

What are the ways we can increase revenues as a business owner? There are really only three primary ways, and all the other ways are subsets of these three primary ways. The three ways are:

1. Get more customers to buy from the business
2. Increase the profits from each sale
3. Increase the sales to existing customers

No matter which form or combination of marketing venues a business uses, the Return on Investment (ROI) should always be considered and monitored. By tracking the ROI, a business can determine the effectiveness of its current marketing campaign and how small or large changes affect the increased revenue.

One of the factors in ROI analysis is making sure a business understands its lifetime value of a customer. The lifetime value can easily be determined by an owner or manager via answering the following questions:

- What is the average purchase of each customer?
- How many times does a typical customer purchase goods or services from the business per year?
- How many months or years does a customer typically stays with the company?
- How many referrals does a typical customer make to your business each

year?

Let's take an example of how this works out. The example is Dr. Jane's dentist office. Dr. Jane is a good dentist and takes care of her patients each and every time they come in for a check-up or other dental service. Let's say that Dr. Jane's average patient bill each time they come into the office is $1,000. The average patient comes in twice a year and stays with Dr. Jane for an average of 42 months. Since Dr. Jane is always concerned with her patients and encourages them to make referrals to her, the average patient refers two new patients every year.

Here is the lifetime value of a patient for Dr. Jane: $1,000 (average bill)

Number of visits per year = 2 (number of visits per year) x $1,000 = $2,000

Months or years patient stays with Dr. Jane = 3.5 years (42 months)
$2,000 times 3.5 (42 months patient stays with Dr. Jane) = $7,000.

Each refers an average of 2 new patients each year which is 3.5 (42 months) times 2 = 7.

$7,000 times 7 = $49,000 lifetime value of one patient for Dr. Jane.

Now, each business or company needs to determine their average lifetime value using their own numbers. The value will surprise many owners. One factor that all business owners and managers should analyze or have an expert assist is in determining how to increase any of the figures in the lifetime value of a patient/customer/client. Any change will have a dramatic effect on the overall revenue with limited effort or expenditures by the business.

By determining the area of the business you want to impact

- Driving more customers
- Increasing profit per sale
- Increasing the frequency of purchases by existing clients

You will have a focused effort that can measure the ROI and impact the Lifetime Value of a Customer.

The general marketing efforts of a business are divided into six distinct areas:

- Radio
- Television
- Print
- Telemarketing
- Direct mail

- Online/digital

All of these marketing areas and their sub-categories need to be constantly monitored and updated. Living in a constantly evolving world means that the capabilities and systems to impact your marketing campaigns are in a constant state of flux. While there are many sub-categories within each of these areas, the highlights of each are as follows,

Radio and television are still viable, but normally require large expenditure of marketing dollars to get the bias points needed to reach the demographics of the business. With cable television, electronic recording devices, and online movie and show services, it is getting harder and harder to reach your targeted market.

Print, such as newspapers, yellow pages, and magazines have had a significant decline in readership over the past ten years. Many of the major print outlets are working hard to establish a digital presence, since that appears to be where all of their new customer base is coming from today. Since distribution is down with print sources and rates have increased to handle the overall operations of these organizations, a business is reaching far fewer customers than in previous years. Where do you go to get current events or information about a specific topic? About 80% now use the Internet for at least some form of your news and research.

Telemarketing allows for a human interface with a customer or prospect. The challenge is that many people within the United States have put their phones on a "Do Not Call" list that keeps telemarketers from engaging with them.

Direct mail is a good source when properly used. The challenge with direct mail is developing a proper campaign that hits your targeted demographics multiple times with a powerful message. Traditional response rates for direct mail is 1-3%. Businesses need to determine what offer is going to make sure that they are getting a payback from that low of a return. Also, most direct mail needs a good copywriter to produce a sales page that gets higher response rates.

Online or digital marketing services is the new frontier for business. Most business owners think of a website with online or digital marketing, but the areas are much larger.

Why are online or digital marketing services so important to a business today? Some of the common Internet search facts that everyone should understand,

- About 95% of Internet searches never go beyond the first page of a search engine's results.
- Within the United States, almost 92% of people state they research or find more information about a product, service, or company on the Internet before purchasing or going to the business.

- 72-90% of those who see a negative or no review about a product or service will not purchase that good, service, or from that company.
- 46% of all United States adults own a smartphone. This percentage is much higher in many other countries, and the United States percentage keeps getting higher.
- 64% of the time, smartphone users use the device to shop online.
- About 47% of smartphone owners use the device to search for a local store.
- 84% of small businesses with a mobile presence reported an increase in new business activity due to mobile marketing efforts – (Source: Web.com).
- World Internet usage when compared to population shows over 34% use the Internet.
- Over 78% of North Americans use the Internet – (Source: Internet world stats).

Let's explain some of these larger areas, and then the focus will be around mobile marketing for a business.

The business website is the first basic tool that all businesses should have to allow for clients to know about your business and the services or products you offer. Today, a recent survey by StaticBrain shows that over 70% of businesses still don't have a website. This site must be current and trendy to what is happening within the marketplace today. Most websites need to be updated or be completely redone every three to seven years.

Search Engine Optimization, or **SEO**, is the process of getting the search engines like Google, Yahoo, Bing, and Ask.com to quickly pick up a business's online presence when a customer types in a search for your business or the products or services it provides. SEO in its most basic sense is the optimization of the internal parts of business websites.

Areas that are a must-have on your website to maximize your search engine optimization:

- XML Sitemap – This displays all of your content pages so that search engine bots (crawlers that capture your website data) can read this data.
- Make sure you have Robots.txt in your root directory – this file allows communications between your site and the search bots.
- If you have 404 Error pages, make sure that the viewer is linked to another relevant area of your site.
- Make sure that your URL structure is less than 100 characters.
- All page titles should be descriptive of what is within the page. These titles should be concise. The best title length is between 70-100 characters.
- The site speed is important to not only your users, but to the search engines as well. Use a tool to regularly check the speed of your site.
- All photos or images should be properly labeled and optimized.

Search Engine Marketing, or **SEM**, is the expansion of customer searches so that the search engines believe your business and online presence are the most relevant to the searcher's request. The primary goal of a search engine is to return the exact results a searcher is looking for on the first page. SEM is the off-site of a business's website optimization that can contribute to increased search rankings. Very few searches go to the second page of a search to find what they are looking for on that search.

Make an effort to routinely do these SEM activities:

- Write content and post on a blog or on your website
- Use social signals to increase the traffic to your website
- Constantly add new content to your website
- All of your images should have tags and links
- By using video marketing, you are impacting the SEM of your website and rankings
- Monitor your Google Analytics and determine where on the Internet you can increase your visibility

Video marketing is quickly becoming an important digital asset to a company. Many people prefer to get their information about a product, service, how-to, or business with a video. The video is a multimedia tool for a business owner that can impart clarity and value to the client. Since it is a multimedia source, it has been proven in multiple studies that the viewer will retain the information much better and for a longer period of time.

Your business should do these actions with its videos:

- Create a YouTube video channel for the business
- Keep videos between 30-120 seconds in length
- Make sure that you determine how your video will be used
- It is much easier to get to your customers' hot buttons with video, so make sure you have determined which button is being "pushed" for each video
- More short videos are better than one long video
- Host and maintain your videos on sites where you maintain control of the customer
- Don't use Flash
- Make sure you have optimized all of your videos with titles, tags, and descriptions

Social Media is one of the top buzzwords or activities today. Everyone is doing it, right? Facebook has over one billion active users. When used properly, social media can be one of a company's great assets online. A company must remember that social media is designed to be an active exchange or engagements between people and not a sales source. Social media is becoming the phone service of the 21st century.

Social signals from social sites are the #1 ranking factor for Google for a business's private content, according to a Google insider. The larger search engine monitoring services indicate that the top things you should accomplish with your social media marketing are:

- Post to multiple channels or social media sites. Content that is published to at least three or more sites will increase engagement by 30% or more.
- Engaging or posting to social media channels should be done during the best times (these times should be your customers' local time):

- Monday from 12:00 to 1:00 pm
- Tuesday from 4:00 to 5:00 pm
- Wednesday from 2:00 to 5:00 pm
- Thursday from 1:00 to 4:00 pm – This appears to be the best day of the week for a single post
- Friday from 12:00 to 2:00 pm – Highest volume of posts
- Saturday from 11:00 am to 11:00 pm – Best day of the week for overall engagement
- Sunday from 11:00 am to 6:00 pm

Mobile marketing is the engagement of customers on their devices that they carry with them.   These devices include cellphones, smartphones, wireless receivers, tablets, and proximity devices. Over 96% of cell phone users have them with three feet 24 hours a day.

What are the first steps to using mobile marketing successfully within a business? First, you must optimize your website for mobile. Mobile-optimized is sometimes called "fat-finger-optimized." It allows customers to easily navigate your online presence on those smaller mobile devices. It places the critical data in front of the customer so he/she doesn't have to scroll all over your site to call or get directions.

Second, a business must create an offer. Businesses should create a compelling offer that is viewed on mobile devices and spread through the use of SMS text messages.

Third, businesses must take advantage of the local shopping sites and all of the search and social sites' location services. Businesses should also consider a mobile application that stays directly on their customers' phones so that they can easily engage with customers. The business must have a reason for the mobile app that would encourage the customer to keep the app on his/her smartphone.

Fourth, use Quick Response (QR) codes and text message flyers to allow mobile device customers to quickly get the relevant information they are looking for today. These must be used to get what the customer wants, not what you want them to see.

An example of a QR code being used incorrectly was when a regional bank had a new mobile application created to allow customers to more easily access their account information on the go. This regional bank had a QR code created and placed on much of their print material that told the customer to scan the QR code to get the new mobile app. The problem was that one of the marketing staff thought that since the bank was getting the customer to scan it, they could market some of their other services on the main page of the bank's website. The QR code directed to a non-mobile-optimized bank website where the new app link was not on the home page. This caused the mobile app to not be integrated as quickly with customers, and as a result, was a bad mobile experience for the bank's customers.

Proximity Marketing is the finally mobile area a businesses should take advantage of otherwise known as Wi-Fi marketing. More and more businesses are offering free Wi-Fi at their locations, but fail to monetize or take advantage of it. Wi-Fi marketing allows businesses to quickly grow their email lists and Facebook fans, instantly increase customer loyalty, and capture social data for intelligent ad retargeting, contests, and more. This leads to vastly increasing the amount of sales to current customers. By using proximity marketing services you can engage in social channels, send surveys out to customers to get ready for the next season, request reviews of their experience while in your store and send coupons or specials to them.

What if you could collect the demographics of 76% of the people that walk into your business just by offering free Wi-Fi? The right service of Wi-Fi marketing does exactly this and when coupled with advanced retargeting methods you can keep your business going even after your customers have left your location!

- "86% of consumers age 21-24 & 35-44 are highly influenced by the availability of in-store Wi-Fi" from Jwire
- 75% of smartphone owners use Wi-Fi on their devices
- 79% of mobile consumers are influenced by the availability of in-store Wi-Fi when deciding where to shop
- 63% of US adults use the Internet wirelessly on a smartphone, tablet, laptop, or ereader

While proximity marketing and retargeting mobile devices is a relatively new digital channel it appears to be the leader in increased revenues and engagement with a business's customer base for the near future. TransMedia Hotspot is a leader in bringing this emerging technology to businesses and the place to check for the latest trends.

Email marketing is the digital replacement for direct mail. Using a customer or prospect's email and sending a message, voice broadcast, or video can be a very effective tool. The largest challenge with email marketing is getting a customer to open the email.

Business actions for email:

- Get your customer's email address
- Develop a regular contact with your customers through emails
- Offer free versions, samples, or trials of your goods or services to get their email address and put them on a separate email list
- Develop a series of email copy that can be input into an email autoresponder – these can include a video series, newsletter, or announcement of new services or products
- Get an email autoresponder for the business

Pay Per Click (PPC) is the online advertising method for many sites. These online sites charge you for getting your short message clicked on and the viewer to read your more detailed message. You can find these types of paid advertising on many of the major sites like Google, Facebook, or Yelp, as well as on many of the smaller sites. This is a quick way to get your presence seen online. Generally speaking, spending money on a site like Google or Facebook for advertising will not improve your standing in their site rankings. Many organizations consider it the online version of "rent versus own."

Using PPC for your business:

- Identify the keywords that your customers search for
- Develop a short compelling message to get them to click
- Each day, monitor the PPC campaign and adjust
- Try multiple messages at the same time on PPC to get quicker clarity of what is working and, thus, drive costs per click (CPC) down

Local/Maps/Directories are sites that give either a community or a specific business type increased exposure to users. Some of the more common sites include Yelp and Foursquare.

Press Releases in the digital world are a little different than what most people consider a traditional press release. Since many of the newspapers and magazines are going online, they rely on information from the Internet. Businesses, individuals, and organizations can have newsworthy information published online to get greater exposure. Once published online, it can be picked up by associated press, local print outsourcers, and major networks. This is a way to get significant attention quickly, provided the press release is part of a cohesive marketing strategy. It's important to keep in mind that one press release alone is not going to get your business noticed.

Reputation Marketing is your business's online word-of-mouth. It is how your business is viewed online by potential customers or patients. Google defines online reputation as

"Your online identity is determined not only by what you post, but also what others post about you – whether a mention in a blog post, a photo tag, or a reply to a public status update." - Google

All businesses and many individuals have an online reputation. Since most business owners state when asked where you get new customers from, they state via referrals. As a result, you need to take your online reputation seriously.

To conduct a quick check of some of the more common sites that keep comments or reviews about your business, go to http://www.getmyonlinereputation.com.

These are just the highlights of your options for marketing your business on the Internet via digital marketing. While an overall marketing strategy and campaign should be developed for each business and category of a business, it is critical that it is implemented. Then, the ROI of each component must be constantly evaluated. In today's constantly changing environment, a business must always be seeking to improve on its successful actions and reduce or eliminate activities that do not add to its revenues and keep it ahead of its competitors. Too many business owners think that once they get their websites to the first page of the search engines, they can stop doing what it took to get them on the first page. This is totally untrue. A business must be constantly innovating or it will die a slow death.

Your business should have an expert marketing strategist/consultant on the team. TransMedia Powerhouse is a one-stop digital media strategy firm that assists business achieves multiple channel business presence. The marketing strategist must understand the business's specific position, goals, and actions it is taking to gain revenues and market share.

Your business is what is providing you the answer to your dreams, whether it is more freedom, ability to travel, serving the community, or having more things. Make sure you do everything possible to achieve your dreams and desires through your business. We wish you all the best in your business and life.

Jeff and Dustin Yoe
Digital Media Strategists
TransMedia Powerhouse
405-562-8494

www.ingramcontent.com/pod-product-compliance
Lightning Source LLC
Chambersburg PA
CBHW070027100426
42740CB00013B/2614